D1076288

CM10001258
03/11
£20
796.522309 Faw

RON FAWCETT

Rock Athlete

RON FAWCETT

Rock Athlete

with Ed Douglas

VERTEBRATE PUBLISHING

Vertebrate Publishing, Sheffield
www.v-publishing.co.uk

RON FAWCETT
ROCK ATHLETE

Vertebrate Publishing
Crescent House, 228 Psalter Lane, Sheffield, S11 8UT
www.v-publishing.co.uk

First published in 2010 by Vertebrate Publishing, an imprint of Vertebrate Graphics Ltd.

This book is a work of non-fiction based on the life, experiences and recollections of
Ron Fawcett. In some limited cases the names of people, places, dates and sequences
or the detail of events have been changed solely to protect the privacy of others.
The authors have stated to the publishers that, except in such minor respects not affecting
the substantial accuracy of the work, the contents of the book are true.

A CIP catalogue record for this book is available from the British Library.

ISBN: 978-1-906148-17-1

1

Every effort has been made to obtain the necessary permissions with reference to copyright
material, both illustrative and quoted. We apologise for any omissions in this respect
and will be pleased to make the appropriate acknowledgements in any future edition.

Typeset in Palatino by Vertebrate Graphics Ltd, Sheffield.
www.v-graphics.co.uk

Printed and bound in Padstow, Cornwall by TJ International.

CONTENTS

ILLUSTRATIONS

COVER
Ron climbing *Cave Route Right-hand* (E6 6b) at Gordale Scar, UK *(John Beatty)*

REAR COVER
Ron on Froggatt Edge above the River Derwent, Peak District, UK *(John Beatty)*

INSIDE REAR COVER
(John Coefield)

SECTION ONE
Dad with the milk wagons at Uncle Jeff's farm in Embsay *(Fawcett Collection)*

Mum and Dad at Bridlington *(Fawcett Collection)*

Grandad and Grandma Bate in their garden in Embsay *(Fawcett Collection)*

Alison, Richard, Clifford, me and Dad at Flamborough in 1966 *(Fawcett Collection)*

The first ascent of *Small Brown* (E4 6b) at Crookrise *(Al Evans)*

Following Arthur Champion up *Dental Slab* (Severe) at Rylstone *(Arthur Champion)*

Me and Gibby at Brimham Rocks *(Al Evans)*

Gill, with Bill the dog, walking in to Malham Cove *(Fawcett Collection)*

The first ascent of *Moonchild* (E4 5c) at Chapel Head Scar *(Al Evans)*

Astroman (5.11c), Yosemite *(Fawcett Collection)*

Pichenibule (F7c) in the Verdon Gorge *(John Beatty)*

Yosemite Valley *(Fawcett Collection)*

Me and Gibby in the Verdon *(John Beatty)*

Me with Jerry Peel in the Verdon *(John Beatty)*

The late, great Pete Livesey *(Brian Cropper)*

Gill following the top pitch of *Chrysalis* (F7b) in the Verdon Gorge *(John Beatty)*

Illustrations

SECTION TWO

The first ascent of *Milky Way* (E6 6b) at Ilkley *(Fawcett Collection)*

Also at Ilkley, the first ascent of *Desperate Dan* (E7 6b) *(Fawcett Collection)*

Paul Williams in El Chorro, Spain *(Fawcett Collection)*

The West Face of El Cap, Yosemite *(Fawcett Collection)*

Gill on top of El Cap *(Fawcett Collection)*

On and off *Strawberries* (E6 6b) at Tremadog *(Leo Dickinson)*

The first ascent of *The Cad* (E6 6a) on North Stack Wall, Gogarth *(Fawcett Collection)*

The crux section on *Cave Route Right-hand* (E6 6b) at Gordale *(John Beatty)*

On the top wall of *Lord of the Flies* (E6 6a), Dinas Cromlech *(Paul Williams)*

High on Martin Atkinson's route *Pierrepoint* (F7c+), Gordale *(John Beatty)*

Bavarian Reality, Germany *(Fawcett Collection)*

The late Wolfgang Güllich *(Fawcett Collection)*

Revelations (F8a+) at Raven Tor *(John Beatty)*

Playing the 'Rock Star' role in Japan *(Que Handa/Fawcett Collection)*

Climbing the *Edge of Extinction* in Japan *(Que Handa/Fawcett Collection)*

The cliff in the Crimea where the speed climbing competition took place *(Fawcett Collection)*

The dodgy top-rope winch in the Crimea *(Fawcett Collection)*

With John Long in Joshua Tree *(Bob Gaines)*

SECTION THREE

Making the first ascent of *Master's Edge* (E7 6c) at Millstone *(Fawcett Collection)*

On top of High Tor after soloing *Darius* (E2 5c) live on daytime TV *(Al Evans)*

With Sid Perou in the Verdon *(John Beatty)*

Gill and I dressed as H.M. and Martha Kelly at Laddow Rocks *(John Beatty)*

Preparing to paraglide in Snowdonia *(John Beatty)*

Cutting loose high on *The Prow* (F7c) at Raven Tor *(Fawcett Collection)*

Sid films me climbing *Chrysalis* (F7b) in the Verdon *(John Beatty)*

A proud moment: me with Natasha on the day she was born *(Fawcett Collection)*

Dad with the girls in Embsay *(Fawcett Collection)*

With the girls in Australia *(Fawcett Collection)*

Hanging out on the 'collapsing ledge' high on the Aiguille du Midi *(Leo Dickinson)*

With Brian Molineux in a snow cave on the Eiger *(Leo Dickinson)*

Running up Ringing Roger in the 2007 Edale Skyline race *(David Holmes)*

Climbing *Not To Be Taken Away* (Font 6c) at Stanage *(Pete O'Donovan)*

With the girls in the Ardeche *(Fawcett Collection)*

vii

PROLOGUE

A Century of Extremes

DOWN IN THE VALLEY, lights were coming on as dusk deepened into night. I reached into my chalk bag for the cigar I'd stashed there before leaving the house, got it lit and lay back on the flat gritstone summit, exhaling. The smoke rose straight as a pencil into the air. There wasn't a breath of wind. My eyes closed and my tired muscles began to relax. Just across the dale was the little cottage where I lived. I could use a bath and needed a pint. The air was beginning to cool. But for now I was happy not moving for a few minutes and enjoying the warmth of the rock against my back. Finally, I was at peace.

It had been a long day. I'd parked that morning under Froggatt Edge, the partly quarried gritstone crag that fringes Big Moor, overlooking Derbyshire to the west and with the city of Sheffield at its back. It was a clear, autumn day and the beaches and oaks below Froggatt were golden. In the sun the air was warming fast, it would be a hot one, but the crag faces west and so for the time being was still in the shade. There was nobody about. I put my hands on the rock and felt at once that the friction would still be good after a cold night.

I sat down and changed my shoes, lacing up my rock boots and trying not to think of what I was proposing to do. The scale of it was vast – one hundred Extreme grade routes in a day. I hadn't made a list, and I hadn't thought too clearly about where

1

to find the most routes for the least amount of effort. I really just wanted a reason, some kind of target, to keep me out all day, to test my body, to find out what I was capable of doing.

There was no ulterior motive. I wasn't there for sponsors. I didn't care whether what I was doing would be reported in climbing magazines. I just wanted to find that edge I felt I'd lost. For almost twenty years I'd spent every waking moment either climbing or thinking about it. My body was honed by a relentless training regime that I had started to resent: hundreds of press-ups each day and seemingly endless top-rope sessions where I would do laps on routes I had once found hard. I'd given pretty much everything I had to the sport. What did I have left?

I started as I meant to go on, soloing up *Downhill Racer*, the flawed masterpiece of my old friend Pete Livesey, crimping on its chipped hold and then moving on, a gem of a route. I climbed down *Long John's Slab*, the easier Extreme to its left. Two down, ninety-eight to go. Moving leftwards along the crag, I continued, climbing routes I'd done so often that I knew each hold before I reached it. I could feel the momentum building and shut off my mind from everything but moving up rock.

Back at the slab, I collected my gear and moved right to the blanker, neighbouring slab where the routes were even more committing. I've always been a bit of a thug, more comfortable on steeper routes where strength comes into play. But I would save myself a lot of energy for later in the day by climbing these slab routes, even if they were dangerous. I squeaked my boots, rubbing my palms across the soles to clean off any loose dirt and padded upwards, adding five to my tally. Further right the crag got steeper and I felt a small twinge of apprehension. The last time I'd been here I'd suffered a bad fall while soloing and broken my leg. Today there must be no mistakes.

So casually had I taken my plan, I'd brought nothing to eat. Now I was hungry. I should have continued along the edge of the moor to Curbar Edge and another batch of routes to solo, but instead I dropped back down the hill to my car and raced down to Hathersage. I sat in a café half-watching two pretty waitresses move among the tables. I wanted to stay and maybe start a conversation. How could a compulsion to climb push me around like this? And yet, there I was, back on the street, getting into the car and taking the road up to Stanage.

I'd never enjoyed the texture of the rock at Stanage all that much. It didn't compare favourably with the gritstone I'd grown up with in Yorkshire. I found it lichenous and insecure, and as a consequence I didn't know the routes I was planning to climb nearly so well. Starting at the right-hand end of the crag, I tried out an idea to speed my progress. I'd brought my oldest pair of sticky rock boots, now stretched and consequently loose on my feet. I could walk comfortably in them between routes, and by wrapping carpet tape around the uppers, I hoped they would stay solidly in place for when I was climbing.

Starting around *The Dangler*, I moved left, cursing whichever guidebook writer had decided to describe the crag from left to right. Where was I? My boot idea wasn't working either and I soon changed into my regular pair, putting up with pinched feet to save time. I was fed up. An old boy in breeches and floppy big boots latched on to me as I moved along the crag, trying to engage me in conversation about the good old days, the time of Joe Brown and Don Whillans. I didn't want to be rude, but I was busy and getting frustrated. Things weren't coming easily anymore.

I had the motivation to step up a gear when climbing the harder grades, but that left me vulnerable on under-graded routes where I thought I wouldn't need to struggle. On an innocuous-looking climb called *Fern Groove* I found my feet and fingers greasing off the holds, my eyes scanning the rock ahead, flummoxed at what to do next. It was only E1, the easiest grade that qualified as Extreme, but I found myself backing off it. I felt

3

shaken. I was losing momentum.

A little further along, I came across two climbers I recognised, Johnny Dawes and Martin Veale, practising desperate unclimbed routes with the safety of a top-rope. Here was the next generation hard at play. I might have abandoned my plan right there, and joined them for the rest of the afternoon. It looked like fun. But I felt shy with them, and the burden of my target was settled on my shoulders. I pressed on. But the kind of Extremes I was searching for were now becoming thinner on the ground.

I soloed a slab called *Wall End Slab Direct*, and then the gorgeous, unprotected arête of *Archangel*, pushing to the back of my mind the thought that I might be in any kind of danger. I'd more or less forgotten I wasn't roped. But I still felt under pressure. Ploughing through the waist-high bracken, turning bronze with the season, I began to fret about the time. I'd probably get more routes done at another crag. The sections of cliff on Stanage were becoming more isolated and further apart. After soloing *Count's Buttress*, I decided to run back along the top of the crag and down to the car park, now half a mile back up the road. My tally was up to fifty-six.

Reaching the car, I slotted in a Lou Reed album and sped off up the hill, then down past Higgar Tor and around to the small car park below Burbage. The climbs here were shorter and the friction much more to my liking. The crag doesn't catch the sun until evening and so the rock was still cool. I moved up a gear climbing short but awkward problems several grades harder than *Fern Groove*, but I felt secure and strong, full of confidence again, the momentum back with me. There were lots of hard routes close together and I felt strangely inspired by the route names: *Above and Beyond the Kinaesthetic Barrier, Pebble Mill.*

It must have seemed crazy to those climbers I met that day. Jogging from one route to the next in some kind of frenzy. They weren't to know that I'd been doing things like this for most of my climbing life. When I was young, and often on my own, I taught myself to climb this way, soloing on the crags around my childhood home in Embsay, a small, tight-knit village outside Skipton. In those days, my appetite seemed insatiable. I would run back from school to go climbing. I felt most at ease moving on rock. It was where I was meant to be. Later on, I would stay at the crag to climb a bit more when everyone else had gone to the pub. I was utterly driven by my passion for climbing.

The day was wearing on and although I'd pushed my total up to the mid seventies at Burbage, I didn't have much more than a couple of hours of daylight left. I might have been older and wiser now I was in my early thirties, but I hadn't changed my habits. It was, however, getting harder to find the spark that once had come so easily. My life felt less secure than when I was a lad, driving my parents up the wall with all the scrapes I found myself in. My first marriage had ended a few months before and I wasn't sure where I was going. Everything seemed uncertain. Maybe that's what I was doing up here, trying to make sense of things in the places I knew best.

Back in the car, I had a choice. Nip down the road to Millstone Edge, a gritstone quarry that I knew well and was close at hand, or drive a few miles back to Curbar, where I'd been that morning. Millstone might have been nearer but it was taller than Curbar, meaning I'd need to do more climbing. With twenty-odd routes still to do, I didn't think I'd have either sufficient time or energy. So I headed south.

Crags have their own character, and Curbar is no exception. It's a tough place, often steep and intimidating, more so than its neighbour Froggatt. The first big wall is tall and slightly leaning. I started on a famous Joe Brown route called *Right Eliminate*, an awkward, off-width crack. When I was a young climber, with a hemp-line round my waist tying into a hawser-laid rope, a route like this was about the hardest thing in the country. Brown had been one of the heroes of my youth, a legend to my generation of climbers, coming of age in the late 1960s. What's more, he was a working-class hero, from a background like mine. I hadn't come from a wealthy family who could indulge my eccentric passion for climbing. My dad drove a wagon for a living and my mother worked in the local mill.

Moving along the crag, I ran into John Allen leading a friend up his neat little slab route *Kayak*. John was a gritstone master who had amazed the climbing world as a teenager in the mid 1970s, a genuine *wunderkind*. A little younger than me, he seemed more relaxed these days, just out for fun and not bothered about where it was going. I stopped for a chat but I still had almost twenty routes to go. I needed to keep moving. The evening was wearing on and the midges were out, chasing me along the crag.

My brain ached with the tension of so much soloing. I looked at my village across the valley and yearned for home. But I wasn't finished yet. By the time I reached *Apollo* the lights were on in the valley. I stripped off my shirt, stashed my gear and jogged down to the *Deadbay Crack* area, half-climbing, half-falling down the crack itself and then back up the groove.

After sprinting back up to the *Apollo* area, the last few problems I needed to do there were all favourites. I felt the finishing line was close. The sun was long gone, but I knew now that I was going to come through. When I added them all up, my one hundred routes totalled 3,957ft of climbing. I'd also walked and run more than twelve miles moving between crags. My legs ached a little from it. The skin on my hands, after decades of climbing, was unbroken.

When I was climbing hard, people often used to ask me what I would do next. It's a question many athletes must sooner or later come to dread. And it's a question people stop asking after a while, when they begin to think that for you, there is no next thing. I didn't mind. I had plenty of other things to do when

I stepped aside. Looking back now, it seems like another world, especially when I was just a kid, growing up in Embsay. But I can still remember the excitement I felt, daydreaming at school, desperate to be outside, up on the moors again, climbing.

ONE

The Milk Round

MY FATHER WAS NOT A GREAT TALKER. Even when I spent all day with him, we almost never spoke. He was one of those Yorkshire Dales blokes who just got on with it. His job was driving a wagon round local farms collecting milk for the Milk Marketing Board. In those days, the mid 1960s, milk still came in aluminium churns. Dad would climb down from the cab and help the farmers load them onto the back of his flatbed wagon. I loved to go with him. I can still see his handsome face with its broad lick of hair over his forehead studying the road as the day began.

In the school holidays, when I could nag him into taking me along, Dad would get me up at around 4.30am, the crack of dawn in summer but pitch black in winter. He'd set the fire first. Dad loved routine. I can still see him laying out the newspaper he'd rolled the night before in the grate, and positioning the sticks, all the same length, carefully on top and then just the right amount of coal. The fire would warm the house and heat water for when Mum and my sister and brothers got up, a few hours later.

Then he'd make coffee. He was, from what I remember, the only person in the village to drink coffee. It seemed incredibly exotic. He ordered it from the village shop and it was brought in especially at great expense. And this was ground coffee, not instant. He spooned it into a jug and then filtered it with a tea strainer. No one else was allowed to touch it. I can smell it now, the aroma spreading through the whole house. He'd drink a cup straight away and make a flask with the rest for his second breakfast. I always wanted to ask why he drank coffee and not tea like everyone else's dad, but I never did.

Summer mornings were best, though, with dawn just breaking as we moved around the kitchen. For breakfast I'd have a jam sandwich and a cup of tea, and take another jam sandwich for lunch, and we'd set off. Dad would take the back road from our home in Embsay to the north of Skipton and then up the Grassington road to the west of Crookrise and Embsay Moor to Rylstone. I got to know all the farms: Grange, Raise Gill, Buckden. There was a three-legged dog at the farm on the road between Coniston and Kettlewell, and a sign at Oughtershaw, in the back of beyond, that read: 'Beware of Snakes.' I suppose these trips were my first adventures.

It's hard to explain how much these places mean to me. From quite a young age I was exploring on my own. I wanted to know what was behind the horizon, the rim of hills that looked down on my world. In Embsay, to the south, was a high limestone ridge, look north and there was Embsay Crag and Crookrise. My parents didn't have a car, and we rarely went exploring. I loved wandering the fells; I'd go out to Deer Gallows and not come back until I was tired or hungry. I just loved being outside, in nature, watching wildlife and content to be on my own. When I started climbing, although I loved it and knew I was good, it was first and foremost just another way to be up on the moors.

We'd get back from the milk round at five in the afternoon and Mum would have tea on the table. If Dad was quiet, Mum was the opposite. She liked a natter. Dad just wanted a quiet life. He was up early six days a week and by the time he got home he was exhausted. He'd just sit down and read the paper. On Sunday he'd do maintenance on the wagon. The regular pattern of days meant everything to him. People sometimes ask me if my dad was into sport like me, but he was too tired to do anything else but work. When you've grown up with people who worked that hard, it's hard to think of going climbing as a job.

Mum was more open, and loved being sociable. They were so different, and they fell out sometimes because of it. She was an only child and her dad, Billy, had come from Culcheth in Lancashire around the time of the Great War. Billy ran a market garden and sold fruit and vegetables and other groceries from a small shop in his house. He was tall with a broad, open face, an impression made only stronger by his wife Winnie's tiny stature. Winnie, my grandmother, was local, from Skipton. They were generous folk. I can still recall as a young teenager crying my eyes out on their garden bench the day after Winnie died. Billy had a taste for offal and was always offering me strange meals, like brain stew baked forever in the Rayburn, or raw tripe, seasoned with salt and vinegar. He'd say: 'Try some of this, Ronald, it'll put hairs on your chest.' Wanting to be a man, I ate it, but I'd cover the stuff in vinegar to hide the taste.

Billy loved to talk as well. He'd be out in the garden working, and anyone walking past would be buttonholed for a chat. I'd watch people jump over the wall and dodge round the back of his house through the fields so they wouldn't get caught by him and have to listen for the next hour. He had this fantastic accent, predominantly Yorkshire, but with a bit of his original Lancashire left.

All of us lived close by, not just my Mum's family but my Dad's too. My whole universe, when I was little, was within a few hundred yards. Embsay is a small village that was getting bigger when I came along. There was an old cotton mill that was still operating when I was growing up, and where my mother worked, though she took a break for a few years when the kids were small. I worked there as a young man and can still remember the gossip and banter the women shared. It was the perfect place for Mum to hold court.

Like her parents, she was a great one for cooking and baking. Coming back from school as a young lad, I'd come in the kitchen and find her baking: scones, cakes, bread. She was very physical, and would give me a hug if something had gone badly. Dad wouldn't touch me at all, except to give me a crack across the back of my head if I'd done something wrong.

Sometimes I try and explain to my daughters what the world was like in those days, growing up in the late 1950s and early 1960s in rural Yorkshire, and I'm very aware I sound like an old codger. But life was so different. The Second World War was only a decade finished when I was born in May 1955 and there was still a strong feeling of austerity and thrift around. Money was tight. If I wanted something then I had to earn the money to pay for it.

Then again, there wasn't much to buy. Billy Bate had a car, but my other grandad didn't, and Dad only had the lorry. We didn't have a telephone when I was young and the black and white telly had two channels. Televisions were rented in those days, presumably because they were less reliable and too expensive to buy. Walking through Skipton you'd see television sets waiting on the doorstep of people who couldn't make the payments, waiting to be repossessed. Dad would have his paper, and each week we got the Victor comic which Dad would get to read first on pain of a smack. I loved reading about Alf Tupper, the Tough of the Track. He was working class like me, and despite the best efforts of the sporting establishment he always won through.

Going into Skipton was as cosmopolitan as life got. It was a prosperous place in the early 1960s, hordes of workers flowing out of the factory gates like a tide, before all the mills closed. But we never went to the theatre and I was never one for the pictures. I'd never been in a restaurant until I went to the States for the first time. Mum and Dad thought pizza was foreign food so a curry was beyond the pale. Working class life in a small Yorkshire village was deeply conservative and I suppose attitudes people had then would be considered deeply prejudiced now. But there was a strong sense of community and people looked out for each other. I experienced that strange northern paradox of living somewhere that was gregarious but at the same time insular.

I remember after a trip to Yosemite, in the early 1970s, coming home after weeks in California, where my mind had been stretched and my body tested, lying on the lawn at the front of the house in the summer sunshine, thinking about everything I'd just been through and how quiet and stable everything in Embsay was compared to America. The most amazing thing was none of my relatives would ever ask me about it. Even if they wanted to know they wouldn't ask. They'd say: 'Been away lad?' And that was it. Not long before he died, I remember sitting with Dad watching the news on television. There was a report about some occurrence in America, and Dad nodded at the screen: 'You've been there, haven't you lad?' There was a hint of pride in his voice. All those years he'd never said a word, but it had all sunk in.

Dad's family were Yorkshire farmers from higher up the Dales. He'd been born in 1929, just over the border in Lancashire's Ribble valley where his dad, Fred Fawcett, was working as a tenant farmer in Bashall Eaves. Following an unsolved murder there in 1934, Bashall Eaves became known as The Village That Wouldn't Talk. My sister has all these old photos from the Victorian era of weather-beaten Yorkshire families looking squarely at the camera outside farmhouses that are probably occupied by office workers now. Grandad Fawcett moved to a house a stone's throw from ours. He'd married a woman from Hubberholme called Frances. Her brother was a well-to-do fellow called Jeff who had bought a handsome old farmhouse and the land on the Skipton side of Embsay. Fred Fawcett had left Bashal Eaves to work Jeff's farm, which was mostly dairy.

Jeff and his wife Ethel – my great aunt – came across as being a bit posher than us. They were moving up in the world.

Ethel always had nice things. None of the other women in the family had nice things. She'd do hats and gloves and 'best'. The other women didn't do best either. In the early 1950s Jeff built some semi-detached houses on a small piece of his land, less than a hundred yards from the farmhouse behind the bungalow where Grandad Bate lived. When they were finished, Mum and Dad moved into one. It was modern but there was no central heating and we only ever lit a fire in the front room at Christmas. If you complained about the cold, you were given a job to do or told to put on a jumper. Nowadays those houses sell for a quarter of a million.

In those days, children didn't ask parents how they had got together and what they liked about each other. They were just Mum and Dad, as fixed in their habits as the stars and the moon. They were just there. If I did wrong, Dad would give me a cuff round the back of the head, and if I was upset or down, Mum would give me a hug. Looking back, it was a very secure, rather sheltered upbringing that gave me a lifelong passion for the outdoors. Although I've lived in Derbyshire for thirty years, I still think of Yorkshire as home.

I knew, however, our family was more complicated than most, even if we didn't talk about it. For a start, there was Uncle Norman. Norman was Dad's younger brother and he lived with their dad in the village. Norman had done brilliantly at school, winning a scholarship to Ermysted's Grammar in Skipton and then a scholarship to Cambridge. He was the first in our family to do anything academic like that. He got a first-class degree and became head pathologist for North Yorkshire police. Then things began to go wrong. He could never talk about what happened. Perhaps the strain became too much for him, or else he was just made that way. He'd entered a world completely outside his childhood experience and perhaps he felt lost between the two. Whatever the reason, his mental health started to crumble. He spent time in a mental hospital and then came home to live with Grandad Fawcett. It was something the family never talked about.

Norman spent my childhood doing odd things, like walking round the village naked, scaring the neighbours in the process. Dad would say he did it so he didn't have to get a job. Others in the family just found that kind of behaviour embarrassing, including me. But for some reason I always got on well with Uncle Norman. He didn't mean any harm. Presumably he was fond of me too, because when he died he left me £500. The rest, including Grandad Fawcett's house, went to several charities, which caused a bit of a stir.

There were four of us kids at home and I was the oldest. After me comes my sister Alison, six years younger than me, and then Richard, now farming in Wigglesworth, North Yorkshire. The youngest, Clifford, is a mechanic with a heavy goods vehicle licence. He's in the vehicle recovery business near Bradford. Both my brothers now have families of their own, and neither of them has ever been remotely interested in climbing.

We also have a half-brother, Bryan, who is five years older than me. We knew Bryan had a different dad but we didn't know his identity and didn't ask about it either. Until I was much older, I never thought about what this meant, or the difficulties and anguish it must have caused. When I was young, it was just an accepted fact. My mother had had a relationship with someone in the village when she was a teenager and got pregnant. Abortion wasn't legal then, and anyway she would have naturally kept the baby. Her parents were amazing folk. Bryan never found out who his dad was. People assume the past was a less tolerant place, but in all honesty, no one ever looked down on Bryan or Mum or gossiped about us. I suppose it helped we had so many relatives in the village.

Bryan lived with Grandad Bate, but he and my Dad seemed to get along fine. When he left school at fifteen, Bryan joined the merchant navy. While he was away I took the opportunity to sneak into Bryan's room and play his records. He was a big rock'n'roll fan, and had a smart pair of winkle-pickers in his wardrobe. I'd try those on too. When he turned up for his six-week training course, they told him he needed a haircut. He told the barber he was a bastard for cutting off his rocker's 'do. So they held him back a week. Pretty soon after he finished training we started getting postcards from all round the world. He'd come back home bringing something exotic like a pineapple. A pineapple! We thought they only came in tins.

By then, Dad had stopped working for the milk board. When they switched to tankers, he was told he'd have to do more training and get a new licence to drive one. Dad couldn't be doing with that, so Jeff bought a wagon and Dad worked for him instead, bringing feed from the docks in Liverpool and distributing it to the same farmers he'd collected milk from. By the time he retired, the business had six wagons and Dad was still working a full day.

I remember driving early one morning with Dad when I was in my early teens, down the East Lancs Road, to see Bryan who was in port and to pick up a load. Bryan showed us round his ship. I'd started growing by then and kept cracking my head on the bulkheads. Dad and Bryan laughed their heads off. 'There he goes again.' Watching my big brother disappear off round the world seemed almost unbearably exciting. He took up photography, became quite good at it, and showed us pictures of places like the Suez Canal. Some of the world's glamour and excitement had rubbed off on him. At some level, I wanted to experience what Bryan had. Trips like that to Liverpool proved a welcome break from life in Embsay. We did go on holiday, but not often. I remember a week at Flamborough Head when I was eleven. And I remember going on the Flying Scotsman when it stopped at Embsay station once. There's a black and white photograph of us four kids outside a static caravan near Scarborough.

I'm sure I had a good time, but I have stronger memories of

family visits to Dad's relatives in Dentdale. Mostly they were tenant farmers, like my Grandad had been, or else working on the Settle to Carlisle railway. There were unspoken rules to family visits in rural Yorkshire in the 1960s. For a start, you didn't go to stay. Folk didn't have a spare bedroom for visitors and even if they did most of our relatives had to be up early the next day to go to work. It would be a real imposition to expect to stay the night. We would borrow Jeff's old Bedford van and go up the Dales for tea on Sunday and come home that evening. Us kids sat in the back, among the tools, careful not to get oil on our clothes.

Visiting Uncle Jack was my favourite. First off, he lived in a wild, remote spot at the top of Dentdale, the kind of place I was starting to seek out for myself. He didn't have electricity, normal enough for those parts in the 1960s, and he still used an outdoor toilet, which made visits a bit more of an adventure. More than that, he did the kinds of things I found most exciting, like poaching salmon. The thrill of getting caught added just the kind of spice I'd developed a taste for. Coming home from one poaching expedition, Jack spotted a bailiff before he spotted us and handed me the fish we'd caught to stuff inside my coat. The bailiff knew Jack's tricks but wouldn't search a young lad. I can still remember trying to look innocent while my heart rate soared.

I have to confess that I took after Uncle Jack in some ways. I was often in trouble. Any chance I got I'd be out, up on the moors or down by the river, thinking up things to do to escape boredom. My best friend and partner in crime was Martin Brewster, the local builder's son, who lived almost next door to Grandad Fawcett. It was hard to say which one of us was more naughty.

My earliest scrambles were part of our adventures, just another way to experience the outdoors. Climbing was just part of what was on offer. We'd sometimes see climbers up at Crookrise, and we'd scramble around the cliffs in our wellies or plimsolls, depending on whether it was raining. Martin never took to climbing;

I remember us scrambling up some limestone slabs and Martin panicking and turning around and running down them straight into a barbed wire fence. He cut his arm quite badly and I had to help him home. Crikey, I copped it from his mum for that one. She immediately told my Dad and I ended up confined to my room. This was the worst punishment for me, restricting me from the thing that made me happiest, being active outdoors. As I got older, I'd nip out the bedroom window and jump down, which only enraged my Dad more. 'What do you think you're doing jumping out the bedroom window? You'll only kill yourself.'

Our biggest scrape was building a pipe bomb. I can't honestly say whose idea it was, or where we got the knowledge to do something quite so stupid, but I'm sure it involved fertiliser, easily found on a farm, and a scaffolding tube. We stuck one end in the ground, lit the fuse and retired to a safe distance. A very satisfying jet of flame shot out of the top and kept burning. Pretty soon though, the bottom of the pipe started to get hot and the whole thing toppled over. That might not have mattered if we hadn't made the mistake of lighting the pipe close to the road into Skipton. It just so happened that the local bobby was cycling past at the moment the pipe fell over and sent a jet of flame across the road. This was not good timing. I got a sharp crack round the head for that one. These days, I suppose, we'd have been arrested on terrorism charges.

Not all our adventures were quite so delinquent. Inspired by Uncle Jack's salmon poaching, I became a dab hand at tickling trout. There's a lot of nonsense talked about this. It's a lot simpler than some would have you believe. It certainly doesn't require any tickling; you just heave them out. Jack showed me a neat trick for catching salmon. They'd stick their heads under rocks leaving their tails exposed and he'd lower a wicked-looking triple hook underneath it and then bring it up sharply, catching the tail and dragging the salmon out. Any trout I caught I'd sell to Grandad Bate for a shilling or two and he'd sell them on from his shop. I could also earn a few pence cutting thistles in the cow pastures for Grandad Fawcett. From time to time, I helped take the cattle along the road to the market at Skipton with a village character called Howard Peel. Howard was known to us kids as Wuggins And The Egg, because he walked round the village with a basket of eggs, day or night, dressed in worn out farm clothes. Wuggins never said a word to anyone until late in life, when he learned to read and write, and made the local news as a result. After that you couldn't shut him up.

Not surprisingly, given how much of my early years were spent outside, school was a bit of a trial. So many climbers, it seems to me, spent their school careers looking out of the window dreaming of freedom. Like most kids in the village I went off to primary school in shorts and a pair of clogs. Lucky for me when I went to secondary school in Skipton I was given a pair of long trousers, because those boys still wearing shorts were ribbed mercilessly, essentially for being poor. Everybody, almost everybody, bought clothes in the same shop in Skipton. If you made a few quid, then you changed shops. That's how people knew you were doing well.

The village primary, where Mum and Dad had been to school, had enough children for three classes and three teachers, one of whom, Mrs Atkins lived next door to us in Brackenley Avenue, where she could keep an eye on me out of class as well as in it. To be honest, primary school was more or less an extension of village life. I did reasonably well, felt secure and happy, and seemed to get on fine with the teachers, even with Mr Shillito, the headmaster.

That pattern continued after I arrived at Aireville Secondary School, or at least it did at first. I can't say I have fond memories of the place. It had opened only a few years before, to increase education capacity for the post-war baby boom. There was already a long-established grammar school in Skipton, but I don't remember ever having a realistic chance of getting in. There were only a few places allocated to children from our village, and I wasn't one of them.

The Milk Round

The teachers at Aireville were a mix of characters, from time-servers to those who really engaged with the children. Included in the former was my physical education teacher. For the five years I went to Aireville Secondary, arriving in the September of 1966, he wrote exactly the same thing in my school report: 'Tries hard'. Technically speaking, this was true. I did try hard. I liked being active. I'd started growing earlier than my mates at school and towered over my brothers. We used to do the odd bit of cross-country running and I loved that. We were told to run from one point to another and back again and then left to get on with it. I enjoyed it for the freedom it gave me. The school had an outdoor activities programme, which included climbing. This was the era of Outward Bound and the outdoors being character building, so I suppose many schools did that kind of thing. But because I didn't shine at more conventional activities like football, in the eyes of my PE teacher, I didn't qualify for climbing trips away from school. It was so frustrating because I knew most of the kids that were taken climbing weren't that interested in it out of school.

The school did organise walking trips to the Lake District, a big mass of mostly reluctant kids stretching like a snake across the fells. In those days driving long distances made me nauseous. I'd puke out the window of the coach after twenty minutes. Then, feeling hungry because there was nothing in my stomach, I'd have to eat my packed lunch, leaving me with nothing but fresh air to keep me going when we reached the Lakes. But I loved being in the hills. One of the young walk leaders drafted in to help was Brian Swales, who was a couple of years ahead of me at Aireville. Brian was a big, friendly lad with a passion for two-litre Ford Cortinas. When we started climbing, he'd drive us at top speed up to the Lakes. We've been friends for over forty years.

I suppose part of growing up involves the painful discovery we all have to make that most people, even most teachers, aren't that interested in you. I was and still am quite shy, and as a young lad was eager to please. 'Conscientious' is a word that crops up frequently in my school reports, certainly at the beginning of my time at Aireville. But society didn't expect much of a country lad at an obscure northern secondary school in the 1960s. Teachers probably assumed we'd end up doing what our parents did, mostly some sort of repetitive practical job, like Dad's. If I was lucky, I'd get the chance to use my maths, the subject I was best at. So I suppose I felt a level of disillusionment at school. That the system was stacked against people like me. When I discovered climbing, this made me doubly anxious to succeed. But I also took the attitude that if they weren't interested in what inspired me then I wasn't going to be interested in what they were offering in return. My last school report for English summed it up: 'Ronald admits his lack of interest and he does not seem prepared to make the necessary effort to improve. His work tends to very slapdash [sic] but his ability is shown when he talks or writes on one of his enthusiasms.'

Judging by this appraisal, my English teacher didn't think my 'enthusiasms' were relevant to my future success. How could climbing mean anything except as a hobby to take the edge off a dull working life? One teacher did encourage me. George Spenceley had been on an important survey expedition to South Georgia led by the actor and explorer Duncan Carse in the mid 1950s. Carse was famous in those days for playing Dick Barton on the radio and his survey work was later useful when British troops landed on South Georgia during the Falkands crisis of 1982. Mr Spenceley taught me geography and I loved listening to stories about his adventures. He gave me articles to read and encouraged me. I felt I was talking to a kindred spirit, even though we came from very different backgrounds. I don't know how much of a climber he was, but in the 1960s there was more of a crossover between climbing and more general exploration. You felt they were connected in a way that perhaps they aren't anymore.

If I'd done something amazing over the weekend, then I wanted to tell Mr Spenceley about it.

So my route into climbing, unlike so many others, wasn't through school or the Scouts, or even an older, more experienced friend. Roaming around the moors near my home, under crags like Deer Gallows or Crookrise, I'd seen climbers in action and was simply curious to have a go. At first there was just me, either on my own, or else with Martin, although after he crashed into the fence and hurt himself he lost interest pretty quickly. That happened at Haw Bank Quarry, in those days owned by the Skipton Rock Company, which, in its heyday, had produced 80,000 tonnes of limestone a year. Haw Bank overlooks Embsay to the south, so I was blessed in having a big limestone crag on one side of the house, as well as some superb gritstone climbing on the moors to the north. Some people assume that I have a particular affection for gritstone, thinking I started climbing on it and because I climb on it so often now, but that's not correct. I loved Yorkshire limestone, which is far superior to the version in the Peak, and I did so from the start.

These days, climbers must wonder about the big hole in the hillside they pass as they drive up to Crookrise or Deer Gallows. But in the 1960s Haw Bank was quite popular with Yorkshire climbers, before the routes got blasted into pieces and made into cement or motorways. Now the quarry's fenced off so it's difficult to know how much is left, but I remember slabs at least a hundred feet high, a rare commodity on limestone. At quite a young age I was soloing the easier routes there – up to Severe in standard – often in my Wellington boots, standard footwear for most outdoor adventures when I was a kid. Not surprisingly I got comments from proper climbers alarmed at the sight of a young lad – I must have been just fourteen at this stage – wandering all over a high limestone quarry in inappropriate footwear. It seems staggering to me now that I did this. It was crazy, really. But it does show that I had a real passion for soloing and the psychological tools to thrive high on a big cliff without a rope. But I must have taken the hint from those startled climbers. I fell into conversation with a lad whose name, he told me, was Arthur Champion. I asked him if he'd take me out and show me how to use a rope and so forth.

Some of the disquiet about what I was doing must have reached my mother, because she started to take notice of my interest in climbing. If I was going to do something so plainly foolish, she decided, then I'd better learn how to do it properly. She approved of Arthur. His mother owned the tea kiosk at Skipton bus station and Mum knew the family. They were keen church-goers, and while my parents weren't, that added a gloss of respectability.

Arthur was a likeable young man, aged around 18, always jolly. He was a leader in the Venture Scouts and had been at Aireville Secondary too, but was now an engineering apprentice in Keighley. Caving was really his passion and he'd just joined the Craven Pothole Club. When he turned up that weekend towards the end of the summer holidays I was struck by how much older he seemed and how serious what we were doing suddenly became. Best of all he had lots of equipment. Somehow this made what we were doing all the more legitimate. This was proper stuff.

We took the bus up the Grassington road to Rylstone. The fell above the village is a wild place, almost eerie, especially at night. There's a lot of history on these moors. William Wordsworth set a poem here, 'The White Doe of Rylstone', based on a local legend about a deer that crossed the hill from the village over the top to Bolton Abbey each Sunday to graze outside the church while the congregation worshipped inside. The legend was connected to a local family, the Nortons, who rose up against Elizabeth I in defence of Catholicism. There's a cross on the main crag and to the north a huge obelisk commemorating local soldiers killed in the Great War. Rylstone has a lot of ghosts.

It all seems so long ago now. Neil Armstrong had walked on the moon a few weeks before, Harold Wilson was prime minister and troops were being sent to Northern Ireland. England was another country. We rattled through the classic easy climbs: *Monkey Puzzle, Twin Cracks, Falcon Crack,* the classic *President's Slab, Chimney Slabs Route Two, Chockstone Crack, Flake Climb* and *Trowel Face.* The last was an Allan Austin route from the 1950s, the man who would dominate the Yorkshire scene before Pete Livesey arrived, but the rest were routes from the early days of Yorkshire exploration in the 1920s.

The highlight of the day was *Dental Slab,* which my old guidebook says is a contender for the best route of its grade – Severe – in the whole of Yorkshire. I don't suppose I knew it then, but members of the Craven Pothole Club, Arthur's club, did the route first, in the mid 1930s. One of them, Sidney Waterfall, lived in my village. He still had the caving ladder he used to stand on while he stripped *Dental Slab* of all its heather and grass. They must have been bold lads, because the route looks a lot harder than it is. It must have been a real step in the dark.

I'd done routes of a similar grade at Haw Bank Quarry, harder probably, but having the rope and all the gear – karabiners, nuts and so forth – made it special. I remember Arthur climbing and the rope going tight, and putting my hands on the starting holds. Rylstone is wonderful gritstone, rough and inviting, even in the terrible footwear we had then. There was a steeper section to start, and a hard pull between two horizontal breaks in the rock, then a step right onto the slab, padding up and across that to an awkward mantelshelf move above another break. There were moments when I looked up and could see little in the way of holds but I soon thought my way round the problem, pushing down and stepping up. It felt beautiful. Then I was at the top, feeling intensely pleased with myself. I felt that I'd done something life-changing. I felt that I'd found my vocation.

TWO

First Steps

I WAS IN DEEP TROUBLE. Strength in my forearms was starting to fade. My muscles felt knotted with blood and lactic acid. The fingerhold I was gripping too tightly was greasing up. It was as though the limestone could smell my sudden rush of anxiety. With my left hand I reached out again with a karabiner and attempted to force it through the narrow eye of the old aid bolt I was trying to clip. Below me the rope stretched in a clean arc for what seemed like miles to some distant nuts wedged in the crack below. They didn't look like they would hold a fall. I could feel the sweat prickling my forehead under my helmet. I fought to subdue the fear starting to creep through my chest. I had to get this bolt clipped. Falling was unthinkable. I could climb this route free, I knew it, but I hadn't anticipated the problem I now faced.

I caught sight of Graham's face, fifty feet below me. His mouth was slack and he looked gripped with fear. I don't suppose he'd anticipated the day working out this way. Graham Summers was one of our gang that met each weekend in Skipton. He was a similar age to me, with a heavy metal haircut, and lived in Leeds. I didn't know him as well as the rest of our group, but Graham was a talented climber. We'd hitched up to Malham Cove that morning in the middle of the August bank holiday weekend of 1971. The Malham Show was on, and the village was full of farmers and tourists admiring sheep. I was sixteen years old.

24

Things might have looked just as they always had in Malham, but on the crag things were changing. While I'd been at primary school, in the early 1960s, there had been a surge of interest in aid climbing, particularly on the steep limestone crags of Yorkshire, places like Malham and nearby Gordale Scar. Recently, however, there had been a shift in attitude, inspired in part by what climbers were doing in the States and in part by a resurgence in an older British ethic. The fashion now was to climb free and not rely on any aid at all. All those stunning, overhanging routes put up with pegs and bolts were being climbed afresh, this time using that equipment purely for protection. I'd been to Malham often enough to know which routes might go free. Where the treasure was. Now it was time to grab it. *Mulatto Wall* was an obvious choice for my first hard new route. The line took a faint groove up a steep blank wall on the right wing of Malham. It didn't have that much aid climbing on it and I was pretty sure I could do the moves. It was just my sort of thing. That said, it's still an intimidating climb today let alone then, and I'd not done a new route of such difficulty.

Just because a route had been climbed first with aid didn't mean the protection was always all you could wish for. Take that bolt on *Mulatto Wall*, the one I was trying to get a karabiner through. I suppose the guys who first climbed the route in 1964 must have put it in. Their surnames were Brown and White, hence the name *Mulatto Wall*. It wasn't the kind of bolt sport climbers use now. Someone had drilled a hole with what was called a star drill, hammering it again and again until he'd made a neat hole, and then bashed in a Cassin drive-in bolt, what we called a golo. The bolt was millimetres thick and barely an inch long. They were designed to take bodyweight, not for falling onto.

None of that was the problem. The size of the bolt's eye was the problem. When it was placed, people didn't use karabiners made from aluminium, they used steel ones. These were much heavier but the steel had a narrow diameter. The new aluminium krabs were fatter and wouldn't fit the archaic bolt's eye. Yet clipping it was now the only chance I had of not taking a monster fall should I fail. Once again I tried to fiddle the karabiner through the bolt so I could clip the rope and press on past the most difficult moves, which, not surprisingly, coincided with the position of the bolt.

That's what we did in those days; or at least, that's what I did: press on. I never really thought about it at the time, but I had this incredible confidence that things would work out if I could just keep going. That's what I felt on *Mulatto Wall* on that August day in 1971. If I could just get this krab through the bolt, I knew I could climb through to the end of the first pitch. I was already half-thinking about the second pitch, which carried on up the right wing, stepping right past an overhang and then up a steep corner. I could see it above my head. I just couldn't wait to get up there and finish the route.

But then, that was another feature of my climbing style that would stay with me throughout my career. Impatience. I could never settle down and concentrate on one thing at a time. I never cleaned a route properly, almost never practised moves until I had them wired. I just wanted to be on the rock, climbing, moving freely and smoothly. It seemed like I was made to cover ground as efficiently as possible. It's ironic, given the stick I took for some of my new routes over the years, but climbing from the ground up wasn't just the most ethical way of doing things for me, it was the most natural. I'd been tall even at primary school and had quickly outgrown all my friends. Now I was sixteen, my co-ordination and musculature had started to catch up with my gangly limbs. I felt more in control of myself. I wasn't whacking into ship bulkheads as I had on Brian's boat. I never got too heavy; my shoulders bulked up a little in my twenties, but even in my prime, despite being six foot three, I was never heavy, and my thighs never thickened much. My fingers, however, had grown into the proverbial bunches of bananas. I have no idea how this happened except that my Dad also had big hands.

More than any physical changes, however, was how easy being off the ground was for me. I felt at home. Even at a young age I felt comfortable at heights. Maybe that was the problem now, on *Mulatto Wall*. Despite the heat, even though I was pumping out trying to clip that stupid bolt, I didn't feel out of control or even that frightened. I belonged up here. The first section, thirty feet or so, had been loose and I'd tossed down some rock away from Graham. Then I'd got a good sling on an old tree stump at 35ft. Above this was a sheltered little corner and I got in some nuts that rattled like old bones. I felt more anxious now, looking at the steep wall above, working out a sequence on small pockets to the bolt. After a few tries at clipping it with the wrong karabiner, I went to clip it back onto my harness.

Then my handhold snapped.

In the Roadrunner cartoons, whenever Wile E. Coyote runs off the edge of a cliff, there's a pause while he turns to look at the camera. It's like he wants us to acknowledge he's doomed before he starts to fall. We know that he knows. That doesn't happen in rock climbing. You start accelerating instantly. After a second you're doing thirty miles an hour and have covered around thirty feet. This is plenty fast enough that if you hit something it will hurt. I felt the grim and unmistakeable 'pinging' sensation of protection failing under my weight as the nuts below me blew out of the crack. I wondered if I was going to stop before I hit the ground. The first thing I hit, however, was the big tree growing at the bottom of the route. Instinctively I put out my left hand and grabbed a branch. This sliced through the web between my thumb and forefinger, leaving my thumb dangling.

Powering through the branches and punching a hole in the canopy, the next thing I hit was Graham – with my head. He'd been whipped into the air by the force of my fall onto the

27

tree-stump. Luckily for me I was wearing a helmet. Unluckily for Graham, he wasn't. The force of the blow left him unconscious and he dropped the rope. We both then fell to the ground. I was winded and my hand was pumping blood. But at least I was still alive. Graham soon came round, and likely had a few sharp words to offer me. Two friends climbing nearby rushed over to help. With both of us in a sorry state, we debated what to do next. I had no money for bus fare but I needed medical attention fast.

From the direction of the village came the sound of the Malham Show, now in full swing. Even in those days, an event like that had a first-aid station, so we decided we'd go and use the facilities. Holding my hand to my chest, I followed Graham's unsteady steps to the foot of the crag and back to the village. We can't have been that badly injured though, because we had the presence of mind to sneak over the wall at the back of the fair rather than pay to get in, thus saving ourselves a few pennies. The St John's Ambulance patched us up and suggested I go straight to hospital and get my torn hand sewn. They even arranged a lift for me to hospital in Skipton. I had to wait to see the doctor who arrived in top hat and tails, interrupted on his way to some posh do. I didn't want him to take it out on me, so I got an apology in early.

'Don't worry, lad,' he said. 'I didn't want to go anyway.'

Two weeks later I was back at Malham, my hand not yet healed, banging in a solid peg near where the bolt was. Then I led the route free. Graham held my rope again. It's a classic climb, *Mulatto Wall*, even though I say so myself. And I've still got the scar.

My trip to Rylstone with Arthur Champion had been in late August 1969. It had been two years exactly since I'd stood on top of *Dental Slab*. I still lived in the same house, and I'd been going to the same lessons at school, but my life had changed for good. It was after I started climbing that my school reports started looking shaky. I'd always felt a bit out of place, but now I had something else to focus on. I was obsessed.

Arthur told me about a group of climbers meeting in Skipton each Friday evening. He'd been caving and climbing with some of them, and thought it the best way for me to carry on from that first day. The bus station gang weren't a club as such, but they knew some of Skipton's Venture Scouts and used their clubhouse, next door to the café in Skipton bus station, run by Arthur's mother. They'd doss down there for the night and then go off in the morning on the first bus to whichever crag had been agreed on. I doubt we ever drank anything stronger than tea but since we weren't officially allowed to use the place, I'd often find myself, as the skinniest in the group, climbing through the toilet window to gain access. We were always fearful of a knock on the door from the police.

There was a lad from Leeds called Mick Hillas, with ginger hair and beard. Mick liked a laugh and a pint. Paul Trower, who became better known than Mick, was from Keighley, along with his mate Phil Webb, known as the Gordale Gob because he was never short of an opinion or the urge to express it. Both of them had been aid climbing with Arthur and were responsible for several important routes, like *Yosemite Wall* at Malham.

It was autumn now, so the main focus was on aid climbing. That's what people did in those days. Climbing walls were only just in their infancy, so in the winter months we either went caving or aid climbing. The weather was usually atrocious, it was physically tough and the process of pegging up steep limestone cliffs was often alarming. People think that because you're placing pegs and hanging off gear, aid climbing must be safe but that was far from the case, certainly in the late 1960s.

About a month after I started climbing, Paul and Phil had a terrible experience in Gordale Scar after they got benighted a few feet from the top of a line called *Hangman* as the weather turned foul. Mick and I had spent the day there too, doing something easier in the snow and sleet and had left at four just as it got dark. We said we'd see them back in Skipton. Rain was hammering down by the time we reached town, and we were glad to sneak into the hut and cook some food. As evening wore on, we decided they must have stayed up at Malham after finishing late, and we crawled into our sleeping bags. Falling asleep, I was startled by the heavy exhaust note of a Land Rover right outside the hut. There was a bang on the door. We leaped out of bed, thinking it was the police and got our gear together. Then, glancing through the window I saw Paul and Phil in the back of the vehicle, wedged in among some bails of hay. I opened the hut door to the farmer from Gordale Farm.

'Do you know these two?' he asked, pointing at Paul and Phil.

'Aye,' I said.

'They've had an accident and I'm taking them to hospital. They want to talk to you.'

Paul and Phil were in a terrible state, still in their helmets and their harness, pegs hanging off their waists.

'We've just had a right epic,' Phil said. 'I've bust me legs.' Before I could say anything, he continued. 'All our gear, everything, is still on *Hangman*. Will you go and get it before it's nicked?'

This sounded like a dying man's last wish so I said we would and the farmer drove off to the hospital. Standing there in the driving sleet, Mick and I decided to catch the boozer's special, the last bus, to Malham. That took the last of my cash but a mate's a mate. Once there, we walked into Gordale and tried to find somewhere dry to doss for the night.

It was a hopeless task. The wind and sleet was howling down the gorge. It's said that the scar was scraped out by melting water from the ice sheets that once covered Britain. I could believe it that night. My sleeping bag – £3 from Woolworths – couldn't cope with this and I turned all night on the stony ground. Mick, who could sleep anywhere, snored his head off. In the grey light of morning, we could see a frayed end of rope swinging in the wind 35ft above the boulders at the start of *Hangman*. The other end was tied off 20ft from the top of the crag along with sets of etriers and pegs.

It was still a bit of mystery as to what had happened, but they told us later that they'd taken too long on the route and become benighted. Phil had led the top pitch through a series of roofs but in the bad weather and muck couldn't see where he was going and decided to belay. Later they realised they were almost there, but in the chaos of the storm, their bodies wet and freezing, they decided to abseil back to the ground. Phil went first, but the rope became hopelessly tangled and his cold hands couldn't free it. So out came his penknife and he just cut the mess away, immediately falling as he did so, and breaking both his legs on the boulders beneath. The noise of the wind drowned out his cries of pain.

Paul, who'd felt the rope go suddenly slack, concluded Phil was down safely and abseiled after him, shooting off the end of the rope without warning and breaking both his wrists. They were in a terrible state and made for the farm, Paul moving more quickly as Phil crawled down on his knees. When he reached the farm door, however, Paul couldn't use his hands to knock, so banged on it with his head.

We climbed to the top of Gordale and abseiled in to retrieve the lads' gear. I don't mind admitting I was terrified, as most fourteen-year-old boys would be. I'll never forget the weight of water pouring down Gordale that night. It seemed unreal, like a dream.

Not long after, I had a close call of my own on Kilnsey Crag's gigantic main overhang, just to the north of Gordale in Wharfedale. We loved it there, but it was awkward to hitch to and often we'd end up walking the last four miles from Grassington. It was usually dry under the roof, however, and I'll never forget my first time swinging in etriers as I hung from the stance on the *Directissima*. Paul Trower reached me and climbed through towards the roof, hauling himself on what we dubbed the 'suicide cord', the rotting slings, which graced the first section. These creaked and groaned even under Paul's meagre weight and he was glad to reach the stance.

Then we saw the last bus pass us, heading up to Kettlewell a few miles up the dale. Once there it would turn around and come back. If we weren't standing beside the road by the time it came through Kilnsey again, then we'd be walking. So I launched myself up the pitch, trying the fakir's trick of climbing rope that doesn't seem to be attached to anything solid. Once I reached Paul, we set up the abseil off some fixed pegs tied through with some ragged, ancient tat that didn't look up to much. But needs must, and so we slid nervously down the ropes, and while Paul packed the rucksacks I tried to pull them through. Our ropes were the old hawser-laid type, and horribly stiff. I just couldn't shift them. So Paul came and lent a hand. Under our combined weight the ropes suddenly gave way and we crumpled to the ground. The tat through the pegs had simply broken. We didn't have time to think about it, because the bus was coming. We were still wearing our harnesses when we stepped onboard.

Rescuing gear come what may might sound excessive but to anyone from my background who started climbing in the 1960s, there was absolutely no choice. Gear was expensive and it took a lot of bloody hard work to afford it. We weren't going to leave gear as booty for someone else. Of course, if we found abandoned gear we were cock-a-hoop. Sometimes we went out specifically to see what we could find.

As soon as I started climbing seriously, I needed a bit of gear, and that meant finding some cash. I'd always earned a few bob selling trout to Grandad or picking mushrooms, and herding cattle occasionally. Now I took on a couple of paper rounds and ran to school to save my bus fare, a couple of miles each way. That kind of thrift came naturally to me. It was an extension of my home life, which was no different to others in the village. A lot of people round us would grow their own food, and not because it was a fashionable thing to do. It never occurred to me to think otherwise. As a kid, if I wanted something, I worked for it.

Starting out, I suppose I wore plimsolls, but pretty soon I spent £3 on a second-hand pair of specialist climbing boots known as RDs, after the climber who developed them, René Desmaison, the controversial French alpinist then at the height of his powers. Those boots meant no school dinners for a long while. They had brown suede uppers and were smooth soled like modern climbing shoes, but designed for climbing long alpine rock routes. They were consequently more comfortable but also much stiffer. I could have cried – in fact, I think I did – when, having left them by the fire to dry one night, the sole of one boot melted off the upper.

Starting out in such indifferent footwear had a big impact on my climbing. Without access to modern climbing walls, it took longer to become strong. That saved me from overtraining injuries, which climbers would begin to suffer from as walls were built. More than that, a climbing wall is no place to learn footwork because the footholds are always obvious. As I learned how to climb, concentrating on where my feet were going was essential. You had to be so precise, especially on grit where inflexible soles were a real handicap. There was no choice but to figure out your next move carefully rather than stick a foot on and hope. That bred a kind of mental flexibility. It's the same with the French climbers who specialise on the sandstone boulders at Fontainebleau near Paris. They never say they can't do a boulder problem. They just say they don't understand it yet.

The rest of my gear was fairly rudimentary too, certainly in comparison to what became available in the late 1970s and early 1980s. I got a helmet after six months, which proved handy on *Mulatto Wall* but wasn't something I stuck with. I remember also having a hemp waistline into which I'd clip the climbing rope. On aid routes you'd have a chest harness and you'd tie the rope into that as well, and stand in stirrups. Fall off onto a waistline, of course, and you'd suffocate quite quickly as the rope compressed your lungs. There were no belay plates to catch a fall on either. You took the rope around the waist and wrapped it a couple of times around your arm. Hawser-laid nylon ropes, however, were stiff and slippery, and awkward to manage. Holding any kind of fall was uncomfortable and a long one would burn your flesh as the rope slid through your hands.

Equipment had improved since the 1950s, with the development of nut protection, but things hadn't changed that much. When I started, climbers were still using nuts with their thread reamed out and threaded onto nylon cord. We still call modern wired wedges 'nuts' for that reason, but the protection offered by the original variety was a lot less reliable than modern protection. We knew that if you fell off there was a good chance you'd hit the ground. Compare the equipment I was using at the start of my climbing career, and what I wore on my last new routes in the mid 1980s, and you'll appreciate how important a part improved gear played in the revolution that transformed climbing in the 1970s.

If affording equipment was difficult, then travelling was even more so. My overriding memory of those first years was always being hungry because I didn't have enough money. To begin with, I went everywhere either by bus or by hitching. Despite my height, I often managed to get on buses to Malham for half-fare and on longer trips I either stuck out my thumb or shared a ride with older friends who had a car. If the weather was bad we'd hole up in the Beck Hall Café. They were always kind to me there. I'd sit watching the rain, getting endless top-ups of hot water for my teapot. I think my record from the same bag stood at sixteen. If things got desperate then I'd put some sauce into a cup and pour hot water on that. If we had a few bob, I might have half a pint at the Buck Inn at Malham, which would take the edge off the walk to whichever barn we'd chosen for the night. We slept in Malham Cove itself if the weather was good, sheltering under the steep white bank of rock above our heads, or in the caves up on the terrace, high above the beck. I'll not forget my sleeping bag rolling off in its bag one evening as I was unpacking my rucksack and falling free for a couple of hundred feet into the water. That was a cold night.

If it was raining, and it often was because we climbed right through the winter, then we sheltered in the barn near the crag. We called it the Rat Barn for reasons I'd sooner forget. The place was crawling with them, and more than once I woke up to find one of our not-so-little furry housemates helping itself to our food. Mick would be snoring his head off as the rats ran over his sleeping bag while I tossed rocks at them to drive them away. When the rats got too bad we moved up the road to a barn near the youth hostel that was rodent free but usually full of cows. It was really two stone walls and some corrugated iron. If we were lucky, there'd be straw in it. Some of the lads would sneak into the hostel to lift any food they could lay their hands on.

Being so accessible, the crags at Malham and Gordale proved a big magnet for the bus station crowd. But Yorkshire limestone was a tough school to learn in. I became quite proficient at aid climbing, regularly doing the big routes up the centre of Malham until we could do laps on them, repeatedly climbing the same thing to get fit. When I arrived in Yosemite I found that there was less to learn about aid climbing there than I imagined. Yosemite aid climbing certainly felt safer than the big routes at Gordale, where difficult pegging and loose rock made things dicey. You could easily strip a pitch there. But it gave me an encyclopaedic knowledge of Yorkshire limestone climbing.

I did team up with Arthur again after my first day on Rylstone but he had always been more interested in caving. Oddly, it was a caving trip with Arthur that caused my parents their biggest fright, and not climbing with my new and riskier friends from the bus station. Arthur invited me on the Gaping Gill meet, still run by the Craven Pothole Club, that winches members of the public into a cavern bigger than St Paul's Cathedral. It's 365ft from the top to the bottom and you descend through a waterfall lit by the slanting light in a strange, Heath Robinson contraption reached by a gangplank to where it dangles over the abyss. At the bottom of the cavern was a sea of lights, as the assembled cavers dispersed down different passages. Arthur taught me how to light my carbide lamp, which seemed impossible to get right to me, and then led the way into the dark. We spent a long day squeezing, crawling and shuffling along on our knees through all kinds of formations. I remember particularly the Sand Cavern where some lad had set the world record for living underground, and then going on to Bar Pot and an impressive series of pitches where hordes of cavers were abseiling further into the system.

At the end of the day, after twelve hours underground, we made it back to the main cavern, which was now dark. Night had fallen. I was slowly winched back up, the cold water pummelling my wet body as I slowly froze, to discover it was 11pm. Arthur was planning on staying at the cave for the whole weekend to push some exploration being done at that time. I had no lift back. I was going to be in big trouble.

It was fifteen miles from Gaping Gill across the moors to Skipton along a route I didn't know that well. I managed to find my way across the fells to Trow Ghyll, an eerie place of trees overhanging a sombre gorge, which was far more frightening than being lowered into Gaping Gill. I managed, through a piece of amazing luck, to hitch a ride with a farmer for the rest, but it was still the early hours when I walked up the lane from Skipton to Embsay. There was only one thought in my head all the way home: I'm going to be in deep trouble. I must have been barely fifteen at the time, so I can't blame my parents for being worried.

I turned on my carbide lamp to see more clearly – the road was still lit with gaslights in those days – and saw a figure coming towards me. Someone just as daft as me, I thought. It was Mum walking down the lane to meet me. She was worried sick.

Climbing was bad enough, but going underground was even worse. It was only a few years after the Mossdale Cave disaster, when six lads from a group of ten were drowned after a sudden sharp thunderstorm flooded the passage they were exploring. It was the worst loss of life in British caving history. Hundreds of men worked for eighteen hours to rescue the missing cavers, and hopes were high they'd be found alive before the bodies were found. Mossdale Cave was sealed off and even now those involved find it difficult to talk about what happened. It left an impression among the public for years afterwards that caving was for madmen. Predictably, Dad went absolutely berserk. I spent a lot of time in my bedroom after that.

Caving and aid climbing, the two main activities that first winter, never interested me that much. I soon became focussed on free climbing. I remember early trips to the left wing of Gordale, which was full of desperate VSs and HVSs. I remember soloing an HVS called *Riddler*, just to finish off the day, when a hold snapped at the top and the route nearly finished me off instead. I hit the steep slope at the bottom and slid over a smaller crag to land near some tourists enjoying a picnic. I'd cracked an ankle, and was covered in cuts and bruises, but I managed a smile. They gave me a sandwich, which was nice. When I got home I told Mum I'd fallen off the bus, and she chose to believe me.

When I started climbing at Malham, the routes I aspired to were the more recent, largely free routes, like *Carnage*, put up by the Barley brothers, Tony and Robin, who lived over near Brimham Rocks, where I'd see them quite regularly. Eventually, I'd free *Carnage* of its aid point, but even then I wanted to do as much free as I possibly could. After our *Mulatto Wall* adventure,

I went back to Malham with Graham Summers to try to free climb the soaring overhanging flake of *Yosemite Wall*. It was crazy really, especially as the gear was so bad. I eventually did it in the early 1980s at around E5.

Once I had a good bank of Yorkshire climbing experience behind me, I was keen to join the bus station gang on a trip to the Lake District. More often than not at school I had my nose in a guidebook or Joe Brown's autobiography *The Hard Years* so I had a list of routes I wanted to do up there. I hitched up the A65 with Paul, and finally reached the Salutation Hotel in Ambleside, full of bearded men in jeans and tartan shirts knocking back pints of beer. I dumped my rucksack on the pile, and joined the crowd. That night, like so many that followed, was spent in the open shelter in Waterhead Park where you vied for space with the occasional tramp down by Lake Windermere. More than one lad got tossed into the water still inside his sleeping bag after a heavy night in the pub.

In the morning we walked back into the village for breakfast at Mrs Dunlop's café. She was a formidable woman, Ma Dunlop, who served nothing but greasy breakfasts and wielded an enormous teapot. No one was allowed to touch it. I'll never forget sneaking over when she was out of the room to fill my cup just as she walked back in. I got a clout round the back of my head for my trouble and never did it again.

That first morning it was pissing down with rain, and because I'd heard that Castle Rock stayed dry in the wet thanks to its steep angle, Mick Hillas and I hitched round there to have a look. We reckoned that a Malham Very Severe was worth a Lake District Extremely Severe, and we weren't going to mess around working our way up through the grades. So we settled on *The Ghost*. Now E3, in those days it was graded simply XS and had a fearsome reputation. The weekend before Chris Bonington had pulled a flake off the crux and made it even harder. 'Probably impossible,' was Bonington's verdict.

Of course, I didn't know this until an older lad shouted across to me with the news. This was Al Evans, who'd come to Castle Rock with Dave Parker, although with more sense they were on *Overhanging Bastion*, which really did stay dry in the rain. Al comes from Sheffield but was studying photography in Morecambe at the time – he went on to work in television news and on *Coronation Street* – so the Lakes' crags were his local area. He was an ebullient character, full of jokes, and good company.

'It'll be alright,' I called back, thinking anything but. The first pitch had been okay, even in the wet, but at the stance I faced a big, looming wall. Leading off, I felt scared but got in a couple of good runners before making a nasty, rightwards traverse onto some good holds that deposited me onto a ramp that was running with water. My rack of equipment was so antiquated and meagre that I didn't have anything to protect the next moves. All I could find was a thin piece of cord draped over a small blunt spike, and with the confidence it gave me, I launched myself, feet skidding, up the hard moves.

At school the following week, I told Mr Spenceley after our geography lesson that I'd done *The Ghost* the weekend before. He was polite enough to sound impressed, even though I imagine he didn't know anything about it. Al, on the other hand, knew exactly how hard the route was, especially in those conditions, and invited me to drive down with him to the Peak District the following weekend to climb at Stoney Middleton. I was excited, but also nervous. These days Stoney has rather fallen from fashion, but in the early 1970s it had some of the hardest routes in the country, many of them the work of Tom Proctor. Tom pretty much owned Stoney. We had similar backgrounds too, growing up in farming communities on the rural fringes of big towns, Tom outside Chesterfield in the Derbyshire village of Holymoorside. Like everybody else, when I got to know him, I found Tom to be a great bloke, modest and easy-going, but immensely strong from training his fingers with sprung steel wrist exercisers. From a distance, he looked formidable.

Like all teenagers with an obsession, I pored over any published material I could find about rock climbing. That was more limited in the early 1970s, but I could still get a sense of what was happening around the country, particularly in *Mountain* magazine. The free climbing revolution that dominated the mid 1970s was just beginning and standards were starting to climb. To a fifteen-year-old climber, the people featured in magazines seemed like gods, and their exploits beyond the reach of someone like me. When we arrived at Stoney I felt reluctant to get straight onto Tom's routes. So Al led me up a route called *Boat Pusher's Wall*, done by another of my heroes, Jack Street, in the mid 1960s. Like *The Ghost*, it's a route that's now graded E3. When I found it easy, Al decided I was being too respectful and needed pushing a little. He took me up onto Windy Ledge and showed me *Our Father*. Proctor had graded this HVS when he climbed it in 1968, but it's now a tough E4 with a boulder problem roof to start. It got its name from Tom's second Geoff Birtles reciting the Lord's Prayer as Proctor muscled his way boldly up the steep leaning groove in a wildly exposed position. Al had watched the first ascent done, and the second as well, the only two ascents *Our Father* had had at that point. Some climbers, many of them from the Peak District, regarded it as the hardest route in the country. To be honest, I thought *Wall of Horrors* at Almscliff was harder, but then, I am a Yorkshireman.

Al told me afterwards he'd contacted the influential editor of *Mountain* magazine, Ken Wilson, that night to tell him he had just seen the future of British climbing. Wilson wasn't impressed. 'I've seen them come, Al,' he said, 'and I've seen them go.'

Within a couple of years my circle of climbing friends had grown beyond the bus station gang. Brian Swales, who had guided my school walking trips, was the focus of another local group who styled themselves the Sadcocs – Skipton and District

Climbing or Caving Society. Terry Birks is still a friend from those days. Pete Gomersall was also associated with this group, and later on so were his friends Joe Healey and Phil Davidson from Liverpool. Both of them were tremendous climbers, Phil making the first solo of *Right Wall* on Dinas Cromlech. After I left school, I'd hitch down to Pex Hill in Cheshire, to meet them at their local crag, and climb until my fingers ached. I loved Pex and found it great training and really technical, rather like my bridges at home. In the age before bouldering mats, it was serious too. You could easily snap an ankle. But it was somewhere I could reach with my thumb if no one was around to offer me a lift.

I remember an early trip to Gogarth that was also typical. I must have been fifteen or just sixteen. I hitched down with Phil Webb and we slept at South Stack in an old concrete bunker – an air-raid shelter I suppose – that was damp and cold. The weather was grim, not raining too hard, but blowing like we were off Cape Horn. In those days, the café at South Stack was a charitable place, so we took shelter there and they gave us regular top-ups of hot water for our pot of tea. While we were idling through the day, Al Evans and Dave Parker, as arranged, walked through the door, having hitched down from Blackpool. They looked exhausted. 'Do you have any nosh, lads?' Al asked.

We took them back to our air-raid shelter and stoked up the fire we'd lit to keep warm. I had several pounds of oats I'd brought from home, which I hoped would last me for the week. Al called it muesli, but it was the kind of stuff you'd give to horses. We'd also been collecting limpets off the rocks down by the sea, but they were buggers to cook and remained chewy however long we left them over the fire. Compared to the mushrooms and trout I could find at home, eating at the seaside was an unknown proposition.

As a student, Al got a grant, and so had a few shillings in his pocket. Clearly taking pity on us, he took us into Holyhead for some fish and chips and then we headed to the pub. That was another feature of climbing in the early 1970s and no doubt had been for several decades. Everybody drank and everybody smoked. Except for me, that is. I wasn't bothered. It seemed like a fast way to piss away whatever money I could scrape together. Why waste money on beer when I could be climbing? Later, after I married, I'd have the odd cigar but that's about as far as it went when it came to intoxicants. Which was good news for Al and Dave, because after they'd drunk all their cash, I had my five shillings for the week's food left. 'Don't worry lads,' I said, 'we'll be alright.' Next day, the weather eased a bit and I went down to Gogarth's Red Walls, a crag I never liked much because of its loose rock.

Al was a great catalyst for exploration. He did plenty of his own new routes, but if he found something he wasn't sure he could manage, he'd draft in someone to lend a hand. I benefited myself from his largesse, after he discovered the potential of Chapel Head Scar, a superb, overhanging limestone crag unlike anything in Yorkshire, near his student digs at the southern end of the Lake District. Chapel Head had tufas and pockets, quite different from the edges and pinches at Malham. We did a fantastic new route there, discovered by Al, called *Moonchild*, which has gradually crept up the grades over the years.

Being a photography student, Al was keen to take a lot of pictures of me climbing during those early years. He took a shot of me on one of my earliest new routes at Crookrise, near my home in Embsay, which I must have done when I was eighteen or so, a short but fiercely technical problem called *Small Brown* that still gets a grade of 6b. It was a Joe Brown climb, but he'd used some tension from the side low down to get past the crux. Thin gritstone problems like that were a real handful in EBs. Al's photographs meant I started appearing in climbing magazines myself, initially for the new routes I was doing in Yorkshire like *Small Brown*. The first edition of *Crags* even had a free poster that featured me in a picture of Al's climbing *L'Horla* at Curbar in the Peak District.

Yorkshire was my daily bread in those days, despite my urge to travel. I was still at school and had almost no money, so I made the most of what I had. I fell into a pattern of going on the limestone at the weekend with the bus station lads, and climbing on the gritstone after school on my own, doing long circuits at my local crags. If it was raining, then I walked down to the railway bridges in front of Haw Bank Quarry, to traverse their vertical limestone blocks back and forth, often for hours. You can still make out my rubber boot marks under the cobwebs and dust of forty years. When I started I could hardly do a move, but gradually I pieced together sequences and then a whole 30ft traverse, the width of the bridge. Eventually I could do twenty-four repetitions. Not much homework got done. But if my teachers had seen how disciplined I was they wouldn't have said I couldn't focus. Using the railway arches was all about finding something convenient that I could use everyday to train my finger strength. And my inspiration for that came from the Leeds University climbing wall.

Don Robinson, a lecturer in physical education at Leeds, had built what is widely recognised as the world's first climbing wall in 1964 in the sports centre corridor, but for reasons I've never been able to fathom, it wasn't used much until a few years later. I guess it was just ahead of its time. And many climbers still regarded rock climbing as simply preparation for mountaineering. Why would you train for it? But then a group of young rock climbers appeared on the scene who fully understood the uses of Robinson's idea and began meeting there regularly. Leeds was too far for me to reach easily, which was why I found something similar close at hand. But I was in awe of the regulars, who were only a few years older than me but seemed grown up and worldly.

John Syrett was one of them, a bold and talented climber,

whose dedication to the Leeds wall had accelerated his ability. Al Manson and Pete Kitson were also inspirational. Al was technically one of the best climbers I've ever seen. Pete was more down to earth than Al and John, who were cerebral characters, and so more approachable. I learned a lot from those lads, watching them at Almscliff, one of their favourite crags, overlooking Lower Wharfedale. In those days, they'd be there almost every day, working out new routes or new problems of fiendish difficulty. I could soon solo *Wall of Horrors* or *Western Front*, and did the second ascent of Pete Livesey's *All Quiet*, but then I'd get on one of Al's problems and not be able to touch it.

Syrett's repeat of Allan Austin's climb *Wall of Horrors*, the most famous route at Almscliff, had galvanised rock climbing in the early 1970s. Austin had been an icon in Yorkshire rock climbing and here was a young kid boldly despatching his most famous route. Syrett hadn't been climbing a year. Despite this, John was gentle and modest about his own routes. He gave his new route *Propeller Wall* at Ilkley the grade of VS, below the top Yorkshire grade of HVS. It's E5 now.

Pete Livesey was another character coming to the fore and benefiting from this new interest in training. Pete would have a deep impact on both my life and my climbing, and while he wasn't a regular at the Leeds wall, he saw what was going on there, and as a talented fell runner knew the value of training. He'd climbed since the early 1960s, but it wasn't until his probationary year as a teacher spent marooned in Scunthorpe that he started training for climbing. Then in 1971, the year I did *Mulatto Wall*, he did some free ascents that rivalled Syrett's Almscliff coup, in particular a climb called *Face Route* at Gordale. And while the lads using the Leeds wall were most interested in technical difficulty, at first anyway, Pete was looking for stamina.

That was my plan, training every day on the bridges outside Embsay. I had no sense that climbing would lead me anywhere.

There was no career or money to be had from it. I knew I was good at it. Not in the sense that I thought I was better than everyone else, more that it felt right to be doing it. I was at home. Having discovered the thing that motivated me, school inevitably became a waste of time. My grades dropped off and while I did finish with a few qualifications, I didn't have enough to continue my education. I didn't want to either. I'd found a way to experience the world, as Bryan was doing, travelling round the country discovering new crags.

Mum must have wondered how I was going to make a living, but despite the broken bones, I can only hope she didn't disapprove too much of my climbing. I never thought about it at the time. What sixteen-year-old does? But looking back I can appreciate she was desperately worried. I suppose she was right to be.

During my last term at Aireville, I'd arranged to go climbing with an older friend called John Allott. It was the day of my geography 'O' Level, and so I said I'd catch the bus as soon as the exam finished in the late morning and meet him at Gordale. I handed in my exam paper, picked up my rucksack and caught the bus to Malham. When I got to near the entrance of the gorge, just above the village, I saw Brian Swales waiting for me. I was surprised to see him. 'You can't go up there, Ron,' was the first thing he said, and he put his arm round my shoulder. John had decided to spend the time before I arrived soloing the formidable aid climb *Cave Route*. He'd attached a prussik loop to protect himself on the rope as he climbed up. When he fell, however, the knot slipped and burned through the thin cord. John fell. No one blamed me, but at the funeral I felt guilty, for not being there to hold his rope. Small wonder my mother was keen to see my enthusiasm properly channelled.

Towards the end of that early period, hanging out at weekends at the Venture Scout hut in Skipton, I got to know another climber who would become my most regular partner through the 1970s. Chris Gibb was a little older than me, and already married with a young daughter. He worked as a television engineer for Slater's, the rental company, and consequently had a van for work, a Ford Escort, which he adored. He had a narrow face and a full, straggly beard, and was always smiling, a cheerful, snaggle-toothed grin. Gibby loved socialising and had no hesitation in chatting to anyone, quite the opposite of me. He was like a social bulldozer, and I followed in his wake. Being so outgoing, he'd come to know most of the top climbers in the north of England, people in the north Lakes like Pete Whillance, Dave Armstrong and Rob Matheson who were at the front of a resurgence in standards there.

Originally from Lancashire, Gibby was big mates with climbers there too, people like Ian Hayes and Jack Firth, which is how I came to know them, and other Lancashire climbers like Jerry Peel and his climbing partner Barry Rawlinson, both of whom I had tremendous respect for. Thanks to Gibby, I felt at home in lots of different climbing scenes. Even better, Gibby was very keen and hugely strong but more than happy to follow rather than lead. It's too easy just to look at training schedules or body shape or personality when analysing why someone is a great climber. Sometimes it also comes down to who is tied in to the other end of the rope.

THREE

Yosemite Ron

It was 11pm. Another shift was over. I rinsed out the sink, dried my hands and put the tea towel on the rack. I've had some dull jobs in my time, but washing up in a hotel in Skipton had its compensations. For a start, there was always food left over from the restaurant, which supplemented my diet. I even got food for weekend climbing trips. But the main thing was I had a few more quid under the mattress and my dream of going to Yosemite in California was that bit closer to becoming reality. Flying anywhere in the early 1970s was an expensive business. A flight to San Francisco cost around £200 in an era when the average weekly wage was £32. And I wasn't getting that much washing pots.

Leaving Aireville, I had no real idea of what I wanted to do with my life, other than go climbing. I'd had the usual desultory meeting with the school careers officer. He wasn't that interested and I wasn't that bothered, but because I loved being outside I told him I fancied working as a builder. If it was good enough for Joe Brown, it was good enough for me. He told me I was too bright to work as a builder, but if I wanted to be in the trade then he could find me something working in a builder's office. My parents were keen I settled down to something steady so I decided to give it a try. I have never been so bored in my life, before or since. After four days I'd had enough and walked out. The thought of spending the next forty-odd years doing something

47

like that made me feel ill. Still, I could hardly remain a burden to my parents, not bringing in any money.

I spent the next year working casually, starting as a labourer for a building firm in Grassington, ten miles away. I worked as a plasterer's mate, and since the plasterer was 65, it was usually easy work on farmhouses across the Dales. The hard part was hitching to Grassington each morning. Then, disaster struck. Gathering up some loose scraps of felt on a flat roof one day, I stepped through a skylight that had been accidentally felted over and shot through into the room below, breaking a couple of ribs and my collar bone and cracking my skull. It took me a couple of months to recover and then I started at the cotton mill in Embsay. Finished cloth came off the looms and was inspected and put into lengths. My job was managing the machine that did this, which was pretty dull but the machine wasn't so noisy that you couldn't talk while you worked, and since everybody who worked there came from close by, we all knew each other. The lad who worked the other shift to me hated getting up in the morning, so I worked exclusively from six until two. Getting up so early every day was a shock at first, but it left the afternoons free to climb. They were always looking for people, so I could jack the job in to go climbing for a month and then come back. Dad never said as much, but he thought me a bit of a wrong 'un for doing that. He wanted me to get something steady.

I also worked in a bath factory in Addingham. Brian Swales was chief engineer there and got me the job. I worked alongside Pete Gomersall on the production line. Baths would come off the machine having been pressed into shape. The first bloke would drill the plughole; the next would drill holes for the taps. Gommy and I were so competitive that without discussing it we became the fastest hole-drillers the factory had ever seen. We got so quick, we ended up doing twice as many holes as anyone else, earning ourselves the unqualified hatred of all the other workers.

It was winter when I started at the bath factory, which was also the best time to be going down caves. Gommy wasn't just a great climber, he was a very neat caver too. I remember doing Langcliffe with him, a notoriously gnarly trip, and at the time many of its vertical pitches hadn't been climbed. Cavers relied on ladders to get up and down these sections but because there were only two of us, carrying all the gear required wasn't possible, so we decided to climb these pitches instead. It was terrifying, picking our way up damp, greasy limestone in the dark.

To my parents, work kept you from the shame of reliance on the state and a descent into abject poverty. To me, work was just a way to go climbing. Still, with few qualifications I didn't have many other options. It's not like I could go to college, which would have been the ideal way to keep climbing as much as possible and make things easier on my parents. So when a climbing friend called John 'Doc' Hammond suggested I go back into education at the school where he was teaching – Greenhead Grammar in Keighley – to retake some exams, I thought about it seriously. If I passed, then I could apply for college and get a grant for the next few years. John had also introduced me to one of his climbing partners, Pete Livesey, who was at teacher training college and making the most of the long holidays. Doc and Pete enjoyed more security than me and still had time to go climbing. I told my parents I'd be going back to school.

With my future more settled, or at least postponed, I was free to concentrate on what interested me most – climbing. With routes like *Mulatto Wall* and *Our Father* under my belt, I felt confident about taking on greater challenges. Inspired by photographs I'd seen in *Mountain* magazine, Gibby and I decided to go to Yosemite to explore the Californian free climbing revolution that was getting underway. No climbers we knew had been there. According to *Mountain* magazine, the future Everest mountaineer Doug Scott had aided some big walls there, and the

Scottish climber Rab Carrington was rumoured to have done some free climbing there on his way back from an expedition to South America. But where in California Yosemite was we barely knew, let alone what we'd climb when we got there. There were no guidebooks, or the Internet, but it seemed like the perfect adventure. If my brother Bryan could sail off to Africa, why shouldn't I fly to California and go climbing? I don't think I was particularly mature for my age. It just seemed like a good idea.

Everything about America was mind-boggling. I was a shy, gawky teenager who'd grown up in a small Dales village, and now I was in Los Angeles, watching the biggest cars I'd ever seen easing along the freeways under a Californian sun. I had the sense that anything could happen. There were beautiful women everywhere I looked, tanned and smiling. I found myself falling in love every three minutes.

Mostly, it was hot. It was the middle of summer, perhaps not the ideal time for your first trip to the Valley, as it was called, but I'd had to finish my exams at Greenhead first. And this was real heat, never experienced in Yorkshire. These days, climbers visit Yosemite in late spring or early autumn, but in those days most climbers were still aid climbing, and any free climbers were doing 5.10s and easy 5.11s, not grades where the temperature was critical. It was in California I discovered my inner sun-worshipper.

'Come on,' said Gibby. 'Let's go to the pub.'

The plan was to catch a bus to the fringes of L.A. and then start hitching, but we both figured it would be easier after a beer. Gibby walked into the first bar we came across and approached the bar.

'I'll have a beer please,' he told the barman. There was a pause while the guy stared at Gibby, trying to figure out how old the bloke with the big sideburns might be.

'I.D?'

'Aye, lad, I'll have a pint of I.D.'

An hour or so later we hit the road. Even in the early 1970s, hitching in California was a scary business. I remember sleeping by a railroad, listening to the train horns all night as wagons full of peaches rolled slowly past. In the shadows, dodgy L.A. types you wouldn't find in Skipton lurked around us. I didn't sleep much, and kept a hand on my wallet; it held all our money for the trip.

Reaching Camp IV, Yosemite's infamous dirt-bag campground, felt like reaching the Promised Land. No climber, however experienced, can come here for the first time and not be changed by it. I'd never seen so much rock. I was blown away by what I was seeing but at the same time couldn't wait to get started. Although at first, the climbing felt a little alien. Having been heavily glaciated and baked in the sun, Yosemite's granite is highly polished and I needed to adjust. Footholds were often negligible, and I had to learn to relax and trust my feet. Luckily, having grown up climbing cracks on gritstone, I soon came to terms with jamming on granite.

Gibby and I didn't do anything startling that first trip. To be honest the climbing wasn't unduly strenuous. There was nothing too steep, with most free routes being vertical or just off vertical. It was more sustained than bold, with lots of cracks to take our trusty Moac nuts or Clog wires. We were just in love with the whole scene. Everything and everybody was larger than life.

In 1973, Jim Bridwell was the bandit king of Yosemite climbing. 'Bird', as he was known, held court on the section of Camp IV reserved for volunteers on the Yosemite Search and Rescue Team, living in a kind of party tent, the focus for the freaks, hippies and adventurers that made climbing there so memorable. In his bandanna and waistcoat, and a Camel cigarette dangling from his lips, he looked every inch the counter-culture hero, which is pretty much what he was – Billy-the-Kid in rock shoes.

The court that gathered around Bridwell ebbed and flowed over the years, but a key member was John 'Largo' Long, the larger-than-life muscle man whose climbing stories have made him a best-selling author. John was a brilliant bloke, full of humour and very friendly to me. This was one of the best things about going to California at such a young age. In Yorkshire I'd felt people thought I was a bit strange, even allowing for how shy I was. Here I felt I could relax and be accepted. John played a big part in that.

The group of climbers that hung out with Bridwell – John Long, John Bachar, John Yablonsky, Tobin Sorenson and their like – dubbed themselves the Stonemasters. Long and Bachar were heavily into training, and Bachar developed an outdoor training facility he called Gunsmoke, doing sets on a rope ladder with plastic rungs eventually dubbed a Bachar ladder. Those boys loved working out, even if they didn't much care for working. Climbing was their job, and they took it very seriously.

One evening round the campfire, Long, sitting next to his extravagantly beautiful girlfriend, confided in Gibby and me. 'I don't like to share a tent with a woman before a big climb. I need to focus on my health. I need the air to be fresh, not stale. I can't breathe someone else's air.'

'I tell you what,' said Gibby, who was a bit pissed, 'I'll step in if you like.'

The Stonemasters had made several other modifications to the campsite to suit their needs. They'd brought in a swaging machine so they could make their own wired nuts. They'd also managed to run a cable from the lights in the Camp IV toilet block to the boom box in Bird's tent, so party nights had a soundtrack. I can't pretend that large amounts of exotic chemicals weren't taken, although not by me.

I was always quite reticent to get involved in anything that I didn't understand. It's in my nature to study things first to see how they work. I'm cautious like that. Some of the characters in that scene were wild, and the drugs didn't help. They'd be off their faces for days. Years later, I was persuaded by one of the Stonemasters to do a couple of lines of coke at his house in Los Angeles, but it didn't go well. I was awake for two days straight and was then wrecked for the rest of the week, not capable of climbing. I thought: 'Bugger this!' And never did it again.

Where I really profited from their experience, however, was in the fine art of scamming. The Stonemasters might have worked hard at climbing, but it didn't pay the bills, at least, not then. People would dine out on the legends of those days, but that happened later. In the meantime, we all had to eat, preferably for free. In her autobiography, Lynn Hill says she managed to survive the several months of her first trip to Yosemite on $75. The three months I stayed during my first visit in 1973 cost me a little more than that, but not much.

First off was camping for free. To be honest, I hadn't fully prepared for the complications of camping in Yosemite. It's not like we didn't know about the bears. How could we not? There were signs everywhere warning us to lock up our food in heavy, padlocked bear-proof containers dubbed 'coffins'. But while Gibby had brought a small tent to sleep in at night, I didn't have anything. I just rolled out a sleeping mat on the pine needles and dirt at night and crawled into my sleeping bag.

In the trees behind the campsite were old tins with bear-tooth puncture wounds and shredded rucksacks that had once held food or just something that smelled nice. The bears would eat anything, from soap to shaving foam. Not that either of these commodities were much in evidence at Camp IV. The idea of bears is quite exciting, and I must confess to a bit of a thrill at having to lock up our food to stop it being eaten. But lying in the dark in the middle of the night and sensing big, furry shapes snuffling past my bed left my heart fluttering a little.

To escape campsite fees, if not the attention of bears, I volunteered for the rescue team with the National Park Authorities, which offered climbers free lodging in return for future services rendered. Since there were very few rescues at that time, I never had to get involved. Then there was the tradition of 'scarfing' at the cafeteria in Yosemite Village, falling on half-consumed meals abandoned by tourists who couldn't clear their plates.

If you spent a bit of time chatting up the girls behind the counter there was a bonus to this scam. You'd hand over a dollar for a .25¢ cup of coffee, and whoever served you would hand back four quarters. You'd then take several packets of crackers given out free at the condiments desk and settle in to wait. Bus loads of tourists were best, because the driver would tell his passengers he was about to leave before they'd finished, forcing them to abandon half their lunch. That's when we moved in. For a shy lad like me who blushed at the chat-up game, this took some nerve, but needs must.

It didn't always go well. On a later visit, when Yosemite had become popular with Brits, John Syrett and I walked into the cafeteria at breakfast to see a half-eaten breakfast and a folded newspaper abandoned on one of the tables. John slid into the seat and picked up the paper while the pair of us got to work on the bacon and eggs. Not being absorbed in reading, I noticed the bloke whose food it was first. He was standing over us, looking cross.

'John,' I said.

'Hang on, Ron, I'm reading.'

'JOHN!'

It was a bit embarrassing, as we explained to the police who came to arrest us. Luckily they let us go with just a warning. We were more careful after that.

For cash, I joined in the classic Yosemite wealth-creation scheme of recycling soda cans for a penny a go. Trouble was, all of us were at it, so there was fierce competition for the right sort of soda cans, those bought in the correct jurisdiction with an unmistakeable purple stamp on them. Those cans without the stamp, brought in by visiting tourists, weren't worth anything and were discarded by the can-hunters. The following year, on my second visit, Jill Lawrence arrived with Pete Livesey, bringing with her some eye shadow that turned out to be an exact match for the ink used to mark the cans. It didn't take us long to counterfeit a stamp and start our own production line, converting the worthless cans into one-cent winners. We cleaned up, in more ways than one.

We didn't do anything remarkable together on that first trip and Gibby, having a job and a family, headed home after a couple of weeks. I had no reason to rush back. I was waiting on my exam results to see if I'd done enough to get into college. Meanwhile the Stonemasters could use a Brit who seemed to know what he was about, so I found myself sharing some of their adventures, like the *Central Pillar of Frenzy*, a classic 5.9 on the Middle Cathedral.

My next outing with John Long was altogether more ambitious: the *Nose* of El Capitan, 3,000ft and over 30 pitches long. What's more, he wanted to see just how fast we could climb it. When the *Nose* was first climbed in 1958, Warren Harding, Wayne Merry and George Whitmore took 47 days. Two years later Royal Robbins, Joe Fitschen, Chuck Pratt and Tom Frost cut that to seven days, mostly by climbing in a continuous push and dispensing with the siege tactics Harding and his partners used. Times had continued to come down, but no one had managed to climb the route in a day.

The first guy to contemplate doing so was a climber called Frank Sacherer, who had been responsible for lots of free ascents in the Valley in the 1960s. Sacherer was a physicist working on particle accelerators who ended up working at CERN in Switzerland in the late 1960s and 1970s. It says a lot about Sacherer's reputation at the time that when he suggested the idea of climbing the *Nose* in a day, nobody laughed, because if most other climbers had suggested the idea, Camp IV regulars wouldn't have taken them seriously.

Sacherer and Bird discussed the route and in 1965 did a reconnaissance of the lower section of Stoveleg Cracks – named because sawn up stove legs were used to aid them on the first ascent – to see if they'd go free. Sacherer believed that if you could climb this section fast, then a single-day ascent might be possible. According to Bird, Frank hated sleeping on big walls and liked the idea of avoiding a bivouac on the *Nose*. After Sacherer left for Switzerland, Bird freed the Stovelegs and then moved on to other things.

I'm not quite sure why John asked me to do the *Nose* with him. I'd been doing a lot of climbing and was in great shape, but I'd never done a pendulum in my life. In retrospect, I felt he wanted to weigh up the likelihood of climbing the route in a day and took the Limey along because he had no intention of pre-empting Bird's stake in what would be a momentous achievement. We took a 200ft 9mm rope to climb on, another older bit of rubbish for the pendulums and a third line to haul the bag. We didn't take a hammer but did take pegs, kingpins we could just slot in with our fingers into the old peg scars.

We started at first light and just went for it. The Stoveleg Cracks aren't that hard, but we did a lot of free climbing on the route, up to 5.10 and some 5.11. But the basic point was speed, so when we started to slow down we'd just start pulling on the gear. Henry Barber had recently done the *Nose* and freed more sections of it, including the Pancake Flake just above the huge feature known as the Great Roof – the twenty-third pitch. This had really cheesed off the locals, because Henry wasn't very popular in the Valley at the time. Henry wasn't much older than me, and swung between being too quiet and too brash. When he did the first ascent of *Butterballs* in 1973, a really awkward finger crack that's now graded 5.11c, things got worse. An East Coast kid had done arguably the hardest free route in the Valley. The locals were, as they say in America, pissed. So when John and I appeared to be making fast progress, friends came onto

TOP Dad with the milk wagons at Uncle Jeff's farm in Embsay. MIDDLE LEFT Mum and Dad at Bridlington, with Flamborough Head in the distance. MIDDLE RIGHT Grandad and Grandma Bate in their garden in Embsay. BOTTOM Alison, Richard, Clifford and me, with Dad in the doorway, at the static caravan at Flamborough.

TOP LEFT Making the first ascent of *Small Brown* (E4 6b) at my then local crag Crookrise. TOP RIGHT My first roped climbing experience, following Arthur Champion up *Dental Slab* (Severe) at Rylstone. MIDDLE RIGHT Me and Gibby – young guns – at Brimham Rocks. BOTTOM Gill, with Bill the dog, walking in to the spectacular Malham Cove in the Yorkshire Dales. OPPOSITE The first ascent of *Moonchild* (E4 5c) at Chapel Head Scar. OVERLEAF The east face of Washington Column in Yosemite, with me leading at around the halfway point on *Astroman* (5.11c). The 'Harding Slot' is just right of centre, in the top half of the page. Neither Pete nor I particularly wanted to lead this pitch due to its reputation, and the way we were swinging leads it should really have been my pitch. Instead, I ran the two pitches below it together so it fell on Pete's lead. He wasn't very happy when he realised!

OPPOSITE High on *Pichenibule* (F7c) in the Verdon Gorge. TOP Yosemite Valley. El Cap towers above the valley floor on the right. MIDDLE RIGHT The big guns! Me with Jerry Peel in the Verdon. BOTTOM RIGHT Me and Gibby, a little older and hairier, in the La Palud campsite in Verdon. BOTTOM LEFT Just as I remember him – the late, great Pete Livesey. He always had that manic grin; you never knew when he was being serious, or planning his next prank. OVERLEAF Gill following the top pitch of *Chrysalis* (F7b) in the Verdon Gorge.

the meadow under El Capitan to cheer us on.

It was a real pleasure climbing with Largo. We couldn't have been more different in shape. I was tall and compact, with thin legs. John was beefy, with muscular arms and a broad, heavy frame. But his footwork was immaculate – delicate and precise. He didn't just rely on power to get him through hard climbing; he relied on excellent technique. I envied him his outgoing nature, the way people warmed to him because he loved to entertain. He'd do things like write poems and then read them to climbers hanging out in the parking lot at Camp IV. Still, he had a temper. We did the south face of Washington Column together, now an entry-level big wall around eleven hundred feet long that goes mostly free at 5.10, but in those days a route like that would take up to three days. As we set off up it, some human shit landed near us. Looking up, we could see two guys near the top of the route laughing and shouting at us, clearly amused by their direct hit. John clearly wasn't amused. Later that day I arrived at a stance near the top of the route to find one of the climbers belaying his mate. He turned white. 'I think you'd better come down!' he shouted. His mate seemed annoyed. 'What for?' The belayer could see Largo steaming up the pitch I'd just led. 'I really think you should come down!' By now the leader had figured out what was happening. Looking as contrite as he could manage, he encountered Largo at the height of his wrath.

At Boot Flake, the top of the sixteenth pitch of the *Nose*, we had to lower down and then make a giant pendulum swing left on the rope into a new crack system. Climbers call it the King Swing. Sorting out the ropes can get complicated doing that kind of manoeuvre. I suppose I was a little nervous too, anxious not to slow John down. But in trying to speed up I dropped the third rope, the one we were using to haul the bag when the climbing was too hard to carry it. It wasn't tied into anything and I just let it go. Watching it whipping down the cliff, I thought, 'Oh shit.

I've dropped it.' I was so worried about what John would say I thought I'd not mention it. Maybe he hadn't noticed? Nothing was said but John must have known. He just carried on regardless.

By mid afternoon we'd passed the Great Roof, freed the Pancake Flakes and climbed a few more pitches. We were moving fast. But when we reached Camp VI, John called a halt. I still wonder if we could have reached the top that night, but I certainly didn't begrudge his decision to stop. Instead, we settled in for a bivouac. John had many theories about how an athlete should maintain his body to achieve the best performance. Losing salt in the hot Californian sun could leave a climber dangerously dehydrated so to counteract that, he put salt in our drinking water. A lot of salt. Sitting on the ledge I took a swig and nearly retched. It was undrinkable. John shrugged.

'Dehydration's really bad, man. You gotta have salt.'

Having taken a swig, he took out a hard-boiled egg from a bag full of them. Eggs were his other theory. 'Protein, Ron. You gotta have protein. Eggs. Eggs and salt.' And having eaten a couple to go with his salty water, he proceeded to roll himself a spliff and settle back on the ledge. So there we sat, on a narrow granite ledge more than two thousand feet off the ground as the wall moved into shadow, John a bronzed and slightly stoned Californian dozing contentedly, and me, a long way from Embsay, contemplating a bag of very smelly hard-boiled eggs. I took great pleasure in throwing them off the ledge, seeing how far I could get them away from the wall.

A few years later, John introduced me to his new girlfriend, Lynn Hill, who had just started climbing in the Valley. She seemed very much in John's shadow at that time, and very young. Literally in his shadow, given how small she was next to him. But she was friendly and not fazed by living in the weird, testosterone-fuelled world of Camp IV. She was also clearly a brilliant climber. Everyone who saw her at work said the same thing, once they'd picked their jaw off the floor: 'Who's that girl?' She was like a bomb going off, one that destroyed a lot of prejudices in the minds of male climbers about what a woman could do. In 1993, Lynn was the first climber to free the *Nose*. That news just blew me away. Not that I was surprised Lynn had done it because she is so talented. It was more that I had in my mind the memory of those sections John and I couldn't free, the thin cracks that just wouldn't take my chunky fingers.

I loved climbing with John. But it was with Pete Livesey that I matched the rapid rise in Yosemite climbing standards that gathered pace from the mid 1970s onwards, led by young newcomers like Ron Kauk, one of the nicest and most gifted climbers I've known, and John Bachar, whose soloing exploits were so inspiring. I was back in the Valley the following year when Pete turned up with Jill Lawrence. Pete was essentially on the run from his own wedding, in the middle of his year off between college and taking up a teaching job back at Bingley College. It was the year he did *Right Wall*, and he was clearly in good form.

That summer of 1974 in Yosemite was one of the great times of my climbing life. Pete and I did a stack of great routes, both new and early ascents, gobbling up the rock as fast as we could. We repeated *Space Babble*, a 5.11 put up by Ron Kauk and Kevin Worrall, which takes a beautiful line of weakness up one of the finest buttresses in the Valley on Middle Cathedral. When we got to the bottom, Pete said: 'I've forgotten my harness kid, you'll have to lead it all.' I didn't mind. Apart from one pitch of 5.11 face climbing out of nine, the route was pretty straightforward, although quite bold.

We also repeated Henry Barber's instant classic *Butterballs*, on the popular Cookie Cliff, although we had trouble finding it. I launched myself up a fierce finger crack in the right part of the crag but struggled fearfully to make progress. Still, I stuck at it and was starting to make some headway when someone called across to us: 'I thought you guys were doing *Butterballs*!'

'So did we,' I called back. *Butterballs*, it transpired, was round the corner and I was halfway up what became a route called *The Stigma*, a 5.13b done by Todd Skinner in the 1980s with a lot of top-rope practice. Perhaps I should have stuck with it. We did, however, do the first free ascent of *Crack-A-Go-Go*, one of the best finger cracks in the whole Valley.

The climax of those early years in Yosemite wasn't a new route but our early ascent of *Astroman* on the east face of Washington Column. This was a staggering achievement, the first big-wall route to be done free and a pointer to how climbing in the Valley would develop. The controversial tactic of yo-yoing was used, climbing free until you fell and then lowering off but leaving the rope clipped in place. But Ron Kauk, John Bachar and John Long who did the first ascent in 1975 created a masterpiece, and a difficult one at that. To put it in context, when *Astroman* was first done free there were around a dozen pitches of 5.11 – around E4 – in the whole Valley. *Astroman* had six in one route, and five of 5.10 as well. In the two years following the first ascent, the route had three more ascents, but in each case the second jumared up the rope rather than follow each pitch, and one of them was a speed ascent by Bachar and Kauk, who clearly knew the route well.

The east face of Washington Column is an imposing cliff and the line of *Astroman*, soaring up cracks in a recess almost on its prow, nagged away at us as the obvious challenge. We stocked up on beer and 7-Up at the shop in Yosemite Village and that evening took the shuttle bus to the Ahwahnee Hotel just below the Royal Arches, the huge feature neighbouring Washington Column. The bus was packed with smartly dressed diners and us, in our cut-off jeans and ragged t-shirts and all our gear.

Walking along the trail towards the start of the route I spotted a half-eaten melon lying in the dust. Free food, I thought, and went to pick it up, only to find myself in competition with three bear cubs. Alarmed by my dash for the melon, they skedaddled up some nearby trees, but where there are bear cubs, there's usually a mother and so it proved. I suddenly found myself looking at the business end of a disgruntled grizzly. It was time to act, so I mentioned I was from Yorkshire, and she wandered off quietly to see how her cubs were getting on up the tree. I quickly grabbed the melon and legged it after Pete. A mile or so along the trail, we found the base of the route and lit a fire – quite illegally – to prevent another visit from my new bear friends. Then we tucked into the cans of beer and watched the stars in the clear night sky.

Next morning, I could tell it was going to be a hot one. We had a couple of cans of 7-Up and prepared ourselves for the ordeal ahead. We took a couple of water bottles each, a rack of nuts, some tape in case our hands got too trashed and tied the ropes on our backs for the first pitch, an easy but long 5.7. Above our heads what had looked like small overlaps from a distance had mushroomed into gigantic roofs. *Astroman* somehow found a direct line through these, like a ship sliding past icebergs.

We roped up for the next pitch, and I raced up a 5.10 lay-back in five minutes. Then Pete led a fierce peg-scarred crack by lay-backing off his fingertips. He had tiny hands, and I found myself having to miss holds as I followed him because they were too small for my thick fingers. Above was a beautiful crack an inch and a half wide with several pegs already in place. Boosted by the fixed gear, I roared up it, pulling two of the pegs out with my fingers. Two more slithered out of their own accord. So much for the fixed gear. Still, we were making good progress, and as I set up a hanging belay at the top of the pitch, the sun struck my face. I took off my shirt and tied it into knots, tossing it off the crag to be collected later, only to watch it catch in the top of a tall pine about a hundred feet off the ground. Pete's landed on our bivouac site.

The temperature soared, but luckily the next pitch was inside a cool chimney that was far from the usual horror show Yosemite can throw at you. The relief was short lived. My next lead was another 5.10 pitch but I missed the belay and carried on up the next 5.10 pitch. After about 220ft of climbing I came to a huge flared flake stuck to the wall and realised that Pete had been following me. Worse, I couldn't figure out what to do next. He fished the topo out of his pants and told me to stop dithering because he could see from where he was how to do it: just chimney the thing. Of course, once he got there he realised he was talking rubbish and lay-backed up to the stance.

Then Pete led up a 5.11 crack into the infamous Harding Slot, done almost free on the first and otherwise heavily aided ascent by Warren Harding. Anyone who assumes Harding couldn't free climb should try his luck on this monstrously awkward vice. Graded just 5.9, it turned into an ordeal for both of us. Pete actually removed his harness after he disappeared into the depths of the chimney, tying it across his shoulder to keep his hips free, wriggling slowly, gaining only inches at a time but eventually popping out at the top. Being a little bigger than Pete I became stuck fast in the damn thing, shouting 'Yer bastard!' into its bowels just as I felt an overwhelming urge to puke. I had to swing out to release the pressure and was then faced with the outside of the slot, about eight inches wide at this point, and a quite hideous off-width.

There were still five pitches to go, and I now had to lead a tough 5.11 layback in the full heat of the sun. My mouth was sticky and we were fast running out of water. At least the grade eased for a bit after Pete's next lead and we finally landed on a ledge beneath the last pitch. We were now out of water, dizzy from the heat and desperate to be finished. But I still had to climb the last 5.11 pitch to the top and it looked hideous, a sparsely protected face in complete contrast to the nice safe cracks below. Just below the first section was a vicious-looking granite spike, which would intercept my falling body should I come off the first hard moves. After dithering for a while I reached a large angle peg sticking a long way out of its crack and filling the only foothold. Pete called up that given the peg was in the way, I should stand on the thing. But I didn't, despite Pete saying I did when he came to write up the climb for a magazine article. I just cranked through it. Just above was another peg and feeling more secure the rest of the pitch went more quickly. I spanned the width of an overhang and reached into the bottom of the final slab and was soon standing at the top, barely able to swallow, my face grimy with sweat and my body exhausted. It was the best feeling in the world.

Astroman wasn't the last time I climbed with Pete in the Valley. I teamed up with him again three years later, and we did a number of hard routes, including the new 5.12s Ray Jardine had added in the meantime. Jardine, inventor of Friends, the revolutionary camming device, was deeply controversial, mostly because his brilliant engineering skills were sometimes applied to rock, including a chipped line of holds on the *Nose*. Not long after, he quit Yosemite altogether. But his routes were certainly getting a lot of attention. I'd made a pretty routine ascent of the famous roof crack *Separate Reality*, in the days before an earthquake did for its lip and made the route much easier. Pete and I also did one of his harder lines, *Hangdog Flyer* on the Royal Arches, a mean, overhanging finger to hand crack with little for the feet.

By 1977 I knew Pete well, and had a clear sense of the width of his competitive streak. But our repeat of *Crimson Cringe* at Cascade Creek was a salutary reminder. The route was one of the first 5.12s in the world, climbed the year before by Jardine. It's two pitches long and the first, which I led, is pretty easy up to a semi-hanging stance. Then followed a thin finger crack, something Pete was good at, but it flared a little and the jams got more awkward. Pete looked uncomfortable, working at the crack, trying to find something that would stick. Eventually he gave up on it and handed the lead to me. I felt much happier on that kind of ground and made short work of it, bringing Pete up on the top rope. He wasn't best pleased. The top of the crag was steep scrubland and looked hard work so Pete announced we would be abseiling off one of those strange mineral excrescences you find in granite called chicken heads. There was a fat, head-sized one near the stance and he draped the rope over it. 'Hold the rope in place so there's no danger of it slipping off,' he told me, and then abseiled back to the stance. Then he shouted up: 'Come on, it'll be alright.' I eased myself slowly into space and then gently slid down the ropes, praying they wouldn't slip off the chicken head, until I reached Pete. It was his way of warning me not to cruise things he'd backed off. We did climb together a few more times after that. But Pete was beginning to lose the impetus that had taken him to the top and soon he would move away from climbing into other activities. Yet he remains for me one of the most compelling individuals that ever tied on a rope.

FOUR

For Pete's Sake

PETE USED TO SAY TO ME: 'It's dead easy to be a hero in your own backyard, kid.' At the time, I assumed he was giving me advice, perhaps because he saw a danger in me being too wedded to my own patch in Yorkshire. Given that I'd taken myself off to California aged eighteen, I didn't think there was much danger of that. Not that I minded him saying it. He looked after me in the early days, taught me how to grow up. I never chatted with Dad much so I needed some guidance, being talented but uncertain how to use that talent. Pete was that bit older than me, in his early thirties when I turned twenty. Aside from that, he just grew up more worldly wise than me, and I benefited from his experience. There's no question I owe him a great deal. John Sheard wrote of our partnership: 'The wise old man and the young virtuoso make a formidable combination.' That's certainly what the story became, and there was a lot of truth in it. Pete's version was more tongue-in-cheek, but there was truth in his verdict too: 'I knew from when I first climbed with him that Ron was better than me. The thing was, not to let Ron know that.'

In retrospect, I can see in Pete's warning to me a reminder to himself to keep the edge that made him feel alive. Not to get complacent. I'm not sure I'm the one to do him justice, but Pete seemed to me an anarchic soul. He loved to take the piss, but it was more than just fooling around. If someone had pretensions, then

Pete was merciless in exposing them. His passion was winding people up for fun, and you can only do that if you can see their weak spots. He would think up nicknames for everyone, more to get a reaction than out of affection. I was Tap, to begin with anyway, as a pun on Fawcett. He said himself he only used it when he thought I was doing better than he was.

With maturity, I can see his need to grate against the world came from something within him but at the time it was quite unsettling. I wanted the world to think well of me. I didn't want to be thought of as a bad man. Pete didn't really give a damn. He went ahead and did the things most of us only think about doing. Some of it was quite funny. People would turn up at the house he shared with Jill Lawrence – who was nicknamed Florrie – and they'd be sitting around without any clothes on, like climbing versions of John Lennon and Yoko Ono. It unsettled you, because you didn't know how to respond.

If you're good at climbing, there may not be any money, but people still want a piece of you, whether they want to use you to uphold their idea of the sport or to sell magazines. Even if you're shrewd, that can be a difficult path to tread, but I was just a wide-eyed kid from a small Yorkshire village. If it hadn't been for Pete, I might not have got so involved in the media and wouldn't have got the sponsorship I did. It's true I picked up some bad habits, particularly the kind of petty – and not so petty – thieving that was common in some parts of the climbing community then. This would eventually get me into serious trouble, but that wasn't Pete's fault. He didn't force me. I have to take responsibility. Gibby would never have pinched anything, despite hanging out with the same crowd.

It took Pete a while to admit to being a climber. First off, he wasn't going to be defined by a label, and second, he wouldn't miss the chance to set you up for a sandbag. That extended to his appearance, which was scruffy and unkempt. He peered at you from behind thick-rimmed specs, his teeth were wonky and he wore a woolly hat on his head. He looked the typical caver, just one more of the sports that he excelled at and had spent most of his twenties pursuing to a high standard. But he'd done quite a lot of climbing before he decided to concentrate on it in the early 1970s, with repeats in the mid 1960s of climbs like *White Slab* and *Troach* on Clogwyn Du'r Arddu, both impressive routes of their time, and in 1967 the second ascent of the *Rimmon Route* on the huge and serious Troll Wall in Norway. His regular climbing partner John Sheard, writing in *Crags* magazine, described his style as 'dictated by knobbly three-inch kneecaps and a permanent awareness of a rear end thrust out as far as possible.' He had thick legs too and would have made a strong mountaineer, if he'd chosen that path.

Still, most climbers have done most of their best new routes by the age of thirty, certainly in those days, whereas Pete was just starting. What motivated him? How and when did he realise that he could excel at this? Because Pete needed to be the best, whatever he was doing. He was deeply competitive. It was never just about the climbing, there had to be a mission. If he called me, it wasn't to chat. He'd regard that as a waste of time. He was always looking for the biggest, the hardest, or the newest. It was typical Pete that when he quit climbing at the start of the eighties, he was soon top of his class in his new sport, orienteering.

Before meeting Pete, I was happy to go with the flow, just get along with people and fit in, go up to Crookrise and do a circuit – or do a fast ascent of El Cap, if that's what was on offer. Maybe I could have spent my climbing career doing that, just meandering along. Pete showed me how to pick routes and be professional. Not to waste time. There were small but important ideas he showed me about climbing that I'd never come across anywhere else. Like racking gear. Pete would put the smallest wires at the front of his harness and then work backwards through the sizes to the biggest. It sounds blindingly obvious now, but in the early

1970s this was an innovation, and a useful one. I'd certainly seen no one else doing it. Pete also saw the advantage of using longer ropes than usual, sixty, even seventy metres long – a habit that served him well on his classic Lake District route *Footless Crow* on Goat Crag, which has a notoriously long pitch. He was always re-evaluating how he did things, looking for an advantage over the competition. And he understood the value of information too, producing an early guide to free climbing in the Valley and the first English guidebook to reveal the huge potential in the limestone regions of southwest France. When the moment came for me to put some steel in my climbing, it was partly from watching and listening to Pete that I knew how.

Not only did he have to be the best, he had to be so on his own terms, and that meant having a laugh, subverting the very thing he was trying to overcome. Like the time he soloed the awkward Tremadog route *Tensor* – in a pair of Hush Puppies. He had that theatricality about him, favouring the grand but mocking gesture, like when he dangled a banknote to lure Chris Bonington up *Footless Crow* for a BBC television programme. He'd snookered Bonington, who could only laugh at the joke played on him.

Pete did something similar to me during an international climbing festival organised by the British Mountaineering Council. It was 1976 and I'd just turned 21. We were doing a route called *Cream* at Tremadog, up the dramatic headwall of Bwlch y Moch. There were loads of people watching from behind us, at the top of the neighouring buttress, and a film crew set up to record it all for posterity. Pete was leading the top pitch, and when he passed the crux, a long reach to a finger-jam, he reached back down and slotted a wire into the crucial hold, tugging it downwards so I couldn't flick it out from below. There was no way anyone could do the move with the wire there, so I fell off, in front of all those people. He took the piss out of me for years over that. He could be ruthless, he bent – broke – the rules, and he was focussed.

He defined the phrase 'winning ugly'. But he was always a laugh. It's not surprising that a scene grew up around him, partly because he was so entertaining but also because people felt Pete knew where he was going.

On the subject of footwear, John Sheard said – perhaps tongue-in-cheek – that when Pete's old RDs finally wore out and he bought the new EBs we were all now wearing, he'd realise how much harder he could climb. That may have had something to do with it. Even Pete would admit that he was not the prettiest climber technically, but he was very effective, really good at steep walls, where he could use his immense finger strength and plug away. His psychological control meant he felt at home on bold stuff. Loose stuff. A route like *Mossdale Trip* at Gordale was typical of Pete at his best, one of the country's first E6s and named after the caving tragedy in Mossdale Cave when six people died, two of them good friends of Pete. Long, sloggy and steep with poor gear, *Mossdale Trip* is not a route to fall off. The individual moves may not be as hard as some of the top routes from that period, but it's hugely demanding and pointed the way to future ascents on the crag.

Stamina was part of the key to Pete's sudden emergence in his late 20s as one of Britain's best. He'd seen what people were doing on the Leeds wall, and noticed that climbers there were focussed on technical difficulty, not stamina. It was the equivalent of bouldering now. He must have realised that blokes like Al Manson or John Syrett were more stylish climbers but the amount of effort Pete could put in on a route was in his own hands. He'd been doing an outdoor education course at Bingley College and having qualified had to serve out a probationary year working in Scunthorpe. Marooned in the flatlands of North Lincolnshire, he spent the time traversing, doing endless laps of the climbing wall there. Later we trained together at the new Rothwell climbing wall, built by Don Robinson in a sports hall that was worryingly high. Pete had worked out a huge traverse and there'd be a dozen of us slogging backwards and forwards along it. If you dropped off you had to go back to the beginning and start again. Sometimes we'd go to the wall at the Richard Dunn Centre in Bradford, and then we'd head down to Manningham Lane for a curry or a pint in one of the depressing pubs near there with the obligatory bored-looking stripper.

We did do weights, but nothing structured. I never climbed with a weight belt. Didn't own one. I did a lot of press-ups, but that was about it. Later on I'd see a lot of young climbers with elbow and shoulder problems from getting strong too quickly. They'd started training as teenagers after not doing much with their arms before. I'd worked hard as a kid, haymaking or working outside. Growing up in Huddersfield, Pete was running from quite a young age and later became an expert canoeist. He might have represented his country at both. He already had a lot of stamina before he started climbing and those long sessions spent traversing only increased it. In the mid 1980s, climbers saw the limitations of pure stamina training and began to focus more on raw power, so I suppose you could say that the Leeds wall approach won out in the end.

As for myself, I wouldn't say Pete influenced me hugely on training. I had my own methods in place when I met him. I had been traversing for years on the railway bridges at home, going back and forth for hours at a time, polishing the holds for posterity, much as he had done during his exile in Scunthorpe. But I shared Pete's view that the best training for climbing was climbing, mostly because that suited how I wanted to live. I climbed every day I could, which was basically when it wasn't raining too hard. Once I could do a route, even if it was quite hard, I'd do it again and again, building it into an existing circuit. The mileage I did on rock was incredible and if there was no one to climb with I'd simply go out soloing. I spent so much time on the crag, that I began to forget where I was and the danger I was in. Soloing a classic slab route at Crookrise with Al Evans, I was so relaxed I momentarily lost concentration and turned to say something to him, taking my hands off the rock. I immediately started falling towards a jagged pine trunk at the base of the crag, but had the presence of mind to flip onto my back, avoiding impaling myself and sliding to a halt on the steep bracken to the side.

John 'Doc' Hammond had introduced me to Pete. His girlfriend shared a flat with Pete's girlfriend at the time, and we called in there one day before going climbing. Perhaps John thought Pete could use someone else to take up the horror shows he did at Gordale, where even the second needed to be steady. I knew all about him, and had gone out of my way to repeat his routes, like *All Quiet* at Almscliff and *Flakey Wall* at High Tor in Derbyshire, which Pete had done free that year, bar one rest point. I'd hitched down to Matlock with my friend John Heseltine on two occasions just to do this one route, getting hassled by police as we dossed in the bandstand to escape the rain. Finally we got a dry day and flashed it, dispensing with the final rest point. The quality of the route had blown me away.

Although our names have become linked in the way that Brown and Whillans are, Pete and I didn't climb together all that often, especially in Britain where if he knew he could climb something he'd keep me out of the picture in case I nicked it. We'd always lead through, and I suppose he was worried he'd miss out on a pitch he really fancied. Mostly he'd be climbing with Jill Lawrence or one of his friends like John Sheard or his brother Alec. We'd come together when he felt he needed me, like on our attempt to free *Cave Route Right-hand*, one of the huge aid routes in Gordale. This was in 1975, the year after Pete had added some of his greatest creations, routes like *Right Wall* on Dinas Cromlech in North Wales. He'd taken a year off before starting teaching at Bingley College to see how far he could take things – which turned out to be a long

71

way indeed. Climbs like these were in their turn a step up from the routes he'd done in 1971 to announce his arrival on the scene, like *Face Route* at Gordale. Now he wanted to take things further still.

The Cave Routes were well known to aid climbers. The left-hand version, put up in the 1950s by John Sumner, often required a bivouac in the cave itself. We'd both done them, although after my first winter's aid climbing I had concentrated purely on free climbing and training in the winter. That's how we knew all about the loose rock and doubtful pegs. We'd also spent a lot of time traversing along the bottom of the Cave Routes area and would boulder out the starts of both climbs. The left-hand route is harder overall but *Cave Route Right-hand* has a more awkward starting move. Get past that, and I found I could get rests, lay-backing between them and then bridging out to take the weight off my arms. Although we didn't free it on that attempt – we still needed three points of aid – it was clear it might be done. It wasn't the climbing that had stopped us. We could do the moves. It was the stamina to do them all in one go. It was the same with the big aid lines at Malham Cove. I could climb sequences free but couldn't piece them all together.

Then there was the issue of gear. Cave Route was covered in rusty pegs with flattened eyes, knackered stud bolts like the one that had done for me on *Mulatto Wall*, and one huge bolt made out of steel, like a Victorian coat hanger. I put bits of sling and old rope on these to make them easier to clip and placed the odd nut as I climbed, but it was still an intimidating lead. You weren't sure how good any of this stuff was. Resting or aiding on it was okay, but would any of the fixed gear take a long fall? I wasn't prepared to pre-place a nut either. That seemed like cheating. But I suppose if I had it would have made a free ascent more amenable.

Ethics were on the cusp of change in this period, which made climbing new routes with Pete – a man born to test boundaries – especially interesting. It's not that he didn't know about climbing ethics, he just didn't care about them. His transgressions are well documented and some of them were pretty dreadful. When I saw *Downhill Racer* after Pete's first ascent, it was clear what he'd done. The holds were obviously improved and the route substantially easier. He did something even worse on *Guillotine* at Ilkley, a beautiful gritstone arête that sprouted a useful three-finger slot around the time Pete did the first ascent. That one irritated even me, let alone everyone else. I have to say I never fell out with him about anything he did like that. It was just part of who he was. In France, of course, they'd been chipping holds for generations and would continue to do so. Our more purist approach was a cultural thing that we'd developed for ourselves, and Pete had little time for limits imposed by society, especially his own.

Some of it was just done for a laugh. We'd travel countrywide in search of a project that would hit the headlines. I remember he wanted to free climb *Athanor* on Goat Crag in the Lake District. So we went up there on a day hit and he got stuck trying a little corner that was quite dirty. But he kept at it. He was up and down, up and down, clipped a peg but still couldn't do it. So he took hold of the peg, stood in a sling and carried on. I seconded it free but it didn't count. Later in the pub we were asked what we'd done. Pete said we'd freed *Athanor*. I said, 'Did we 'eck. You stood in a sling.'

Despite his own tricks, Pete could see all the hypocrisies and shortcomings of what everyone else was up to, especially those who accused him most loudly. He took great pains to show how the Yorkshire Mountaineering Club's parochial attitude had held back progress in the Dales. The top grade was still HVS in the early 1970s, although plenty of climbers saw that as a good joke. As late as 1974, when the new Yorkshire Limestone guidebook was published by the YMC, they were still recording the aid points on routes that had been done free, as though freeing a route wasn't an improvement in style. Pete reviewed the book in *Mountain* magazine and tore it to shreds. He took them to task on my account, too. Several of my new routes had been claimed by YMC members and put in the book as theirs, not mine. 'I believe it is customary in Yorkshire to put the record straight twenty years after the event, when no one can argue,' Pete wrote. 'I'm going to do it now.' I guess it helps if, like Pete, you're born in Yorkshire, before you say these things.

I was never one for top-roping or practising moves. I did it very occasionally, but I wanted to keep some doubt in the back of my mind. I preferred to boulder out hard moves, or check holds on abseil, while I was cleaning. Somehow small compromises didn't feel so bad. Pete, on the other hand, didn't care about any of it. He'd practise routes, top-rope them, whatever it took. It might have outraged some people, but his pragmatism freed the logjam that had blocked progress for climbing in general and Yorkshire climbing in particular. Several people had tried to free *Face Route* before Pete succeeded, and perhaps they would have done if they'd practised it in the way Pete did. But it's his name in the book. As for the argument that those who come after should know what the guy who went first relied on, anyone doing a second ascent of Pete's routes would likely know the tactics he used.

John Sheard put it best, in his *Crags* profile: 'He regards potential routes in the same way as he does leftover bits of meat on your plate – if you don't want it, he'll have it.' Within ten years top climbers had followed what Pete was doing to its logical conclusion and sport climbing was born. Now there's a clear distinction between an on-sight ascent and one with practice, and everybody knows the difference, and can climb how they like, a situation Pete would have liked. The irony is that Pete always managed to keep a high level of adventure and uncertainty in his life as well as his climbing, because that's what most excited him. Aid climbing was predictable, and that's why he preferred free climbing.

Travelling to new or little-known destinations was a huge part of Pete's life, something that's sometimes overlooked now.

Before I'd met him, he'd done some wild caving trips to Jamaica and Greece, as well as the expedition to Norway to climb the Troll Wall. In the mid 1970s, alongside his seasons in the Valley, Pete began exploring the rock climbing potential in the south of France. He knew all about it from his caving days, which gave him a head start in knowing where the best crags were and meant that he wasn't far behind the French themselves in exploring their crags. He and his friends in the Phoenix Climbing Club would set off each spring, cramming five people into a Citröen 2CV. That was typical of Pete, packing so many into such a slow car to save petrol. We'd always hide the fifth person under a blanket as we got on the ferry so we wouldn't have to pay for them. Pete really was tighter than a bat's wing. In the end we went so often that Gibby bought shares in the ferry company to qualify for an extra reduction.

So when I came into Pete's orbit it was only natural that I'd join his gang in France. I never had any urge to go to the Alps. I never thought of rock climbing as a stepping-stone to mountaineering. I'd heard too many stories of people sitting in a wet tent in Chamonix doing nothing. I wanted to see the Alps, but I couldn't be doing with not climbing and after my experiences in California it seemed to me you didn't have to. I went to France pretty much every year through the mid 1970s, sometimes for a week, usually for longer. We stopped off on the way south at Fontainebleau, which I adored and would over the next three decades go back to again and again, later on with my daughters. Now that I spend a lot of my time bouldering it seems to me an ideal destination in its own right, but in the 1970s it was simply a fun place to stop on the way to bigger things.

We climbed in the Vercors first, and I remember soloing a route with Pete in the Rochers d'Archiane called *Voie Livanos*, racing each other up the crag in an act of slightly insane competition. The climb must tip the scales at English 5b or 5c and is over 400m high. We started late, a frequent occurrence in

France, and overtook a French couple, that had started at first light. They were stopped open-mouthed as we raced past them unroped. At one stage we had to climb a wide hand-jamming crack, and I remember Pete struggling with his smaller hands to get secure placements and panicking slightly.

Arriving at the Verdon Gorge was an absolute revelation. Here was somewhere close to Britain more on the scale of Yosemite with almost no free climbs. Climbers from Nice and Marseilles, with a background in free climbing at Les Calanque and Baou de Saint-Jeannet, had discovered Verdon in the mid 1960s, but they had largely confined themselves to the small cliffs on the periphery of the gorge. Then in 1968 a team of alpinists from northern France – Patrice Bodin, Patrick Cordier, Lothar Mauch and Patrice Richard – climbed the first big route in the gorge itself, on the Paroi du Duc, a huge cliff guarding the gloomiest northern section, just south of the Pont Sublime. This got the locals going, and that October Joel Coqueugnot and François Guillot climbed *La Demande*, the first route on the gorge's best cliff, L'Escalès. Soon many more climbs were going up, and Verdon developed its own ethic that wasn't quite free climbing but wasn't quite the same as how routes were done in the Alps, where fixed pegs mushroomed and the attitude that anything goes – as long it goes quickly – prevailed.

It's not like we introduced free climbing to France. There was already a long tradition of bouldering in Fontainebleau, dating back to before the Great War, which had started as practice for climbing in the Alps but ended up as an activity in its own right. But no one had seen fully the true potential of French limestone. In Verdon, belays would be fixed pegs, and climbers would predominantly use pegs or threads on the lead, either in the crack systems or in the characteristic *gouttes d'eau*, the water-worn pockets, which characterise Verdon and allowed the blankest looking walls in the most dramatic positions imaginable to be climbed. Local climbers would do a sequence of moves, often hard, and then place a peg and rest – but it was still pretty bold. On that first visit in 1973, I remember a few local climbers were wearing rock shoes, but many still wore the sort of kletterschuhe you'd see in the Alps. All we had to do was what we'd done in Yorkshire and start linking the sequences together and freeing whatever aid points there were. It didn't require us to retro-bolt anything. In fact, I never placed a bolt in all the years I went there. The wholesale bolting of Verdon happened later. Not everyone was pleased. When a picture of me climbing a route called *Le Triomphe d'Eros* appeared on the cover of *Mountain*, some climbers from Marseille added extra pegs to the route to show they had no interest in free climbing. But most local climbers could see what we were doing, and began to appreciate that this was the ethic being practised not just by us but also in Yosemite and elsewhere. I found the climbing suited me perfectly, long pulls off the *gouttes d'eau*, which were big enough to take my chunky fingers and are sharp and positive to pull on.

Life was simple at Verdon. It was cooler in spring and autumn, but without the storms of summer, when lightning can flicker along the top of the gorge. We camped on the village football pitch in La Palud and drank cheap red wine or Pete's favourite, Pernod. Three or four cars would come down, filled with a team that all knew each other, mostly from the Leeds area. In the morning, usually quite some time after a late breakfast – Pete did like a lie-in – we'd head off to the crag. At first, the French stars – Jacques Perrier, Bernard Gorgeon and the Troussier brothers – were a little standoffish. The local climbers didn't know what to make of these badly dressed, often drunk Brits making themselves at home. Getting information out of them was a slow process. The exception was Jean-Claude Droyer, who often hung out with us. Jean-Claude was a Fontainebleau veteran who had climbed in the UK too. He was always friendly and later came and stayed in Britain with me after I married.

Given the French passion for looking good, it's not surprising that once they'd tossed the big boots, the French quickly got to grips with getting fit and dressing for the weather. Patrick Edlinger was right at the front of this new wave of French climbers, and looked the part too, taking Gallic insouciance to the extreme. I had the great advantage of turning brown and was never happier than wandering the campsite in running shorts. We couldn't resist competing with each other. One evening we spotted Edlinger and the others having a training session, hanging off a tree in the campsite. The aim was to find out who could manage a proper one-arm pull-up. Everyone was looking very grim with one or two managing to get one done when Gibby decided to join in. Chris was one of the most naturally strong climbers I'd ever met, and could pull on the tiniest edges. But he didn't look the part and I wonder what Edlinger was thinking when Gibby strolled over, bottle of wine in one hand, fag in the other, more than a bit pissed, and said: 'Let me 'ave a do, lads, let me 'ave a do.' He put the cigarette between his lips and used his free hand to knock off half a dozen. He didn't even spill the ash off his fag.

Climbing in Verdon was almost designed for me, long, flowing pitches of the best quality limestone imaginable. We did explore other areas. There were trips to Buoux, for example, but it never really suited me. Many of the holds at Buoux started life as hidden pockets. Climbers would poke a blade of grass into a thin opening in the rock and wiggle it around to see how big the space behind this thin surface might be. Then, if it proved sufficient, they'd bash it with a peg hammer and expose the new hold. I didn't much care for that, and anyway, my fingers were so thick I often struggled on climbing that required so much pocket pulling, sometimes on a single finger. Later there were access problems and climbing at Buoux was curtailed for a while, so the craze for it rather passed me by.

Anyway, there was so much to be done at Verdon that it hardly seemed necessary to stray too far. There wasn't then the fashion there is now for single very hard pitches, which has changed climbing even on the huge walls of Verdon. Many climbers now are content to lower themselves over the edge of the gorge for a rope length and then climb out. But in the early and mid 1970s, the great appeal was long multi-pitch routes that took in the full grandeur of the place. It wasn't simply a gymnasium but somewhere wild to explore.

Once the initial suspicion had eased a little, a rapport between the visiting barbarians and the locals developed, mostly based around the longstanding climbers' tradition of sandbagging, the presentation of an objective as being easier than it truly is, leaving the victim with a choice between humiliation or not having their efforts given the credit they deserve. Pete was pretty useful at this himself, but the French, being on home territory, held the advantage.

We suffered a classic example of this at the hands of Bernard Gorgeon. While jamming up the crack systems of *Luna Bong* on our first trip, we noticed the superb clean pillar to the right had scraps of tape on it, suggesting it had already been climbed. Bernard told us the route was called *Necronomicon*, named after a fictional book of witchcraft. I wish I'd known there was magic or trickery afoot when Bernard told us the route was 'five and free', meaning around HVS.

Bernard abseiled down with us to put us in the right direction and then took up station where *Necronomicon* traverses out of *Luna Bong* to watch our progress.

'Don't forget,' he shouted. 'Eet's five and free!'

After a few moves, Pete was clinging on fiercely as the HVS romp turned into something more akin to E3 or E4, while trying to appear nonchalant, a façade that gradually crumbled as the climbing refused to relent. Taking over the lead, I pushed on up the final 150ft of the rib, making a desperate lunge for the final holds, calling down to a chuckling Bernard: 'Five and effin' free?' The route was superb, a colossal and perfect white sheet perched in space. There was nothing in Britain I could compare it to. We got our own back later, freeing another superb climb called *Le Triomphe d'Eros* at around E4. 'There you go Bernard,' I told him. 'That one's five and free too.'

Some sandbags were heavier than others. We became interested in a route at the far end of L'Escalès taking a fine pillar and named *Eperon des Bananes*. Though the route came highly recommended we could never find anyone with a firm fix on where exactly it went. Some had spent hours just trying to find the start of the route, returning unsuccessful. Eventually we met the route's originator, François Guillot. With a wry smile, he explained how the topo description of this and other routes in the Verdon Gorge came to be drawn: 'I just mark ze top and ze bottom on a photograph. Michel, ze guide-writer, 'e fills in ze line, divides it into pitches and puts some numbers on it. Zay are creative, zese artists, no?'

Our near-free ascent of the classic route *Pichenibule* was for me the highlight, both of those early trips to Verdon but also of climbing with Pete. Freeing the route was his idea, because it had a huge reputation among the locals for being difficult and sustained. Pull this off, and we'd make quite a splash. In those days it was protected mostly with nuts and pegs, and a few rather doubtful bolts. That made it a much bolder proposition than it is now. As usual, we didn't have a firm fix on exactly where it went or how to get to the bottom of it. That was often the problem with Verdon, and it usually ended with us abseiling nervously into the start of the route. We'd have to figure out the access points for ourselves, and being the junior member, I'd often be sent over the edge first. Sometimes I'd end up in the middle of nowhere, with no stance and have to climb out. I've got an abiding memory of hanging at the end of the rope miles above the distant pines in the middle of a blank white wall and seeing

Pete peering over the edge of the crag laughing his head off. The classic Verdon experience was the *Luna Bong* abseil, straight into space five hundred feet off the deck, a grim memory to anyone who's endured it, and done off trees in those days, not bolts. You'd aim for carefree, and hope the fear didn't show on your face as you committed yourself to the abyss.

Nowadays *Pichenibule* is reached by this abseil, but in the 1970s you walked in from the end of the gorge, through a tunnel dug through the rock for what seemed like miles. The dare was to do it without a headtorch, in complete darkness. As usual we didn't start the route until early afternoon, having left late in the morning and wandered around the bottom of the gorge trying to find the thing. Six hundred feet above us, we could see a French team two-thirds of their way up working across the bolt ladder on the hardest section. They'd started at first light, as they would in the Alps and must have wondered about why the strange pair at the bottom of the crag were mooching around so late in the day.

As in Yosemite, Pete wasn't averse to nudging me into the lead if things looked serious; while there was a lot of aid climbing on the route, it was often quite spaced, and the free sections in between gave a lot of bold climbing. There was a superb crackless corner on the first part of the route, firing two hundred feet towards the terrace halfway up L'Escalès. Above that were seven pitches of pocketed walls, three of them at around E4 or hard 5.11. We didn't bother with the bolt ladder, which I freed with Jerry Peel at French 7b+ – not something the French guidebooks record – but the rest of the climb now went free with moves up to English 6a. The last hundred feet were superb up a sequence of pockets I could barely see until I needed them. We caught the French team just below the top, looking utterly bemused at how quickly we'd caught them.

By the end of the 1970s the French and English climbers had all got to know each other a bit better, thanks in part to some exchange meets organised by the Fédération Française de Montagne et Escalade. At the closing dinner of a meet in France, their bemusement at our strange ways spilled out in a speech given by Jean-Claude Droyer: 'Pete, we are so impressed with your climbing, but a little puzzled. Why, before making a hard move, do you always scratch your arse?' Pete didn't hesitate. 'To make sure it's still there.'

Later on, several French stars were generous enough to acknowledge the impact those years of visits by Pete and the rest of us had on the sudden rise in standards in France. Patrick Berhault, one of the top climbers of his generation in any discipline, said: 'The achievements of Ron Fawcett and Pete Livesey opened my eyes, and the eyes of many French climbers.' Berhault was one of the climbers on the meet in 1978 and later formed a famous partnership with Patrick Edlinger. He was a great alpinist too, but modest with it and didn't play the celebrity like his more famous namesake. Berhault's death at the age of 47 in a climbing accident in the Swiss Alps was a great loss.

FIVE

The Cad

IN THE SUMMER OF 1977, the Sheffield climber John Allen, whose gritstone new routes in the Peak District had earned him the deserved reputation as one of the best rock climbers in Britain, gave an interview to *Crags* magazine, then barely a year old. *Crags* was the cheeky younger brother to the more stately *Mountain*. Rather like Pete, John could say controversial things for a laugh and was being rather dismissive of Pete Livesey's repeat of *London Wall*, which John had freed in 1975. He was defending grading the route at just 5c, technically speaking. Many climbers these days would say its opening moves were more like 6b. The interviewer, *Crags'* editor Geoff Birtles, was asking how it could be only 5c if the great Pete Livesey had taken all day to repeat it?

'Perhaps he's no good,' John suggested.

'You know better than that,' Geoff replied.

'Don't get me wrong. I like Pete and I know he has the best record of top new routes in the last few years – but is he technically efficient? He's not a very inspired climber.'

Geoff was having none of this. 'I would agree that he is not the smoothest mover on rock but my point was that he can dispense with a 5c in better style than he did *London Wall.*'

Then I cropped up in the conversation. 'I suppose you don't think that Fawcett creaming up everything is very good either?' Geoff asked. This sounds quite flattering, but I was a friend of

83

Geoff by this stage, and writing regularly for his magazine. The year before, I'd done a girdle of Raven Tor in the Peak District with Geoff and Al Evans, now graded E5, which he'd called *Cream Team Special*. The word 'cream' meant something. Anyway, friend of the editor or not, John didn't hesitate.

'I prefer Livesey. The climbs he has put up bear his brand of seriousness, stuff like *Footless Crow* and *Right Wall*. He's a frightening climber to make a repeat ascent of. I suppose Ron is but I can't think of any of his new routes.' As I recall, John had been at Raven Tor when we did *Cream Team Special*, taking the piss and sabotaging our ropes by tying off a huge loop of slack that was hanging down to the top of a tree. Geoff had probably been winding John up beforehand to come and watch some proper talent at work.

'Maybe Ron is yet to emerge with new routes?' Geoff countered. This was a fair point, given that I'd only just turned twenty-two, but John had done routes like the beautiful *Old Friends* at Stanage aged fourteen, and *London Wall* itself at sixteen, so he wasn't going to be impressed by that idea.

'He's been around long enough now if he is going to emerge. He's a very good climber and very impressive to watch, but put him on hard technical problems, on actual routes rather than climbing walls. I wonder then how he'd fare.'

I'd always got on fine with John, and continued to do so after this interview came out. He was just speaking his mind, not settling scores, as far as I could tell. As I said, he liked to make provocative statements and might well have been taking the mickey out of Geoff. But he did have this idea that Livesey and I were machines, more interested in training than a route's quality or appeal. True, we did a lot of training, but only so we could climb better and harder routes. The most attractive unclimbed lines in Britain were going to take a big step up in our fitness if we were going to climb them. With more maturity, I might have realised that John's preferred climbing method of long sessions in the café followed by short bursts of brilliance was being undermined by our work ethic. He complained that there wasn't any romanticism in climbing anymore. Pete and I were killing some of the sport's charm.

At the time, of course, I thought all this was unfair but it didn't bother me too much. I'd not long come back from Yosemite, where Pete and I had done a stack of impressive repeats, including *Astroman*, then one of the most desired free routes in the world. I'd done several adventurous trips to France as well, living a life that was, as far as I was concerned, about as romantic as I could have hoped for, recalling the interview with my careers advisor at Aireville. But John's concluding remarks about me stung a little: 'Ron doesn't seem to contribute to new route development as far as I can see. It's not sour grapes. I wouldn't like to repeat some of his new routes – if I could think of one.'

The year before I'd done what has proved to be one of the first E6s in the country, *Slip'n'Slide* at Crookrise. It takes a ramp up a thirty-foot face, starting from a grassy ledge some way off the ground. It was such an obvious line, one I'd looked at regularly as a lad. I'd abseiled down it and cleaned it a bit, and then persuaded a kid called Richard Cox, who just happened to be at the crag that day, to hold my rope. The final moves out of the ramp and up a short wall are on poor smears for your feet. Mess that up and there's a good chance you'll hit the ground from fifty feet. But it's a brilliant climb, done years before sticky rubber became available. It was also, at the time, the most serious new route I'd put up, if not the most technically difficult. Of course, it wasn't in the Peak District, which has routinely regarded itself as the crucible for British climbing standards, but it was close to the quality of John's routes in Derbyshire.

Nor was I confined to one area, as a lot of climbers were in those days, particularly in the Peak. Earlier that year, Pete and

I had freed *Liberator* in Bosigran's Great Zawn, a superb two-pitch route up the right arête of the Zawn's main face. We were always driving off for the weekend on the rumour of some fantastic unclimbed line waiting to be snatched. I freed *Darkinbad the Brightdayler*, a superb wall climb at Pentire Head in a similar fashion with Pete Gomersall the same year. (We did a lot of new routes in Cornwall that year, including one named for an altercation during the walk-in with the espionage novelist John Le Carré, who lives in West Penwith. He'd pulled up in his car as we walked into St Loy, effin' and jeffin'. 'You people make me sick in search of your cheap sport,' he shouted at me. Pete had to hold me back.)

Even so, looking back, I can see some truth in what John Allen had said. At the time I felt myself to be as good a climber as anyone. I'd done a host of repeats, particularly of Pete's routes and often in better style than the first ascent. I'd done lots of free ascents in the Verdon and Yosemite at a time when far fewer rock climbers travelled abroad. And I'd done scores of good new routes. But when you start talking about the truly great rock climbers, there's a lot more to it than stamina or technical ability or even originality. It's something about the new routes they choose to do. Challenges that are both obvious and at the same time a step into the future. Routes that capture the imagination. When John Allen gave his interview, he – and Pete – had done the climbs for which they became well known, in Pete's case routes like *Right Wall* and *Footless Crow*, and in John's case *Prophet of Doom* and the Moon Buttress routes at Curbar Edge in Derbyshire. At that moment, when John gave his interview to *Crags*, the climbs I've done that have been remembered were still waiting for me to show up.

It's not as though what John Allen said changed my life. But there's no doubt that in the mid 1970s my mind was not as focussed as it became later. Climbing was what drove me, but for four years I'd found myself divided between completing my teacher training course at Ilkley College and shooting off round the country to do as many routes as I could. Maybe I was also a little complacent, recognising my ability but not converting it into the kinds of new routes that John Allen was talking about. To some extent I was in Pete Livesey's shadow. Perhaps I was just too easy-going. Whatever the reason, I needed to find direction in my climbing, and a more focussed ambition. I needed to take the lessons I'd learned from Pete and others and stand on my own two feet. How that happened, however, was more complicated that you might imagine.

I can't in all honesty say I was a natural-born teacher. My decision to do a teacher-training course at Ilkley College was prompted more by my need to earn a living and have a good chunk of holiday in which to go climbing. I don't suppose I was the first climber to hit on teaching as a solution, and I wasn't the last. I like kids, and loved bringing mine up, but I can't claim teaching was a vocation in the way climbing was. Going to lectures was a lot easier than plastering or drilling holes in baths and with a grant I wasn't much worse off than I was before.

Living in Ilkley also meant I could spend a lot of time exploring the crags around town. But there was a lot of competition. The same rush for new gritstone routes taking place in the Peak District was in full swing in Yorkshire too. If you got a sniff of an unclimbed line you'd worry someone else would beat you to it. I'd certainly have gone out of my way to pinch a project, something I'd picked up from Pete. In the 1980s the idea grew of climbers somehow having rights to something they were working on. We wouldn't have stood for that. Competition was too intense and ascents didn't require the kind of practise that later became common, or the cost of fixed gear. Everything was fair game, even gear. If someone had seen a line of karabiners left on a route, they wouldn't have said: 'I know, I'll just leave those in place.'

I remember beating Iain Edwards to the first ascent of a route at Ikley, a pumpy horizontal crack climb called *Hand Jive*, soon after I started college, setting my alarm for early in the morning in case Iain got there before me. He was a lovely chap, Iain, a loveable rogue who somehow always ended up in scrapes. He loved tinkering with cars, too. I used to call for him to go climbing, and I won't forget arriving outside his house to hear this strange moaning sound coming from underneath his car. I knelt down and looked under the chassis to see Iain pinned to the floor by the engine block, which had dropped out while he was working under it. Apart from a big bruise on his chest he was fine.

The gritstone legends who had so impressed me when I started climbing – Al Manson, Pete Kitson and John Syrett – were climbing even harder, and had been joined by Mike Hammill, who was sharing a flat in Leeds with Al. Pete Livesey was still adding major new routes, and still bending the rules if necessary. Once or twice, John Allen and his regular partner Steve Bancroft came looking for new lines to equal what they were doing in the Peak District. I remember bumping into Al at Guisecliffe one wet Saturday morning and seeing the shock of recognition on his face. He was probably thinking what I was: What's he doing here? What's he after? It was an exciting time, all these climbers plotting and rushing round trying to pick the best plums before their competitors. Al had been trying a line on Caley Crags, outside Otley, which has some of the best gritstone climbing close to Leeds and some bold, clean lines that had been attracting attention. He'd come close to making the first ascent of *High Noon* earlier in the week, and was worried someone would beat him to it.

Not long before I graduated I did the first ascent of *Psycho* with Iain, at Caley Crags, outside Otley. I loved Caley, but it was a much more attractive crag in those days, before it was overwhelmed by bracken. The area around *Psycho* was full of great lines. Al did the route to the right and called his *Psycho* too, rather graciously changing the name to *Adrenalin Rush* once he discovered I'd already taken it.

My parents seemed happy with what I was doing. They'd worked hard all their lives, and before I went back to school were worried I might drift along. Training to be a teacher had made them optimistic about my future. They didn't mind me climbing, although they didn't really understand what it was about. I don't think they wanted me to pursue it full time. They couldn't see any security in it. To be honest, they were more concerned when I started riding motorbikes, towards the end of my time at college. That really did worry them. These days, most people ride bikes for fun and in good weather. When it's your sole means of transport and the roads are icy it's another matter. I never broke anything but there were plenty of scrapes. I started with a Jawa CZ250, a cheap and nasty Czech import that was legal to drive as a learner. During my probationary year as a teacher, I'd race off to Caley from Guiseley to grab a quick session during my lunch hour. Once I passed my test I sold that and bought a water-cooled Yamaha RD350, popular at the time with new riders but still a bit of a handful. The power would come on sharply in first gear, leaving novices vulnerable to unintended wheelies. This happened to me when Brian Swales begged me to give him a ride. Attempting to show off, I dropped the clutch too hard, the bike reared up and Brian did a somersault off the back.

For most of my time at Ilkley College, however, I simply didn't have the cash to run a vehicle and relied on lifts from friends, particularly Gibby, Pete and other friends, like Steve Foster. In fact, even though I had a full grant, studying and travelling to go climbing put a lot of strain on me financially. My overriding memory of the 1970s was of trying to go climbing while being skint. Still, there were compensations. Ilkley had been a women-only college until just before I applied. That may have been to my advantage in getting accepted and certainly was afterwards. Lots of the girls were doing cookery courses, so there would often be lots of free food available.

I also earned a few quid writing articles for Geoff Birtles at *Crags* magazine. I'd got to know Geoff through Al Evans in the early 1970s, a regular climbing partner of Geoff's. Al had helped set up the magazine with him. The idea of writing articles really came from Pete, who was big on publicity. Although I've often wondered why he wanted to be well known. It wasn't about money because in those days there simply wasn't any. In later days, after he effectively stopped climbing, he wrote a column for *Climber* magazine, but that was more reflective and insightful and not really about Pete. As far I could tell, that's the only money he made from climbing. But he liked to see what he was doing in headlines. I suppose he thought it was all part of the game he was playing.

In the mid 1970s I started climbing with Geoff more often and got to know him better. The catalyst was once again competition for a route. Pete had been at the Peak District limestone crag Chee Tor in March 1976 with another Yorkshire climber called Steve Foster and had come across Geoff and Al trying to free an old aid route called *Mortlock's Arête*. All of them played around on it that afternoon, Pete and Geoff realising that it would go, but both sensing they might need some extra muscle to succeed. Geoff immediately rang Tom Proctor, his regular partner since the late 1960s, while Pete enlisted me, along with Pete Gomersall and his more regular partner Jill Lawrence. Geoff, however, made sure he and Tom made it to the route ahead of us, knowing we'd stop at the Stoney café on the way down. All Pete and I could do was laugh about it and wait for our chance. Geoff wrote later: 'There was not a lot to choose between Proctor, Livesey or Fawcett in 1976; they were the best rock climbers in Britain, among the best in the world in their own ways. Tom had been at it longer and had the power of Samson, Pete had the cunning of [Pete] Crew, immensely fit with enough natural ability to hold his own; Ron had a wild talent which engraved its own legend in due course.'

Tom got to work on the first pitch of *Mortlock's* while all we could do was hang around the bottom of Chee Tor keeping our fingers crossed. It wasn't the first time this had happened. A few weeks before, drinking in the pub on Saturday night, Geoff had overheard Pete planning a trip to the Central Buttress of Water-cum-Jolly, one of those Derbyshire limestone crags now out of fashion. He'd made sure that Tom was firmly in place on the route we were planning to free – *Behemoth* – before we could get there. On that occasion, we got our chance after Tom needed a point of aid, and grabbed the first free ascent for ourselves to give an excellent E5. So we had reason for optimism, waiting to see if Tom could finish off the first pitch of *Mortlock's* free.

Tom was immensely strong, could lift a car up off its wheels, but he was a gentle soul. He never drank or smoked. The lads he climbed with on the other hand would do a route and then head to the pub, where Tom would sit quietly sipping an orange juice. I don't know why he put up with it. Later he went to Cerro Torre and got to within a hundred feet or so of the summit via the unclimbed east face. After that he quit climbing and went underground, literally, digging out caves to find new passages to explore. He trained as a carpenter, and I saw some of the beautiful things he made. Tom was a real craftsman, although on the rock he was all about raw power. On *Mortlock's* he muscled up the initial bulging wall and reached the hanging flake, Pete's high point from earlier in the week. Knowing we were circling like sharks should he fail, Tom gritted his teeth and kept going to the stance at the end of the first pitch. Once Geoff was up, Pete followed.

Even now, it wasn't in the bag. Tom was great on steep stuff but in the awkward leaning groove above the stance he ground to a halt. He didn't fancy pressing on without some decent protection, so he traversed to a tree, from which he abseiled, pulled the ropes through – leaving Geoff marooned at the stance – raced round to the top of the crag, abseiled down the groove and placed a peg. Meanwhile Pete had reached the stance and was bringing me up. It was getting dark by this point, but with the peg in Tom managed to fight his way to the top of the second pitch. Despite the gloom, I could see Pete was grinning: 'Go on kid,' he said, 'show them how it's done.' I followed, trying to climb as neatly as I could, despite the gathering dusk, hard on Geoff's heels. 'A flashing glimpse of his tomorrow,' is how he described it. Pete still tried for the last laugh though, writing to *Mountain* magazine claiming we'd done the first ascent because Tom had messed around so much on the top pitch.

After *Mortlock's*, I spent quite a lot of time with Geoff. He was very sparky and sociable, quick-witted and always one of the lads, holding court in the café or pub, putting himself in the middle of the top players. Running a magazine was perfect for him. I was more like Tom had been, not so interested in the social side, just wanting to be outdoors all the time. But we climbed a lot together during the long hot summer of 1976 and always had a good laugh. A highlight was the second ascent of *Castellan*, the huge roof crack at High Tor that John Allen and Steve Bancroft had done in the spring. Having failed to pull over the roof on the Saturday, Geoff and I went back for a second try on the Sunday, trying to shake off the attentions of Peak District climbing's then paparazzo, John Woodhouse. It seems bizarre now, but John would hang around outside the café waiting to follow us. Halfway up the route, his face would pop over the top and he'd snap some pictures, which he'd then sell to whichever magazine would pay him. It was like having a stalker. The day before we'd had to rescue him when he got stuck trying to find the perfect camera position. So our hearts sank when his blue Mini pulled out as we drove away. When he sent in pictures of my successful ascent the next day, demanding £18 for an exclusive, Geoff billed him £20 for the rescue.

With Al Evans, we also did the first ascent of *Supersonic*, on the main face of High Tor, what I regard as the best bit of limestone in Derbyshire. The route takes the middle of the face, sharing the middle section of *Flakey Wall* before climbing straight up the pocketed wall above. It's a sensational climb, one I'm proud of, and it left an impression on Geoff who put a picture of it on the front cover of *Crags*, along with the text: 'Is this Britain's first 6c?' The short answer to that was: 'No.' No one was more aware of that than me, but Geoff liked to tease his readers, particularly those living outside the Peak District. What people don't know is that Chris Bonington's head was poking into the top right of the photograph used – he must have been on *Original Route* – but Geoff had it removed before publication. 'I'm not having Bonington on the cover of my magazine,' he said, or something like.

Although I didn't think *Supersonic* was really 6c, how the new grading system then emerging worked was something I wrote about in Crags. It's hard to imagine a world now where climbers didn't argue about what grade a particular route does or doesn't deserve, what a 6b moves feels like and so forth. But the modern British system didn't emerge until the mid 1970s. It was an amalgam of technical grades, developed on sandstone in southeast England and transferred to Wales, and the subdivision of the Extremely Severe grade – an idea developed in the Lake District by Pete Botterill – into E1 and so forth.

Livesey was never that interested in grades, unless he was winding up the Yorkshire Mountaineering Club. He'd given *Face Route* at Gordale 'XS' – Extremely Severe – and that was provocation enough in Yorkshire, where the traditional limit was HVS. I'm not sure Pete liked the new grading system, perhaps because it wasn't his idea. (Although he probably said it was.) Change was inevitable, however. Routes that are now considered hard E5 or even E6 had a similar grade in the mid 1970s to routes from the 1950s that were E1 or E2. That wasn't helpful, and could even be dangerous, particularly in an era when protection wasn't much better than it had been twenty years previously.

There were problems as the new system developed, and this accounted for what some regarded as the bizarre grades I gave some of my new routes. This was in part because I put some of the effort a climb required into the technical grade, leaving the adjectival grade purely for danger. Another side effect was how routes were reported. If you don't have a clear grading system with precise and measurable differences in difficulty, then it's less clear which climbers are the strongest, certainly among the general climbing public. The top guys usually have a good idea, with or without grades. Nowadays, using the French sport-climbing grades that became popular in the 1980s, there are websites that rank climbers according to the number of hard climbs they've done. That's the kind of thing you can do with sport climbing. But in the mid 1970s, as I came to the fore, the grading revolution was only just beginning.

There's no question that all these developments changed climbing. When I started, nobody bothered much with numbers or letters. It was the reputation of the route that counted, and whoever first did it. It doesn't matter that, for example, *Sentinel Crack* at Chatsworth is E3. The fact that it's an overhanging Don Whillans gritstone jamming crack says a lot more. But as the number of new routes being climbed around the country increased, along with the number of top climbers doing or repeating them, grading slowly gathered importance. They also allowed the kind of headlines in the climbing media that catch people's attention. 'Charlton Chestwig climbs world's first E13,' creates more of a stir than 'Charlton Chestwig climbs major new route.' If you're trying to earn a living from climbing, then the temptation to stick a big number on something is clear.

I liked the attention I got from appearing in magazines. I suppose I found it flattering. It's nice to be told you're doing well from someone with clout, like Geoff. Pete was a bit wiser than me, being older, and took it all with a pinch of salt. He liked publicising his climbs but kept a respectful distance from the magazine editors. He didn't let a positive write-up go to his head, nor was he bothered if he got slated. A good example was the controversy over the use of chalk, magnesium carbonate, which was becoming more common in Britain during the mid 1970s. Ken Wilson, at *Mountain* magazine, had instantly rejected its use, criticising John Allen's landmark free ascent of *Great Wall* on Cloggy because he'd dipped his fingers in the stuff. 'John Allen free climbs *Great Wall* but uses chalk,' was the headline. Wilson dubbed us the 'Powder-Puff Kids' and demanded that we be challenged: 'They must be barracked remorselessly when they attempt to use chalk on ordinary routes.' A group of mainly southwest climbers, including Pat Littlejohn, formed the Clean Hand Gang to resist chalk's introduction into the UK. It got quite ugly for a while, with strong views on both sides. Once Ken Wilson got fired up about something, that was it, he'd come at you all guns blazing. The end of the world was nigh: 'It would seem that this one-time stronghold of climbing purism and sensitive aesthetic awareness has veered alarmingly off course,' he wrote in an editorial in *Mountain*.

I was probably more of a sensitive soul than Pete and took this more personally. Confrontations hurt me more than they did him. Pete was always careful to stay in Ken's good books, sending him details of whatever he'd done at the weekend and not taking the piss. Like Geoff Birtles, Wilson had his favourites, climbers he thought deserved attention, like Alec Sharp, the Gogarth pioneer. I certainly wasn't one of them. I'd started using chalk in Yosemite and really couldn't see what the fuss was about, but to Ken I was the devil incarnate. Free climbing granite in California without chalk would have been horrendous, and the Stonemasters were using it routinely. They'd adopted it from John Gill, the father of American bouldering. I'm not sure his metaphysical ponderings ever influenced me much, but his use of chalk did.

If I was getting buffeted for my use of chalk by Ken Wilson, and for not doing new routes that met with John Allen's approval, the greatest setback I faced in the mid 1970s was of my own making.

To make my grant go further, beyond scrounging free meals from my fellow students and doing articles, I also stole things, mostly food and the odd bottle of booze. Thieving routes off other climbers is one thing, but breaking the law is quite another. It's something I deeply regret, and not just because I got caught; I'm ashamed of it. But stealing was commonplace among all sorts of climbers in the 1970s, especially abroad when you were trying to eke out what little money you had. For Livesey and some of our group, it was also another way to break the rules and get an adrenalin rush. I felt uncomfortable about some of it, particularly some of our gang thieving in small communities like La Palud rather than large supermarket chains. I didn't do it to make some anti-bourgeois statement. I did it because I wanted to eat and go climbing. I had a student grant, but it never seemed quite enough to travel to Wales or the Lakes.

Having said that, I was perfectly capable of taking things to extremes. The biggest thing I ever took was an expensive stereo from the window of a hi-fi shop in a well-to-do northern town. This thing was gorgeous, like a console from the Starship Enterprise and about three feet long. Pete was with me, so I suppose I was showing off. I walked in, unplugged it, tucked it inside my coat and walked out. Simple as that. It was all part of the brag, but I still can't believe I actually did that. It all seemed such a laugh at the time.

Do something wrong long enough, and you'll get caught in the end. After graduating from Ilkley, I'd started my probationary year's teaching at Guiseley Middle School. After school one day, I went into a supermarket and was spotted by security putting a jar of coffee into my coat pocket. I'll never forget the embarrassment and confusion of those few hours. The security guard took me off to the office in the back and called the police. I was arrested and taken down to the station where I started to panic a bit. The police knew about the coffee, but I had butter and eggs and all sorts down my trousers, and I wondered how on earth I was going to get rid of them. So I asked to go to the toilet and I stuck them in the cistern after prising the lid off it. It's probably all still there.

I was charged and the case went to court. The school got to hear about it. I even got a letter from Shirley Williams, then the secretary of state for education, admonishing me. No pressure was put on me to quit, but I felt my teaching career was over. I felt incredibly guilty and foolish and my embarrassment made it impossible to continue. Getting caught shoplifting had destroyed my future. Worst of all, what I had done made the local paper, the paper my parents read. Next time I went home I had to explain that I'd given up teaching knowing full well that Mum and Dad knew why. We never talked about it. I didn't even talk about it with my sister Alison, the person in the family to whom I was closest. I could, however, almost taste their disappointment. That wasn't something I could laugh off.

There's no question that this embarrassment, which very few of my friends knew about at the time, sent my life in a new direction. Maybe in the long run it even worked out for the best. With my teaching career down the pan, I was free to concentrate on my climbing, the thing I was born to do. I don't think it's a coincidence that around this time the new routes I was putting up not only became consistently harder but also began to include some really impressive lines. It was as though my life had reached a crux. I had made a mess of things with teaching. Now it was time to knuckle down and make something of myself.

For example, at Ilkley in the mid 1970s I did a few new routes, an E3 on the Far Western Buttress called *Carrie* and some routes in Rocky Valley, including *Sunburst Finish* and a hard E6 called *Shock Horror*. Not a bad haul, but the following year I got stuck into the aid route *Milky Way*. This was a well-known challenge, put up in the mid 1950s by Allan Austin and Brian Evans on the Cow, the larger of Ilkley's two squat buttresses, the smaller being the Calf. Pete Livesey had written in 1975 that *Milky Way* was 'too hard for now'. I aimed to prove that things were moving on faster than he realised. The route had a fat wooden wedge bigger than a tennis ball stuck in a pocket at twenty feet offering access to a peg-scarred crack that split an overhang at two-thirds height. I abseiled the line, cleaned some of the holds and bashed out the wedge.

There was a lot of talk about whether the line was chipped around the time of the first ascent. There was certainly a lot of competition from the likes of Steve Bancroft and when people saw me wellying the wedge with my peg hammer they put two and two together and made a crime. To be honest, I'm not sure it made that much difference to the difficulty. It's a bully of a route, with an awkward boulder problem start to an overhanging flake and then a long reach to the pocket. From this a two-finger pocket and a high step got me established in the crack. This turned out to be a brutal business, with few footholds, and had me cramming my fingers into the thin crack, cursing my dad for giving me my thick hands.

At the overhang I got a poor sort of rest in the niche below it. I was already pumped and still had the overhanging crack above to get past. I reached around the roof, put in an excellent nut and eased back into the niche, tucked up like a spider contemplating its next meal. Things weren't going to get any easier. I could see that the crack started narrowly and then widened towards a chockstone. The bottom of the crack was flared and I had to twist my hands horribly to get them to stick. There wasn't much for my feet either. Taking a deep breath, I stuck my foot around the lip but my arms were trashed and I plopped onto the runner, lowering back to the ground.

In a rage, I stormed back up to the niche, powered round the roof and kept going, breathing harder and harder as the crack chewed me up. My whole body screamed with the effort but just as I faced falling again, the jams improved and I was able to go on. As I reached the chockstone I thought my arms would finally get a break, but there was still a sting in the tail. Hands trashed and bleeding, my lungs on fire, I hauled myself onto the top and lay there for a while until I could use my fingers well enough to untie the rope.

I don't suppose *Milky Way* is the best route on gritstone, but it's a very good one, with a great line and powerful climbing. Its status is on a par with Livesey's free version of *Wellington Crack* at the same crag, but much harder. These days it's graded E6 6b, but its reputation as a tough physical challenge requiring a climber's best effort means a lot more to me. That same year I also climbed the left arête of the Cow. Pete Livesey had cleaned it, and the marks the brush had left sent me into a jealous passion. I abseiled down it, re-brushed the holds but didn't top-rope it. I think Pete had realised it was too much for him and he came with me as I bouldered out the start, trying to find the right sequence and sufficient courage to launch up the arête. A fall from the crux would have put me in hospital. Finally, I committed myself and can still feel the surge of relief as I caught the good hold past the crux. *Desperate Dan*, as I called it, isn't pumpy like *Milky Way*, but it's far more serious, and another truly great gritstone line, done in an era before sticky rubber or bouldering mats. It's sometimes given E7 now, although I gave it E5 at the time, making it a contender for the first route at that grade in the country.

You couldn't imagine a more different challenge from The Cow at Ilkley to the blank wall below the old fog-warning station on Holyhead Mountain's North Stack. Just off vertical and covered in small holds, the climbing is much less physical, but it's not a place for the faint of heart. There are few cracks or flakes to put gear in, and in the late 1970s we still didn't have the curved nuts climbers now take for granted. Exploring this wall was going to take courage.

I'd done a lot of climbing over the years at Gogarth and loved the place. I felt completely at home on the Main Cliff, which in its scale and angle reminded me of the big limestone crags in Yorkshire. A whole string of outstanding lines had been done here in the 1960s using a heavy sprinkling of aid. In those days, heads were stronger than arms. The characters involved – Joe Brown, Pete Crew, Jack Street and Al Rouse – were all great exploratory climbers. The challenge of freeing the Main Cliff's classic routes of their few remaining aid points was taken up during the late 1970s as climbers got fitter and what loose rock remained was cleaned off.

The North Stack Wall was a very different sort of challenge. It was all about pulling on thin, friable flakes, spooky rock at the best of times, but with a huge fall in prospect if something should break, it's hardly surprising that it had remained a blank canvas while climbers were drawing lines all over the Main Cliff. Interest, however, was growing. A number of routes were added to North Stack in the summer of 1978, a year of incredible new route activity at Gogarth, but it seemed to me the best line was up the middle of it, starting in a slight groove to a flake and then right to the wall above. But the gear, or lack of it, was terrifying. I abseiled down and gave the line a bit of a brush. I can still remember thinking how dirty it was, and how creaky some of the flakes were. I could do the climbing, I felt sure, but how reliable was the rock? The gear looked atrocious.

Trouble was, I wasn't the only person interested in that blank middle section. It was no surprise to me that the Lakeland climber Pete Whillance had been looking at the same line. The North Stack was almost made for him. Pete was another climber with a terrific head on his shoulders. I'd done a number of his routes in the Lakes, most memorably a bold undertaking on Deer Bield Crag in Far Easedale. I'd gone up there with Steve Foster and we'd more or less ticked the rest of the crag before I got on *Take It To The Limit*. Rockfall later destroyed the route but it was one of Whillance's masterpieces. I had a fearsome time on it, pulling a peg out with my fingers and stuffing it back in because it was the best protection I had. I wasn't sure where Pete had got to with the route on North Stack, but I'd have to get cracking. The angle of climbing on the whole of that wall was his domain.

Travelling down to Wales with Gibby that September, I threw a Troll 8mm bolt kit into my rucksack. I wouldn't have done that normally, so I must have planned to place bolts on *The Cad*. I was aware that it would be controversial but there was an argument in favour of what I did. Parliament House Cave, the deep-set scoop at the end of North Stack, had aid routes with bolts in them. Geoff Birtles and Tom Proctor had put bolts in at Red Walls. It seemed to me a bit like the ethic in Yorkshire. If it had been Cloggy I wouldn't have done it, never in a million years. Ed Drummond had put bolts in on Cloggy's *Great Wall* a year or so before, and was rightly criticised. Gogarth seemed different, but I knew I was testing the ethical limits. Nowadays, people would argue that if you put two bolts in, why not put eight or ten in? That would have turned the line into an excellent sport climbing route at about French 6c. Two bolts – one before the flake and one after – made it safe enough for me, but maybe not for others. And maybe someone would come along and climb it without any bolts. Then again, hindsight is a wonderful thing.

The climb itself is a three-star classic, although at the time I was more concerned about just getting through it. I remember looking down at Gibby to see his mouth slightly agape as he watched anxiously. The groove led up past a small overlap and a good flake. Above that I edged carefully past the first bolt towards the big flake, which boomed hollow when I thumped it. Apparently people have since fallen on it and these days you can get good protection here, but the gear I had didn't feel nearly so positive. I was about 50ft above Gibby by this point and the first bolt felt a long way below. Over to the right the second bolt I'd drilled smiled at me, a little ray of sunshine on a cloudy day. It gave me hope. The sequence off the flake is beautifully technical, stepping nimbly rightwards, not hurrying too much with the promise of safety just off to the side. A thin crux move above the bolt, and the wall eased a bit.

I won't say I have regrets about what I did on North Stack, but the name I gave the route – *The Cad* – told everyone that I was aware of the displeasure I might have caused. To be honest, it was less than I anticipated. Perhaps it's because instead of sloping back to Yorkshire we went to the pub afterwards and told the locals what we'd done. Gibby was often my secret weapon in a situation like that, smoothing the way when my shyness might make me appear defensive.

Despite that, I did feel I'd hurried my preparations. As well as the bolts I drilled, I hammered in a peg above the second bolt that was useless. It proved impossible to reach from the route, and I had to do some awkward moves across to it and then reverse them. I remember climbing up towards it thinking, nice one Ron, you've put this in the wrong place. If I'd cleaned the route more thoroughly and looked more carefully for gear then perhaps I wouldn't have placed the first bolt either. Pete Whillance, who did the second ascent a year later, removed it before he started climbing. A solo ascent was publicised soon after that, although there are doubts about its credibility. Whatever the truth, the second bolt was taken out in 1986 when Nick Dixon did the first ascent without it at E6. By then John Redhead had added his routes *The Bells, The Bells* and *The Clown*, both E7 and both horrifically serious. The world had moved on. All I can say is that

The Cad sees fewer climbers than if I'd put in ten bolts but I'm glad it's such an admired traditional route.

After *The Cad*, some climbers got the idea I wasn't capable of bold climbing. They forget that the same weekend I did *The Cad*, I also climbed a new line on the Upper Tier called *Blackleg*. Also graded E5, it's a serious undertaking, with very little of the gear on it much good. It also went unrepeated longer than *The Cad* did, despite a lot of attention from strong climbers. As Pete Livesey had showed me, spicing things up with a high-profile grand gesture was a sure-fire way to get attention. And as it turned out, I was on the brink of a golden period that would eclipse routes like *The Cad*, a time when the potential I felt I had was finally realised.

SIX

Lord of the Flies

'RIGHT, CHRIS,' I CALLED DOWN, 'WATCH US HERE.' Turning back to the matter at hand, I bunched my shoulders and moved up onto the thin top section of *Lord of the Flies*. I can't remember now whether I meant what I said, and was in reality in any danger of falling off, or not. Filmmaker Sid Perou was always encouraging us to say things to fill the long silences of me performing on the rock and I did the route so many times – more than a dozen at least – that by the end I had it wired. On the other hand, Gibby was the sound recordist, and what with fiddling with his switches and trying to roll fags at the same time, I'm not sure how much attention he was paying to the ropes, which, incidentally, he had wrapped round his forearm rather than through a belay plate.

Sometimes it doesn't matter what you do – how hard you train or how much you climb. Sometimes fate just lends a hand and pushes you along. The film *Rock Athlete* was that kind of moment for me. It got me recognised. For the first time I became well known outside the small world of extreme rock climbing I'd inhabited up to now. It gave me a profile that I could exploit to earn my living and climb full-time, making me in effect the first professional rock climber. It also inspired the next generation of young climbers then taking up the sport. Climbers had traditionally worn thick trousers and sweaters and hung on pegs. Here was a guy in running shorts and a vest, fit enough to keep climbing when it got too strenuous. Gil Scott-Heron warned that the revolution would not be televised, but it turned out that the rock climbing revolution really was.

Sid Perou was a keen caver working as a sound recordist for the BBC at the old Ealing Studios in the mid 1960s. In 1967, he was co-opted onto a film about the Cave Rescue Association called *Sunday at Sunset Pot*, and because of his caving expertise ended up filming underground. The documentary featured the attempted rescue of a caver called Eric Luckhurst who had fallen at the bottom of Sunset Cave in the Dales and died while he was being evacuated. The film had caused quite a stir at the time. Sid quit the BBC and set up as an independent filmmaker, wanting to show outdoor sports like caving, canoeing and climbing for what they are rather than the strange interpretations the media often creates to make them seem more dramatic.

He had just finished a five-part series called *Beneath the Pennines* and having saturated the market with caving films was looking for a new project. Pete Gomersall lived almost next door to Sid, and he knew Gibby too. After talking with them, Sid realised that a sea-change was going on in the world of rock climbing and documenting that would add a narrative structure to a climbing film, beyond simply showing the public a world they had probably never come across before. In a way, he tried to bridge the gap between non-climbers seeing climbing as a strange and frightening phenomenon and a fully realised sport, with its own codes and history.

Sid decided he would focus on what Pete Livesey and I had been doing in the last few years, as leading climbers of the time. Having been commissioned to make a series of three programmes, he divided them between a brief history of climbing from the 1960s onwards, a retrospective of Pete's career and, in the third episode, the first ascent of a new route as an attempt to show the essence of the sport and its future as well. That's where I came in.

First, we needed an objective. Given that the previous two programmes in the series had featured climbs in Yorkshire, the Peak District, the Lake District and Cornwall, it was obvious we should film in Wales. Later, writing in the book *Extreme Rock (Diadem, 1987)*, featuring a pick of the hardest rock climbing from the mid 1970s to the mid 1980s, Pete Livesey suggested that choosing a line on Dinas Cromlech was all his idea. Pete said he had cleaned a line to the left of his own route *Right Wall* in the spring of 1978 and climbed the first crux. Then he'd been forced to traverse off this new line into Right Wall when the route got too heavy. According to Pete, he then told Sid this would make a good project for his television series and seemed disgruntled that Sid had let me loose on it. I don't know whether Pete had got far with the line of *Lord of the Flies*, but neither Sid nor I spoke to him about possible subjects for the third programme. Anyway, plenty of local climbers knew all about a possible line to the left of *Right Wall*.

Sid asked me if he could film a first ascent, but the location he left to Gibby and me. We had a look around Idwal first, on the other side of the hill from Dinas Cromlech, in the Ogwen Valley. I had an idea there might be a gap on Suicide Wall so we explored up there for a while but nothing really suited and Sid wouldn't have been happy about the light. So we switched to the Llanberis Pass, which after the Second World War had replaced the Ogwen Valley as the real focus for exploratory rock climbing in Snowdonia. We were staying at Ynys Ettws, the Climbers' Club hut that sits in the valley below Clogwyn y Grochan, Dinas Cromlech's near neighbour, so the Cromlech was certainly in our minds. The clean open-book corner that forms the cliff's centrepiece is the most iconic landmark in Welsh climbing and I knew it well. As well as the classics put up in the 1950s by Joe Brown and Don Whillans, routes like *Cenotaph Corner* and *Cemetery Gates*, I'd done a very early ascent of *Left Wall* free, certainly before that of Steve Wunsch who used to be credited with the free version.

I'd also done Livesey's own masterpiece – *Right Wall* – first climbed in the summer of 1974, which tackled the huge blank space between the *Corner* and the *Gates*. That was a huge breakthrough, psychologically if not technically. Finding the route on the right wall of the Cromlech is more awkward than on the left, because it's substantially steeper. Lean out on the left wall and you can see where you're heading. On the right wall that's a lot more awkward. Pete was forced to traverse off along the wide ledge that girdles it – having untied from his ropes – solo up *Cemetery Gates*, and then abseil down the line of *Right Wall* to check where he should go next. When it was finished, Pete's creation meandered across the face as it followed the most amenable climbing, but it left an obvious gap for a more direct route to the right of *Cenotaph Corner*. Adding this to the pages of the Cromlech's open book would be substantially harder.

Like most television documentaries, *Rock Athlete* was constructed; glued together from lots of different takes and sometimes hammed up a little, to show what a hard, modern first ascent involved. It looks old fashioned now, turning up in Gibby's Vauxhall Viva and pitching a Vango Force 10 tent. But I think it rings true. Climbers recognised it for being authentic and the public got a sense that this is what modern climbing was all about. The most amazing thing is how all of it – the filming and the climbing – was done on such a shoestring. The opening scenes show me examining my rock boots, their toes worn through, loose chunks of rubber hanging off the last. I don't think young climbers can conceive how hard we managed to climb in such bad footwear. Happily, Sid let me have a new pair of EBs on the BBC's account, to go with the princely sum of £80 I got for appearing in a film watched by millions.

Sid, I think, was a bit unnerved by how quiet I was, and encouraged me to talk while I was climbing. Talking while I climbed was something I did anyway, but it wasn't the kind of chat you could put before a prime-time television audience. I'd berate protection, swear at the width of cracks and dispel any anxiety with a string of admittedly mild profanities. So my on-camera comments, such as they were, were a little stilted. I was both self-conscious and so absorbed in the route that chattering away to camera was beyond me, a fact picked up by the star television reviewer Clive James:

'United in possessing finely tuned physiques, rock climbers are divided in their methodology. Some rock climbers believe that anything goes. They hammer expanding bolts into the virgin rock and link them up with ropes. Given the appropriate budget they would obviously build a marble staircase all the way to the top. A purer breed insists on ordinary pitons as the upper limit of artificial aid. The most pure breed of the lot goes straight up the rock face with no means of attachment except chalk on the fingertips.

'Believe me, if you didn't see this last bunch, you should have. They're *evolving*. Their fingers are long and sensitive, like those of Vladimir Horowitz or certain species of climbing frog. Crouching in space, with fluttering fingertips they search the smooth rock for irregularities, like a blind man reading Keats. Sensitive toes propel them upwards. 'Oof! Aangh!' they say quietly. 'Harf! Ungh! Hoof!' Clearly they have left the English language far behind.'

Clive James was the leading television critic in Britain at the time, so I suppose the fact he noticed the programme at all was good news. I'm not sure he'd be any more eloquent hanging from his fingertips a hundred feet off the ground, but each to his own. I've always thought that one of the appeals of sport is that it takes you out of yourself, away from your thoughts, and so beyond language. Still, I liked the image of a blind man reading Keats. There's certainly poetry on those cliffs.

Anyway, despite his dig at my inarticulacy the few bursts of dialogue in the *Lord of the Flies* film took on a kind of cult status. At one point, finding myself pumping out while I struggled to place some gear, I muttered: 'Come on arms, do your stuff.' I'm not sure where it came from, although it's the kind of phrase I was using at that time in articles I was writing. For years afterwards people would quote that back at me, to the extent I wish I hadn't said it. People learned my unscripted comments off by heart, like they would a Monty Python sketch. Gibby contributed as well, presumably also under instruction to say something – anything – that sounded helpful. 'Is that a big crozzly pocket across there?' he called up, looking alert and anxious for my safety. The phrase 'crozzly pocket' also entered climbing patois after *Rock Athlete* aired, partly because so many were bemused by what 'crozzly' meant – sharp and jagged, as it happens. Crozzle was the mineral crust that formed on top of molten steel and was put on top of walls in northern towns to make them less easy to climb over.

From a climber's point of view, the film looks very different to the kinds of film made these days. Sid was hanging from a rope next to me, climbing up it on jumars when I got above him and then continuing to shoot from the side. Whenever I looked up and left, there was Sid, like a bearded angel on my shoulder. At no stage did he shoot from directly above, although there are some long-distance cut-away shots taken from across the valley. So for much of the route, you can't see my feet, and sometimes even my hands are out of shot. That would be deemed a shortcoming now, when seeing the moves climbers make in their context is what it's all about. But Sid's approach had an interesting consequence that some modern filmmakers might appreciate. The focus falls not on the climb, but on the climber. You can see me completely absorbed by what I'm doing, focussed and lost in it. Shooting from above, you barely see a climber's face. From the side, it's what you notice most. It's mesmerising, watching an athlete performing like that, shorn of everything else that's going on. The only thing I can think of that compares is the documentary that followed the footballer Zinedine Zidane throughout an entire game, focussed entirely on him.

Zidane, however, was playing a regular club fixture, whereas *Lord of the Flies* was a new climb, a unique occurrence, and while the film was a big deal for me, the route itself was ultimately the most important thing. Typically, I rushed the true first ascent. At some stage, Sid filmed me abseiling down and cleaning the holds, but I can't remember now whether what is shown in the film is how it actually happened. I walked up to the Cromlech the evening before the ascent and noticed that the final wall was streaked with water, and then jogged up the route *Sabre Cut* to set up an abseil rope, scaring the pants off a roped party. Lowering myself down the line of *Lord*, I barely glanced at the final moves, thinking they looked straightforward enough. Inevitably, they turned out to be as hard as the crux lower down. At least there was a good nut to protect the last twenty feet. Lower down, I nailed a good peg in below the first crux, which I knew some would find controversial. (Both these pieces of protection are no longer there.) Then I went to bed, hoping the wall would dry out next morning.

There's no question that I didn't do *Lord of the Flies* on-sight – just walking up to the crag and climbing it. I'd abseiled down the line and checked out many of the holds and gear placements, and placed that peg. But *Lord* was typical of how I often did new routes, falling in between the purest on-sight style and practising the thing properly as Pete would have done. Something in me still wanted to do a new route in as pure a style as possible. And, on the negative side, I was still more than a little slapdash in how I went about things.

Better weather next day meant the rock dried quickly and I was soon tying on at the bottom of the right wall. Gibby looks more nervous than I do in the film, chattering away about the rope, but inside I was itching to be gone, to find out what those holds were really like. Starting up thin cracks and then pulling up widely spaced pockets to a good ledge at around thirty feet, the first crux came moving right and up to a thin, fingery section where fiddling in gear was a real chore. That's one aspect of new routing that faded into the background in the 1980s, as climbers did more and more practice and gear improved. In 1979, curved nuts didn't yet exist. The old, symmetrical versions would swivel out of their placements at the first opportunity. Puzzling out the gear was often as taxing as doing the moves.

That whole right wall was a bit of a puzzle. Blank, hard to read and steep, *Lord* took all my effort and concentration to stay on it. Even then, when I reached the girdle ledge two-thirds of the way up, I ground to a halt. This was the section I'd given a quick brush and thought would be straightforward when I was cleaning the line. But I just couldn't see where the holds were leading. I was forced to imitate Pete's tactics on the first ascent of *Right Wall*, sloping off along the girdle ledge to nip up *Cemetery Gates* and down Sid's rope for a quick reminder. Getting the sequence off the girdle ledge was key. With that extra knowledge on board, and a nice fat hexentric nut slotted in above it, I managed to fight my way to the top. I can't remember who came up with the name, but I doubt it was mine. I don't remember liking the book.

Many people now remember *Lord of the Flies* as much for being filmed as for the impact it had in the climbing world at the time. But even before *Rock Athlete* aired in 1980, those who knew about Welsh climbing appreciated what I'd done. Paul Williams wrote in the Climbers' Club guidebook that *Lord* had 'stunned the locals'. Geoff Milburn, writing in that year's Climbers' Club Journal, wondered if I hadn't got the grade wrong.

'This stupendous wall pitch between *Cenotaph Corner* and *Right Wall* was first given an E5, 6a grading and described as being both "harder and more sustained than *Right Wall*." Now that says only one thing to me – if an open-ended grading system is ever to be used sensibly then this is probably the time to have the first Welsh E6 with a technical grade of either 6b or 6c. Whatever the decision there is no doubt that Fawcett is now a head in front of all the other pacesetters, who are trying to create a big impression and this pitch, which must be regarded as a major step forward in Welsh climbing standards, is only the catalyst which will start a chain reaction in the next few years.'

Rock Athlete, on the other hand, despite days of filming, was not yet in the bag. Sid had shot footage of me standing on a large detached block shouting excitedly for the camera. It was to be the climactic moment, the artist celebrating his new creation. When Sid got home and viewed the rushes, however, he discovered a piece of grit had got into the mechanism when he was changing film to shoot the last few feet of the climb, and there was now a continuous scratch through the middle of the scene. The last section would have to be done again.

Meanwhile, a few local 'artists', one of them a friend of mine called Paul Williams, had climbed up to the top of the crag with a car jack and levered the loose block I had stood on off the top of *Lord* in a colossal trundle. 'Christ, it's the size of an asteroid,' Paul said as it fell away, grew smaller and then exploded on the path up to the bottom of the cliff like an atom bomb. The debris at the bottom also frightened off a couple of climbers who'd walked up next day to climb *Spiral Stairs*. Happily for me, it didn't touch any of the holds on my route, but it did mean that the long shots we'd taken of the Cromlech were now out of date. If you look carefully, the offending block is still momentarily visible in the film, preserved for posterity.

The gods were against us. Throughout the summer rain fell, or else the route was wet, or none of us could be in the same place at the same time. It was well into the autumn when we finally met again in Snowdonia, and still there were damp streaks running halfway down the wall. We hung on for a couple of days and finally the weather and conditions came good.

Of course, having committed myself to wearing a running vest and shorts in mid summer, I had to wear them again for continuity. Only now it was November and bitterly cold. My legs and hands were turning blue, so before I abseiled in to the top of the route, we built a little fire in the vegetated area above the wall. Nobody, however, realised my hair was an inch longer, so my 'do magically sprouts towards the end of *Rock Athlete*, and I'm not sure I managed to find the same pair of red socks either. That wasn't all that had changed in the intervening months. Continuity was breaking down in other parts of my life too.

Towards the end of my aborted degree at Ilkley College, I'd started seeing a lass called Carol. She was a lovely girl, and Mum was delighted when we got engaged. After Carol qualified, she got a job in Keighley and so we bought a house together in a nearby village just below Earl Crag, which I came to know well. I loved being able to nip out of the house up onto the moors for a few hours of peaceful soloing.

But it soon became clear that Carol and I wanted different things out of life. She needed someone prepared to settle down and at that stage of my life I couldn't stay still for more than five minutes. I loved travelling, and loved climbing in as many different places as I could manage. I wasn't ready for a mortgage and kids. Mum was fond of Carol and I think she was secretly pleased I was embarking on something that promised some stability after my shoplifting conviction. But I was completely obsessed with climbing. It was how I defined myself, and I wasn't going to compromise now I was finally realising my ambition of being among the very best.

Then, in the autumn and back in Verdon once again, I met a young woman studying maths at Bangor. Gill Kent was clever and funny, and seemed just as at home with the idea of travelling round the world to climb as I was. Although she was seeing someone else at the time, our relationship developed quickly, and soon after I got back, I moved down to Wales to live with her while she continued her course. When we went back up to the Cromlech that autumn to re-shoot the last scene for *Rock Athlete*, it was Gill holding the rope.

After twenty-four years born and bred in Yorkshire, I moved to Wales. Living on the edge of Snowdonia was a big change, and inevitably I developed new friendships. The most important of these was with Paul Williams, whose enthusiasm and competitive streak became an inspiration to me. Nothing pleased him more than sitting in Pete's Eats with a pint of tea after we'd done a new route, writing it up in the special book they kept behind the counter. He also had an encyclopaedic knowledge of climbing history and the journals to back it up. His library was unbelievable. It was his love and it's where he spent what money he had. Lists, league tables, dates, things that could be measured meant a lot to Paul. That's one of the reasons he didn't much care for bouldering. Everything had to have a name and a grade as far as Paul was concerned. That attitude earned him the nickname the Big Tick, but he wasn't some cold-blooded statistician. He was passionate about climbing. And when I was getting to know him, his love for the sport was the one consistent thing in his life at a time when everything else in it was changing. He was living in a beautiful house when I first moved to Wales, but his marriage was breaking up and his wife was moving back to Nottingham. Paul seemed bereft, but he didn't talk about it much. There was a bit of the little boy lost about him.

Paul had served in the Royal Air Force, and had a little Englander side to him, which was more endearing than alarming, as you might usually expect. He was the only friend I had who read the *Daily Mail*, and as long as he had the crossword to do he was happy. We took the piss out of him for that, and one of our friends, the great Gogarth pioneer Jim Moran, used to arrive with a copy of *The Guardian* under his arm, just to wind Paul up. But for all his rightwing credentials, and his noise and occasional sulks, Paul had a heart of gold.

He was funny too, combative and quick-witted, coming up with brilliant one-liners with perfect timing. Climbing near the coast one day, with Paul belaying me, a group of walkers arrived and started watching. One stuffy old boy began a lecture on what I was doing and the history of the sport, droning on authoritatively while talking nonsense. Paul finally had suffered enough, and interrupted.

'Hey,' he said, nodding up at me. 'Do you know who this is?'

'No,' the man replied, looking a little nonplussed.

'That's Charlton Chestwig, the world's finest climber.'

He wasn't the most graceful climber around, being a burly lad with thick, strong thighs, more a rock'n'roller than a Nureyev. Put him next to the great talent of that Welsh scene, John Redhead, and you'd be hard-pressed to find two more contrasting figures. But Paul was a key figure in Llanberis in those years, as much for his force of personality as anything else. He acted like a catalyst, waking people up, getting them out there. Talking about whatever was new. All that enthusiasm was eventually distilled into a number of outstanding guidebooks that caught the flavour of those years.

My previous experience of the climbing scene in Llanberis hadn't been so positive. As a teenager I'd arrived for the first time with Gibby and a friend of his and we'd gone to Wendy's, then the café of choice, for breakfast. In those days, climbers in Llanberis were still surfing the fag end of the 1960s counter-culture and had a reputation for hedonism and the wildest parties. One of the best known from the group was sitting at a table near us when his girlfriend, who worked in the café, brought his breakfast over. He took one look at it, didn't like what he saw and smacked her in the face. The whole place erupted in laughter. The three of us were appalled. Gibby's mate leaned in and said: 'Blokes don't hit women where I come from. Shall I go and smack him?'

I didn't mind that people partied so hard, although it wasn't for me. As one wag put it, when the news broke about this lad from Yorkshire coming down and climbing one of the best lines in Wales: 'We should stop smoking so much dope.' Paul was a little more conventional in his tastes. He liked a pint and was a great one for socialising, but he wanted to climb everything – literally. I could always rely on him as a partner, in much the same way as I could Gibby.

So it was that I found myself back at the Cromlech the following spring with Paul for a sequence of new routes that still remain overshadowed by the impact of *Lord of the Flies* and the film *Rock Athlete*, which aired on the BBC a month later. I'd already done one new route on the Cromlech since *Rock Athlete*, in a freakish spell of good January weather, a sort of more direct version of *Right Wall*, which I called *Precious*. It wasn't a great new route, however, certainly not compared to *Lord* or the routes I did with Paul that April.

On the Saturday morning we walked up to the Cromlech and a line I'd spotted to the right of a classic route, *Ivy Sepulchre*. It took the wall to the right, climbing boldly up a pocketed wall to the same girdle ledge that continues into *Cenotaph Corner*. From there, I reached a pocket and then made a huge lunging reach to a good jug. This we called *Hall of Warriors*, which from this distance in time, I'm guessing was a pun on *Wall of Horrors*, at Almscliff.

With *Hall of Warriors* in the bag, we continued up and across to an upper tier of Dinas Cromlech where a classic Hard Severe called *Horseman's Route* finished up a prominent corner. Here I'd spotted a superb finger crack splitting this final buttress that looked as savage as it was overhanging. Climbing it was like being beaten up. I found it desperately hard, shredding my fingers as I went, every muscle aching as I pulled over the top. Half my gear had fallen out, and I lay on the top fighting to get my breath back. This was so much harder than the route I'd done with Pete in Yosemite that had been set as a benchmark by Ray Jardine – *Crimson Cringe*. Paul shouted up from the belay: 'If you could take in slightly faster than I'm climbing I'd appreciate it.'

I called this monstrous crack *Atomic Hot Rod* and gave it the grade E5 7a, a grade I'd already used a month before for *Strawberries*, a fierce line I'd just climbed at Tremadog. The grading got a lot of attention, particularly for *Atomic Hot Rod*, which was a less well-known challenge than *Strawberries*. You could almost see climbers sitting in grotty cafés around the country poring over *Crags* magazine and scratching their heads: 'What the bloody hell is a 7a?'

It certainly wasn't what people mean by 7a now. I was simply trying to find a way of expressing how much harder I thought this route was than the E5 6bs I'd done so far, particularly in Wales where you'd do one or perhaps two hard moves on the route. *Atomic Hot Rod* was hard all the way up, with a sequence of such moves one after the other, perhaps a dozen in all; I was fighting to get protection in, trying to stay on every inch of the way.

There was a lot of uncertainty around grades at the time, something modern climbers perhaps won't understand. Having started on Yorkshire limestone, I'd grown up dealing with risky climbs where long falls were a real possibility. A route like *Mossdale Trip* at Gordale Scar was really serious but not so hard technically. *Atomic Hot Rod*, by comparison, was relatively safe, but the physical effort and technical climbing involved was far more intense. The grading system didn't cover things like how sustained a route was. Should it go with the adjectival grade – E for effort – or be stuck on the technical grade, which is what I did, grading it E5 7a. Part of me was responding competitively to John Redhead, who'd given his own new route at Tremadog the grade 7a. I went straight down there to repeat it, and found it easier than *Strawberries*. If *Bananas* was 7a, then *Strawberries* was 7b. No doubt Paul, who lived for controversies like these, pitched in with his thoughts too. But mostly I wanted to surprise people into thinking about a problem that still hasn't been completely resolved. The 'E' in extreme still describes effort or risk or both. *Atomic Hot Rod* is now graded E5 6b, although I suspect it's quite a handful at that. Flexible camming devices mean it's a lot easier to protect than when I first did it, which I imagine has taken some of the sting out of it. Maybe having thick fingers meant I suffered more than some on it. But I don't suppose it's got *that* much easier.

The following morning, the Sunday, we were back at the Cromlech, climbing on the left wall this time, filling the gap between *Resurrection* and *Cenotaph Corner*. We named it for the arch-villain of the hit television show *Dallas* – and perhaps also for the maverick brilliance of John Redhead. The gear was horribly spaced, and *JR* has seen some huge falls. I'd now done three routes on the walls either side of *Cenotaph Corner*, but I could still see some gaps. The following weekend Paul and I were back, climbing a rising traverse of the right and then left walls called *Ivory Madonna*. For me, this was the best route of all, better than *Lord of the Flies*, with two beautiful pitches, climbed on a spring day so hot we could see the rock steaming as the final wet streaks of winter burned away. The crux was a fingery thin section traversing across blank rock into *Cenotaph Corner*, a sequence Joe Healey, my friend from bouldering days at Pex Hill, described as being 'Pex 6a' – praise indeed, since this meant good 6b anywhere else. A fall from the last of these moves, after 140ft of climbing, would see you come close to swinging into the base of the route, like a conker on a string, a theory someone tested in the early 1980s, sweeping across the right wall upside down and missing the ground by five feet, before continuing some distance up *Cemetery Gates*, on the wall's right arête. Finally, the following morning, I filled another gap on the left wall, between *Left Wall* itself and *Resurrection*. After the warm, summery weather of the day before, the temperature had plunged, and I found my fingers going numb gripping the holds. The gear too was less than perfect, but the climbing was usually that little bit more amenable on the left wall. I edged my feet carefully along a flake out of *Resurrection*, reached a pocket and then pulled into *Left Wall* before finishing direct up virgin territory. *True Grip* was a good-quality E4 and the easiest of the five new routes I'd climbed on those famous walls, three of them in the space of a week – and my seventh major new route on the Cromlech altogether.

Most of all, I remember Paul's enthusiasm, his passion for what we were doing. It was inspiring. I'd not spent much time in Wales before I lived there, and soon I would move on, to Derbyshire, where Gill and I got married. Although I would still come down from time to time, particularly to repeat John Redhead's routes, my visits were rare. But that spring, with Paul and others, North Wales seemed to me the greatest place on Earth to be a climber.

SEVEN

Strawberries

IT WAS A BEAUTIFUL EARLY SPRING IN 1980. It seemed every day dawned with a clear sky overhead. Midweek, I'd climb on the Yamaha after Gill had gone to lectures and dash down the A487 to Caernarfon in bright morning light. Then I would turn south, the power on, sunshine streaming through new leaves on the trees, leaning into corners, the road dry and grippy. When I reached Tremadog I would park the bike at the café under the crags for a brew, looking up at the sharply angled faces and arêtes across the road and chatting with owner Eric Jones while I drank my tea. Most of the clientele must assume he's just the bloke who runs the café, but Eric is one of the great heroes of British climbing and adventure generally, whether soloing the north face of the Eiger, or base-jumping in Venezuela. He has also kept an eye out for generations of young climbers who show up at his café, desperate to make a name, including me. When I was finished, I'd leave my cup on the counter and go to work.

I loved Tremadog. In those days it wasn't just an excellent place to climb when the weather in the mountains was bad. It was a crucible for some of the hardest routes being done in the country. The first new route I did there was *Cream*, done with Pete during the international climbing festival in 1976 when I turned twenty-one. Pete played his trick of snookering me into falling as I followed him up the second pitch. The following year I'd got rid

TOP LEFT The first ascent of *Milky Way* (E6 6b) at Ilkley in West Yorkshire. RIGHT Also at Ilkley, the first ascent of *Desperate Dan* (E7 6b), a route I'm very proud of. It typifies what I used to look for in new routes: a brilliant line, with hard and bold climbing. BOTTOM LEFT Paul Williams on The King's Way in El Chorro, Spain. It was always a dare to walk this narrow section without clipping in for protection.

TOP LEFT The West Face of El Cap, Yosemite, on the one-day ascent I made with Gill.　TOP RIGHT Gill on top of El Cap after our one-day ascent of the West Face.　BOTTOM LEFT AND RIGHT On and off *Strawberries* (E6 6b) at Tremadog, while filming *Pushing the Limits* for Channel 4 with Leo Dickinson.　OPPOSITE The first ascent of *The Cad* (E6 6a) on North Stack Wall, Gogarth. I'm midway between the two bolts I placed on the wall to protect the climb.

OVERLEAF The crux section on *Cave Route Right-hand* (E6 6b) at Gordale. One of several great shots John Beatty took of me on the Cave Routes, with the image on the book's cover developing a particularly iconic status. OPPOSITE On the top wall of *Lord of the Flies* (E6 6a), during filming for *Rock Athlete*. TOP LEFT High on Martin Atkinson's route *Pierrepoint* (F7c+). The photo shows the true scale of Gordale. TOP RIGHT Not a great photo but it shows just how grim the slimy roof crack of *Bavarian Reality* really is! MIDDLE RIGHT The late Wolfgang Güllich. BOTTOM Repeating Jerry Moffatt's route *Revelations* (F8a+) at Raven Tor.

TOP LEFT Playing the 'Rock Star' role in Japan.   TOP RIGHT The dodgy top rope winch in the Crimea – used for speed climbing competitions.   MIDDLE LEFT The cliff in the Crimea where the speed climbing competition took place. The steel top rope extended all the way to the top of the wall.   BOTTOM LEFT Climbing the *Edge of Extinction* in Japan.   BOTTOM RIGHT With John Long in Joshua Tree. His arms are actually as big as my legs!

of the aid point on *Void*, an excellent new climb on the edge of the powerful looming buttress most famous for Joe Brown's route done in 1960 – *Vector*. But what I loved most about Tremadog was soloing there. The routes seemed to be made for me, long, flowing sequences on routes up to 250ft in length. The first ascent of *Lord of the Flies* is how people remember my contribution to the *Rock Athlete* series, but the opening credits of each programme showed me soloing a route called *Tensor*, on Craig y Castell, just above the village of Tremadog itself. Sid used the footage in slow motion, and in doing so caught something of the strange mixture of feelings you get while soloing high above the ground, of being calm but utterly focussed. I see myself totally absorbed and living intensely; it's what I love about the sport.

My own soloing had started from the early days at Haw Bank and Crookrise, more out of necessity than any addiction to danger. I worked out colossal circuits of routes on all the crags near my home, and would run up onto the moors to get to them. When I moved to Ilkley, I brought that habit with me, and over the years developed a sequence of routes I felt comfortable soloing, like *North-west Girdle*, *Western Front* and *Wall of Horrors* at Almscliff, and something similar at Ilkley and Caley too. Long days at Tremadog were just an extension of this process.

There were times in my climbing career when I did fall soloing. Early on there was the moment at Gordale when a hold broke and I landed close to the group of picnickers. After that, I hobbled up to Malham on crutches and mates would top-rope me so I could keep fit until my ankle healed. Also, there was the bizarre moment when I just let go of the rock at Crookrise, while chatting to Al Evans. I became adept at jumping off, and could get away with the most amazing falls. I jumped off from high on a route at Ilkley once, spraining an ankle, only to discover someone had swiped my trainers while I was climbing. I had to hobble home in my EBs.

Soloing was a big part of the climbing scene in the 1970s, especially in Wales. Eric Jones was just one of several guys doing it regularly, along with his friend Cliff Phillips and other stars like Pete Minks, Richard McHardy and Alan Rouse. It was seen as the deepest, scariest game in town and was undoubtedly addictive. For those routinely using psychoactive drugs, as some in the Welsh scene were, naturally manufacturing your own high through extreme physical experiences was obviously appealing. I can't claim that's what inspired me. I got a buzz from the danger of it, I can't deny that, but most of the time I was in control.

Not always though. I remember trying to solo *Positron* around this time, one of the best-known routes on the steep main wall at Gogarth. It was a crag where I felt completely at home. Gogarth isn't like the limestone climbing I was used to in Yorkshire; it's more open handed, like gritstone, and with my big hands I felt very comfortable on it. I did major free ascents on the main cliff wall around then, *Citadel* and *Mammoth* among them, and in the summer of 1980 the first ascent of an E6 called *The Big Sleep*.

Still, soloing *Positron* was a sobering challenge. Al Rouse had taken a huge fall from it on the aided first ascent, getting into the meat of the third pitch, on the steepest part of the wall, after trying every piece of gear he had behind the flake he was hanging from. Next day he went back with the right size of Moac nut clenched between his teeth, managed to get it placed and then clipped in for a rest. This was the point I reached, only without the Moac and without a rope to clip it into either. Launching out onto that huge, leaning white wall is imposing enough tied on, but with just a chalk bag at your waist it takes a lot of self-control. I'd done *Positron* before and knew I could climb it, but suddenly I was assailed by doubt. I felt my momentum crumble. I knew at once I had to be anywhere but hanging off that flake in the middle of an overhanging wall a hundred feet above the sea. There was just one clear thought looping round my head: 'How the fuck do

I get off this?' Could I possibly survive a fall from here? I looked at the sea, sucking in and drawing back from the base of the cliff. If I landed in the sea would I have a chance? Two or three times I bunched up on my footholds, preparing to jump into the great void below me, but each time couldn't commit. Eventually, I scuttled back down, fingers weakening and a rising tide of panic in my chest, to a large spike just above the belay and wrapped both arms around it. And there I stayed, clinging to the spike like a drowning man hugs the spar of a wrecked ship. Slowly the adrenalin subsided and my arms relaxed. I reached the belay and traversed into *Rat Race*, an easier route, and climbed this instead to its junction with *Cordon Bleu*, which at VS was easy enough for me to down-climb to the bottom of the main cliff. *Positron* was soloed, four years later, by Stevie Haston.

I don't remember anything quite so close to the edge at Tremadog. Once I'd left the café and put my boots on, I would work my way through the card, doing twenty or so routes in the day, racking up as much mileage as I could fit in before wearily climbing back on the Yamaha and riding back to Bangor. I suppose the upper limit was around E2, routes like *Vector* and its slippery crux, thin slab moves on *Silly Arête* and *Pincushion*, and then coming down something easier to do the next one. I just had this unquenchable appetite to be moving up rock.

I certainly had time on my hands. Margaret Thatcher's economic policies were starting to bite and unemployment was rising. Later in the 1980s, scores of climbers would be living in Llanberis claiming benefits, many of them politicised by Thatcher's uncompromising stance. But to me the outside world seemed very distant. For most of the time I lived in Wales I was either on the dole or doing odd jobs. I found it easy enough to manage. I had to live frugally, but was otherwise perfectly happy. The only problem I faced was finding the cash to fund trips abroad. With plans to revisit Yosemite in the summer, I got a labouring job for a few weeks building walls in the hills for a company called Evans, Evans, Evans & Evans, working as a builder's mate, mixing cement for an old boy who must have been in his seventies. He walked with a stick and sang songs in Welsh while he laid blocks, teaching me the words to some of them. Soon we were both at it, him in tune and me mangling a language I didn't understand. I loved being outside all day. It was like my first job after leaving school eight years before. Mostly, however, I focussed purely on climbing, more or less seven days a week. I'd given up any intention of finding something steady, something my parents would endorse. Nothing else mattered beyond climbing. I was obsessed. Looking back I don't regret any of it.

Just climbing all the time wasn't enough though. I still wanted to do the most difficult new routes I could find. The competitive urge was as sharp as ever. I had often thought of myself as being among the very best, and now I was proving it. The most obvious way to continue doing that was to find challenges that everyone agreed were among the very hardest, not just in Britain, but the world.

From the start of the 1980s, however, I began to find how I climbed – the way I approached climbing – was coming into conflict with what I wanted to climb. It felt like I was reaching the limits of what was possible using the tactics I felt were acceptable. I'd always resisted top-rope practice, and was even mocked by climbing partners for not preparing routes properly. All that was because of my deep-seated feeling that what I really wanted to do was start at the bottom and go to the top on-sight. It's how I was made. But what if it wasn't possible to operate at the highest standard and still climb like that? How far could I push things ethically before I felt uncomfortable about what I was doing?

Climbers all round the world would face the same problem over the next few years. The best climbers in any generation will want to climb harder than anyone has managed before. If necessary they'll change the rules to achieve that. My generation was no exception. In the next few years, these arguments would be solved by the acceptance of climbers practising a route and then making what became known as a redpoint, an idea developed in Germany. It was the beginning of a new discipline called sport climbing. I would stay with that new development for a while and then let it go, but in early 1980 these arguments were just developing. And I can't think of any climb I did where this argument was clearer than the route that became known as *Strawberries*.

The headwall of the Vector buttress at Tremadog was just the kind of challenge I needed. It is a slightly overhanging sheet of rock, a blank canvas poised in space above the geometrical angles of the slabs and overhangs that undercut its base. Routes were being found around its fringes, all of them very good and some of them quite hard, but a final, stunning crack-line cutting straight up the middle of it still beckoned. All of us were eyeing this crack. It looked ferociously hard and was shallow and indistinct at its bottom and top. There seemed to be holds that would bring you into the crack from the right and then higher up another sequence that led slightly left, where the crack became narrow again. (Continuing straight up from here, Martin Atkinson created a direct finish, called *Dream Topping*.) Pete Livesey had said it would take another ten years before someone climbed it. That was all the incentive I needed.

I must have first looked at *Strawberries* around the time I did the first free ascent of *Void*. There's a picture of me attempting it on the front cover of Mike Mortimer's 1978 Tremadog guidebook, belayed by Gibby. Whatever the exact date, I didn't spend long trying it, a few attempts one afternoon at most. Nor was I the first to do so. Pete had certainly abseiled down it before me. Paul Williams wrote in *Crags* magazine that the line had been chipped at some stage, but I never saw any evidence that any holds had been improved. If you chip something on that wall, it shows up clearly because the rock at Tremadog is so much lighter before it weathers.

My first attempt taught me one thing: the route was going to be ferocious. Just reaching the crack in the middle of the wall from the stance on *Cream* proved the first crux. Its base was too thin to use profitably, so I reached up and right, the fingers of my left hand pinned to an edge, catching my thumb on a hold and then going again to get a poor jam in the thin crack above. It was all incredibly tenuous. The rock here isn't as rough and welcoming as the rest of Tremadog. In fact, *Strawberries* has more in common with some of the hard 5.12s in Yosemite I've done. There seemed to be less friction, and jams would get horribly greasy as I worked to keep my fingers and hands in them. Although the route is only around sixty feet long in total, it packs in a huge amount of climbing that is incredibly varied – from thin finger cracks to fist jams and face climbing. Placing gear left me exhausted. There was nowhere to pause, let alone rest, and having placed a wire, I soon found myself falling, worn out by the process of getting something in and clipped to the rope. Having been on the end of a beating, I decided the line was too much for me and put it to the back of my mind. There were plenty more objectives for me to try.

The fact I'd had a tough time on *Strawberries* clearly left an impression on my contemporaries. The line was left alone after my attempt, gathering cobwebs. I suppose the argument ran that if Ron Fawcett couldn't manage it, then why should they? So there it sat, a route on the front cover of a guidebook that didn't exist yet. Challenges don't come more obvious than that. Sooner or later some wild young thing wouldn't be able to resist. Stopping for a brew in Eric's café one morning, before a day's soloing, he told me that John Redhead – born in Hull, but very much part of the local Welsh scene – had been up on *Strawberries* recently, trying but so far failing to make any progress. You only had to step outside the café to watch people on the Vector buttress, so news of Redhead's attempt spread quickly.

Knowing that John was now in the hunt concentrated my mind.

It was such a great line and was obviously going to be one of the landmark ascents of this or any other generation. I felt galvanised by the thought someone would beat me to it. So as soon as Eric mentioned it, I was desperate to get back on *Strawberries*, and would do whatever it took to finish things off. The following weekend I brought Gill down on the back of the bike to belay me on an all-out assault. The route, however, had other ideas. It hadn't got any easier in the last eighteen months, and the same problems of tenuous moves and placing gear in a strenuous situation dogged me once again.

I tried time after time, getting weaker with every attempt as I struggled to regain lost ground. Fighting my way up familiar moves, I found them actually harder than on earlier attempts. If I could only get to the top of the crack with a bit more in my arms then I would have a much better chance of making the hard moves left and up to the finishing groove. But by the end of the day I still hadn't managed to climb the pitch without falling. Was there a chance Redhead would be beat me to it? There had to be a way to finish this right now. Gill hated being stuck on a hanging stance right on the nose of the buttress, and wanted done with it. I could feel all my old impatience to move onto the next thing nagging away at me.

So, on Sunday morning, my third day on the route, I abseiled down and replaced the top three runners I'd placed the day before, clipping my ropes through them, so I would have the benefit of a top-rope when climbing the initial hard moves into the crack. Paul Williams, writing in *Crags* after the first ascent, tried to make excuses for me: 'Perhaps this might be regarded as unethical, but as the nuts had been placed from below while climbing, it is only equivalent to a yo-yo – standard practice on some of the harder routes. It will probably be at least ten years before this pitch is cruised on-sight with no falls.'

Yo-yoing must seem a strange term to modern climbers,

but in the 1970s it was common practice and regarded as understandable if not ideal. It meant simply getting as high as you could on your first attempt, aiming to climb on-sight, but, if you fell, lowering back to the last good rest or the belay itself. The more yo-yos you took, the less impressive a first ascent would appear, especially if someone came along and on-sighted it soon after. So while Paul was technically correct in what he wrote about my tactics on *Strawberries*, they weren't ideal. Despite my misgivings, with those runners in place I had the edge I needed.

Moving left from Gill's belay, I reached the base of the crack, the sequence now wired into my brain. Breathing hard, I pulled up, got the jam out right, and then pushed against the fingers of my right hand, levering my body upwards. I brought my left hand to a good finger jam where the crack began to flare. It was a big reach, and I was near full stretch. Heart thumping, I worked my hands against the slick rock, fighting to stay in contact. The buttress disappeared beneath my feet, the road swam below me, faces looking up blurred, as I stabbed my feet against the poorest edges around the crack, moving raggedly up it until I could reach out and left to catch an edge. Here I flagged my left foot behind my right and moved my left hand up again to a better hold. Time to fight in another runner. I was, as always on *Strawberries*, on the verge of falling off, completely consumed by the climbing but needing to remember where I was, conscious that I couldn't get too high without finding another piece of protection. Small wires in those days weren't as positive as they are now and I had to bear in mind that some of the gear might fail. From the left-hand crack I reached powerfully up to a shallow pocket, pumped out of my mind and now desperate to finish. I couldn't bear the thought of failing again so close to the top. I hauled myself up, and made one last thin move to reach good holds before a small groove just below the top. Here I hung off a jug, levering out almost horizontally against my braced feet, while I pulled myself together sufficiently to finish the route.

As I would do a few weeks later with *Atomic Hot Rod*, I gave *Strawberries* the grade E5 7a, and for roughly the same reasons. It was fiercely sustained and I thought this should be reflected in the grade. John Redhead was using a similar approach at this time and gave his new route *Bananas* the same rating as *Strawberries*, although this has been knocked back a little further over the years to E5 6b. I went down to Tremadog with Phil Burke to make a quick repeat of *Bananas*, and while we were there Phil soloed another big route on the Vector buttress – *Mongoose*. *Strawberries* is now given E6 and a technical grade of 6b. This is four or five grades below the hardest routes now being done and yet at the time of writing *Strawberries* still hasn't had an on-sight ascent by a British climber. As far as I'm aware, only the German star Stefan Glowacz has managed that, when he came over in 1987 with photographer Uli Wiesmeier on a book project. At the time Stefan was climbing new routes with the French grade of 8b. If *Strawberries* were made safe with bolts and climbed as a sport climb, it would get around 7b+ or perhaps 7c. So Stefan was clearly on good form, functioning below his limit, and ran out the rope above the crack so he didn't waste time or energy placing more protection.

Some British climbers have come close, like Johnny Woodward, who climbed with Jerry Moffatt when he made his second, cleaner ascent. Some of British rock climbing's unsung heroes have also come close, like the brilliant Dougie Hall, whose speciality was repeating desperate new routes in better style than the guys who did them first. In 1989, Mike Owen and Al Murray both came close to doing the route without falls. Now there are a host of very strong, very fit sport climbers who may fancy their chances. No doubt a British on-sight ascent will be done soon.

At the back of my mind, however, I can't help wishing I'd done *Strawberries* in better style. Alastair Lee, making his film *On Sight*, which explores the problems and attraction of climbing in this style, interviewed me about the route and I couldn't hide the reservations I feel about it. Some people have *tried* to suggest that had John Redhead used the same methods as me, he would have climbed it months before. I'm not sure about that. To be honest, I don't think John's ethics were that different to mine. He was yo-yoing it too. The more important point is that practising routes and then doing a clean ascent wasn't the prevailing ethic at that time. Yo-yoing is what we did. For the day, I think what I did was acceptable, but perhaps at the wrong end of acceptable.

More than anything, I'm just proud to be associated with such a beautiful piece of rock. Jack Geldard, an excellent young climber and journalist, described *Strawberries* as 'one of the very best routes in Wales'. That means more to me than whatever grade it might be, or even that an on-sight ascent has become such a prize. Pete Robins, before attempting his own on-sight ascent, says during Al's film that in Britain, 'You know a route by its name and not its grade.' That's a good way to look at it. It says something about how special British climbing can be. As for any rivalry with John, it's not like he didn't do a whole host of amazing new routes of his own. I think he's probably over it.

Climbing rivalries could become quite ugly, especially after the growth of the sport's media where misunderstandings and grievances could develop more easily and in public. One of the great things about Paul Williams was his ability to bridge the gap between competing climbers. Around the time I did *Strawberries*, in March 1980, he was putting up another excellent new route on the Vector buttress with John Redhead called *Sultans of Swing*. The following month he was up on the Cromlech with me, on the string of new routes I did that April. I don't think he thought about it consciously, but he liked to stay on side with most people and was close to many of the good climbers in Wales. He had been unemployed when I first met him, but got a job working for the hardware manufacturer Clog, heat-treating karabiners. He'd work odd shifts, often getting off work mid morning, which left him free to climb during the day.

Paul was incredibly competitive, even walking up to the crag. You'd arrive at the bottom of the cliff, lathered in sweat, having had to almost run to keep up with him. I remember Paul making us rush up to Cloggy one morning, after he'd boasted to another lad he'd get to the crag before him. This seemed unlikely since Paul was still finishing his breakfast when his rival set off. Nevertheless, we still got there first. The loser walked over to us when he reached the crag. 'Yer bastards,' he said. 'I knew you could climb but I didn't know you could fly an' all.'

We climbed with Jim Moran too that spring. Jim was from Glossop, and had been making a big contribution to new routing in Wales over the previous couple of years. The same year I did *The Cad* and *Blackleg* at Gogarth, he climbed a route on the crag's Upper Tier called *Barbarossa*, climbing with my old friend Al Evans. He clearly had an appetite for big, serious lines. After climbing *Strawberries* in late March, and routes like *Ivory Madonna* in April, the three of us teamed up for a major new climb in May on Cloggy.

Although beautiful, the walk up to the crag was always a bit of a chore, so Paul and I laughed when Jim stuck his thumb out as a train caught us, puffing its way towards the summit of Snowdon with carriages packed with tourists. But we laughed a lot more when it stopped, and the driver leaned his head out of the window and told us to hop on board. I took it as a good omen. Our target that day was a line up The Pinnacle, a huge tower that overlooked the East Buttress, where *Great Wall* is located. On its eastern side, overlooking a gully full of choss and loose rock, is a beautiful clean wall. A well-known Joe Brown route, *Octo*, which he probably rated Very Severe but is now considered Extreme, takes a steep crack on its right-hand side. But no one had so far dared to break straight up the wall itself, or at least, not for real. In jest, the 1960s climber Pete Crew, famous for his first ascent of

Great Wall, had described a route here so preposterous it would make jaws drop before everyone realised it was just a story. He'd called it *Final Judgement.* Now we were doing it for real.

The Pinnacle is an awkward crag to reach. The gully is too unpleasant to contemplate, a lost world no doubt inhabited by species long thought extinct. So we climbed a route up the East Buttress and then traversed across vegetated steep ground to the bottom of the cliff. I soloed to the top of the cliff and abseiled the line while the other two did a route. It was obviously bold, certainly at the time, mainly because we didn't have many small wires. The rock was quite snappy too, and smooth with little friction, almost like slate, so different to the Great Wall. It's an intimidating place and even the belay feels loose and rotten. The wall itself is vertical or slightly leaning, broken with tiny little overlaps and protected with small wires. It was not the sort of place to fall off.

We called the route *Psycho Killer,* which seemed somehow appropriate, since you had to be the former to go on the route in the first place. A few years later John Redhead took things a stage further, climbing a route to its left that he called *Margins of the Mind.* John was always good at route names, an under-rated skill in persuading others to try your routes.

Jim and I combined on another E6 that spring, this time at Gogarth. This was another venue, like Tremadog, where I spent a lot of time soloing that spring, including my epic on *Positron,* and it was clear there were still new lines to be done on the imposing Main Wall. It was great to have Jim along, partly because he was happy to abseil down and clean off loose rock, saving me the trouble for once. But during his excavations a huge boulder toppled off the crag and fell into the sea, just as a group of climbers was traversing under the bottom of the cliff, inches above the water. They were soaked. *The Big Sleep,* as we'd call it, is steep and sustained. It starts up *Dinosaur,* a route I freed around the same time with Paul, breaks left at a peg, comes back right, across the chimney *Dinosaur* follows, and then climbs up just to its right, crossing *Positron* along the way.

Having arrived on the scene a bit too late to grab any of the more famous lines on Gogarth's incredible Main Wall, *The Big Sleep* was quite some consolation. Its second pitch in particular is of a high quality, and the line itself is intricate and appealing. However, it rather faded from view, I suspect due to its being left out of Ken Wilson's *Extreme Rock* in favour of other routes. Editor of *Mountain* magazine, Ken took a strong interest in the development of Gogarth and championed his heroes on the crag, climbers like Alec Sharp, who wrote the crag's guidebook, and Pat Littlejohn, one of the forces behind the Clean Hand Gang. Alec was a well-spoken student at Bangor University at the time, and I imagine more closely fitted Ken's idea of what a great rock climber should look like; Geoff Birtles at *Crags* preferred more working-class heroes. Ken also hailed Pat's route *Hunger* as the hardest pitch in Wales, which had the direct consequence of bringing us down mob-handed to find out if this could possibly be true. I always got the impression that Pat looked down on me a little for being all muscle and no neck, while for our part we found him rather distant. We felt we'd been cast as the bad boys, and rather liked it that way. Ironically, in retrospect, I had far more in common with him than I did with the Peak District climbing scene of the early 1980s, where I would shortly find myself. Travelling round Britain and prospecting for great new routes on as many rock types as I could manage was always important to me, just as it seemed to be to Pat Littlejohn.

In a little under a year, I'd climbed several major new routes in North Wales at or around the E6 mark: *Lord of the Flies, Atomic Hot Rod, Strawberries, Psycho Killer* and *The Big Sleep*. The headline in *Crags* read: 'Fawcett hits top form and blitzes Wales.' I sounded like the Luftwaffe. In the same period, I'd also done the first free ascent of a route at Bowderstone Crag in the Lake District called

Hell's Wall. This was even harder – E6 6c – and judged by modern climbers to be French 7c+. In the past, big Welsh routes often had one hard move while the rest of the climbing was more amenable. The strength and stamina I'd developed in Yorkshire and elsewhere meant that far more sustained challenges could be done on mountain crags and sea cliffs.

There wasn't any plan, and I still couldn't see where any of this was leading, but with the broadcast of *Rock Athlete* in June many more people outside the small village of dedicated climbers started hearing about me. This was something I could use to my advantage. Mountaineers made money, but they inhabited a very different kind of world and were more readily recognised by the public. In the past, top rock climbers had used their fame to open a shop or develop a guiding business. What if it was possible, through sponsorship, to bring in enough income to climb full time and earn a living too? In retrospect, I didn't really have the commercial nous to make that a long-term reality. And it seemed strange to think of selling yourself in this way, marketing achievements you told your mates about in Pete's Eats at the end of the day. I still thought of myself as one of a group, which would take you down a peg or two if you started putting on airs and graces.

A lot of young talented climbers were emerging in North Wales at the start of the 1980s. John Redhead was hitting his stride, exploring the blank rock to the right of Great Wall at Cloggy in an incredibly bold fashion. And while Stevie Haston was wild and inconsistent, he was also immensely talented. It's amazing to me to think of him today as a grandfather, climbing sport routes of 9a. There were many more women floating around the Welsh scene too, certainly compared to the Peak District or Yorkshire, where it was still a resolutely male world with a very few exceptions. Locals spent a lot of time and imagination on all kinds of wildness and hedonism. I wasn't a big one for the famous Welsh party scene, and I don't suppose I'd have stayed if it wasn't for my relationship with Gill, but I still look back on that spring in North Wales with a lot of affection.

When summer came, I quit my job with Evans, Evans, Evans & Evans and flew to California with Gill. I introduced her to people out there like John Long and she was soon at home. We spent months in the Valley, drinking rum by the Merced river and eating ice creams. We even went climbing. I got on Ray Jardine's new classic 5.13, a steep and awkward crack called *Phoenix*. Jardine had pegged out the thin groove that started the route, widening the fingertip holds, which I remember annoyed many of the local free climbers, but it was a good climb and very hard. I spent three days on it with John Long, pushing the ropes a bit higher on each attempt in our usual yo-yo style. I think both of us had real problems with the width of the upper crack. It was just the wrong size for our large hands, and I don't imagine either of us was entirely pleased with the way we climbed it. I was impressed when Peter Croft did the first on-sight ascent.

Gill and I climbed together too, and towards the end of the trip I came up with a secret plan for us to dash up the West Face of El Capitan. Climbed in 1967, by Royal Robbins and T. M. Herbert, the route wasn't as long as the *Nose*, and wasn't really considered on the same scale by the locals, but it still had twenty-four pitches. It also went free, courtesy of Ray Jardine, who had dispensed with its remaining aid the year before to give a handful of pitches at around 5.11, most of them close to the ground. Everyone attested to its quality. By ditching all our bivouac gear and climbing free, I reckoned we could do the thing in a day and be back at Camp IV by nightfall. We didn't have any jumars, and that meant Gill would have to use prussik knots on any pitches she couldn't climb. Since she hadn't done any prussiking before, I promised to give her some lessons before we set off. I was sure it would all work out.

135

Slogging up to the bottom of the route with all the hardware under a midday sun was the usual purgatory but once I'd found the bottom of the route and we'd recovered with a beer, morale began to rise. Standing at its base, the cliff was wildly foreshortened but when I pointed out a team of three climbers adrift on the wall about six pitches up, Gill began to get a perspective on how far we had to travel. As the afternoon wore on and the temperature cooled a little, we climbed the first two pitches, the second the technical crux of the route, in good order, fixing ropes as we went so we could make a fast start next morning.

Back on the ground, we were sorting out our gear when we heard someone – or something – crashing through the trees. We both froze. Instantly I recalled my encounter with the bear cubs before climbing *Astroman* with Pete.

'Bears!' I said to Gill.

Out of the woods, however, came a haulbag, apparently levitating, until I spotted a pair of legs beneath it. Behind the giant haulbag came an attractive young woman with a handbag. The haulbag tilted backwards slightly as it reached us to reveal a pink-faced hippy dripping with sweat. The hippy explained that he and the woman were planning to aid the West Face, hence all the gear. From the haulbag emerged mattresses, huge amounts of food and drink and gear. Once they'd established base camp, the hippy came back and took a long, hard look at our thin provisions and smiled.

'You must be Ron Fawcett.'

'Aye.'

'I heard about you.'

'Aye.'

He then darted back to where his partner was sunbathing. They conferred. Then he trotted back with some large, hand-rolled cigarettes in hand.

'For you,' he said. Gill was keen on her fags, so I said thanks.

'I'm not sure they're actually cigarettes,' she said.

'Anyway,' the hippy continued. 'I was wondering if you wouldn't mind, ah, trailing a couple of ropes for us when you start tomorrow? You know, save us having to aid the first couple of pitches? I mean, the, uh, climbing thing, it's, uh, such a *drag.*'

We spent the night dozing under the stars before the alarm dragged us back to the task in hand. I packed some juice, some beer and a couple of oranges into a stuff-sack and gave it to Gill. Then, to save time, I started climbing up the rope, hand over hand rather than prussiking, hauling Gill up behind me. The thought of being marooned on the wall after dark with absolutely nothing to eat and nothing to keep us warm either was too much to contemplate. We simply had to get up and off before dark.

The route quickly became a blur of feet and hands twisting in cracks and smearing on slabs, the stickiness in our throats only occasionally alleviated by a sip of fluid. At least we were in the shade. At one point, the top of pitch five, we left a beer and an orange to lighten our load, a small present for the pair below us. The sound of a small man hauling a big bag floated up from below. Above, we could see the trio of climbers already installed on the wall a little more clearly now. We were catching up. The next crux was the seventh pitch, a stunning overhanging corner crack with an awkward roof to start. Gill looked flushed when she reached the top and seemed not to be enjoying how fast we were moving so I thought it best not to mention what was coming a pitch or so later.

'Your lead,' I told her at the stance. She could see why. The next pitch traversed sideways along a dike in the wall for a rope length before a few moves led down to a ledge. It made sense for her to go first, since it wouldn't be any more dangerous and then she would have the rope above her when reaching the stance. I needn't have worried. She looked pretty relaxed, despite now being a thousand feet off the ground. A pitch above, we caught the trio we'd been watching from the ground the day before. Gill seemed to think we should stop and wait for them but they had bivouac gear and we didn't, so I butted in.

'Excuse me,' I said, 'I'll just nip up here.' Gill pulled a face, and apologised to the waiting Americans.

'Don't worry,' one said. 'We don't mind waiting. We do enough of it.'

'I'm giving up after this,' said another. 'Gonna stick to dope.'

A few pitches higher, on Thanksgiving Ledge, we shared an orange and a cigarette, all the hard climbing now below us. There was just scrambling from here, and we'd finished the route by 2.30pm, just seven hours after starting. We were back at Camp IV after dark, unfortunately though our sleeping bags were still under the route three miles away, where we'd slept the night before. I put on all my clothes and lay on the ground shivering, exhausted but too cold to sleep – and yet, utterly content.

EIGHT

Head in a Noose

GILL AND I WERE MARRIED IN JUNE 1981 at Christ Church in Burbage, on the outskirts of her hometown of Buxton. Both our families came, and a whole host of climbing friends. It was a beautiful summer's day, perfect weather for a wedding, so I took the opportunity to do some soloing in the morning, nipping over to High Tor to climb *Debauchery* and a bunch of other routes. Properly prepared, I dashed up the A6 in time for the ceremony. Old romantic that I am, our first days of wedded bliss weren't spent on some sun-kissed desert island walking hand in hand along the beach, but hanging off small holds in the gloomy surroundings of Gordale Scar. Gill and I spent our first night of married life under canvas on Gordale campsite – cheaper than Malham, but you had to wash in the beck – and after a wedding breakfast at Beck Hall Café, shouldered our rucksacks and set out to look at the Cave Routes.

Gordale had been one of the first crags I'd visited as a lad, and it could still make an impression on me. Its huge, leaning walls that narrowed as you looked up the gorge, the sound of the waterfall and the way any breeze whistled and intensified in its narrow confines can leave even the most psychologically strong climber feeling anxious. This sense of impending doom is reflected in the route names, particularly on its biggest wall, where the Cave Routes are, *Hangman*, and *Gallows*, which became

139

the free route *Pierrepoint*. They capture the sense that at Gordale you feel like you're putting your head in a noose.

It was six years since Pete Livesey and I had first tried to free these looming, powerful aid climbs. He had managed to climb the right-hand route with three rests on the rope, but the left-hand line was more technically difficult and seemed the greater challenge. I'd been back a few times since then to climb a couple of new routes, an intimidating and steep old aid climb through roofs left of Pete's *Face Route* called *Rebel*, and a more open route to its left called *Nothing to Declare*. Both these were E5, and *Rebel* in particular was of the highest quality, but with a clutch of E6s under my belt in the last couple of years, the obvious challenge of freeing the Cave Routes was now firmly in my mind.

I set to work, abseiling down the top pitch to the cave, and then struggling down the main part of the crag, trying to stay in touch with the wildly overhanging right-hand route, which is joined by *Cave Route Left* where it gets easier. Just preparing the route turned into a bit of an epic, as I fought to clip into gear to stop myself from swinging free into space and unable to get back onto the rock. I managed to replace most of the old tat and bits of sling that littered the climb, making it possible to clip them while leading, and inspect some of the pegs and clean off what loose rock remained. It took more than two hours to get this tedious work done, but by the time I got to the bottom I was too impatient to wait until next morning to give myself time to recover.

Having followed Pete up the route in 1975 without falling, I knew the climbing itself wouldn't be the problem; the problem would be doing it all in one go and placing and clipping the protection. Even so, *Cave Route Right* has the harder start, a fiddly sequence of lay-backs and bridging, before a series of steep pulls and a move left round an overhang led back into a niche – more of a hole in reality – where I could wedge myself in and get a good rest. In fact, there are several places on the route to recover, and I found that after each hard move I could usually get a semi-rest. Once I'd made the hard move above the niche, past a huge coach bolt and a peg, things eased considerably. I just had to keep working hard and the route was in the bag. The second pitch doesn't get done anymore, which is a shame because while it's only E3 it's amazingly spectacular with two roofs, the second of which is huge. Luckily, the holds are enormous and you can swing around in space looking brave.

Cave Route Left, I knew, wouldn't go so smoothly. The day after freeing the right-hand route, I repeated the exhausting palaver of abseiling down and cleaning its left-hand twin. This time the process was even more awkward, because the rock leans out further at this point, making *Cave Route Left* even more wildly overhanging than its neighbour. At least the start was easier, but the crux, again around forty feet up, was desperate. Gasping and muttering to myself as I normally did when things got hard, I worked my fingers into a couple of poor jams using two old peg scars as undercuts – I think I had to excavate a broken peg out of one of them – ran my feet up and then tried to reach into a poor finger-jam. It was hugely powerful climbing, my shoulders bunched with the strain, but despite all that eye-popping effort, I was off. Gill lowered me back to the ground, and I shook my arms free of lactic acid until my forearms could function again. Typically, I would get back onto routes sooner than I should, before my arms had properly recovered. I was always in a hurry. As sport climbing began to take over on steep limestone crags, techniques and knowledge of how to go about preparing a clean ascent of a route like *Cave Route Left* would become far more scientific. But in 1981 I was still climbing as I had for the past decade or so – step aside and let me at it – and if that failed, then I would yo-yo the route until one of us gave in. Yo-yoing, however, did have its rules, at least as far as I was concerned. Once I'd fallen, I'd lower straight back down. I wouldn't hang around to practice moves. And while there was a lot of fixed gear on both these routes, if I needed a wire I would place it on lead, not on abseil. It was just another of those strange little compromises I made to preserve the idea that what I was doing now was just a continuation of what I'd always done. To my mind, placing nuts is a real skill, and one that adds an extra dimension to climbing and I would fight hard to preserve it.

Not everyone, however, was pleased about the developing free climbing revolution. As more free routes began to appear on this ludicrously overhanging wall, the odd new bolt was added, usually to replace an old peg that wouldn't hold a fall. In the early 1980s there were still a few aid climbers around who resented their challenges being treated in this way. They thought unnecessary bolts spoiled their challenge, and wanted them left alone. Things got heated for a while, and bolts were removed. The young Yorkshire climber Martin Atkinson came in for more flak than I did, even though I was also placing bolts. I didn't want to fall out with those lads. I'd started out pegging, and could understand their point of view. But to my mind free climbing was better. Aid climbing seemed like something from the past. It was all fairly academic anyway. There weren't so many aid climbers left to kick up a proper fuss about it. The world had moved on.

It took me a few tries to figure out the crux on *Cave Route Left*, and it didn't get much easier above. The route is more of a crack climb than its twin, and a lot of the moves are off poor finger-jams. I found myself making a sequence of desperate moves, fighting my way up to where the two routes merged and things got easier. To be honest, I can't now remember what grade I gave *Cave Route Left*. While I liked to climb as hard as I could, and push limits, it was even more important to me to climb good routes, to create climbs people would want to repeat because of their quality. Both Cave Routes are three-star classics. The left-hand version is now given E6 6c, or French 7c+ in sport-climbing terms. Ten years before, I'd done my first new route, *Mulatto Wall* at Malham Cove, which wasn't far off the upper limit of what was being done at that time. Things had moved on at an incredible pace. I'm not sure I knew it at the time, but I was starting to come up against the upper limit of what was possible simply by being fit and climbing all the time.

Mostly I felt incredibly proud. When Livesey and I had looked at the Cave Routes in the mid 1970s, the feeling was that they were targets for the next generation. Someone had written into *Mountain* magazine suggesting that a monkey could be encouraged to free Cave Route by wedging a banana in the crack every six feet. Only a few years later, back on the crags where I'd first started climbing, I'd broken through those barriers. A whole new vista of difficulty was opening up.

It didn't occur to me, when I did the Cave Routes, that anyone else would beat me to their first free ascents. In 1981, there didn't seem to be anyone else climbing new routes at that standard, certainly not in Yorkshire. During visits to Gordale or Malham in the early 1980s, I'd often see Pete Livesey out running. I'm not sure that he'd completely given up climbing, but he had clearly stepped aside from the fierce competition he'd enjoyed a few years before. I felt I had completely escaped his shadow and was now out on my own.

That situation wouldn't last long. In 1981, the Lee brothers, Daniel and Dominic, were climbing fierce new limestone problems in the Peak District. They were lovely lads, but kept themselves to themselves and didn't seem fussed about being known. By 1982, Jerry Moffatt and others were breathing down my neck, with Jerry repeating *Cave Route Left* at the end of that year. When I came back to Gordale in 1984, Martin Atkinson was adding some stupendous lines to the right of the Cave Routes, like *Pierrepoint*, which I was pleased to repeat in good order, and then added another of my own, *Defcon 3*, a route which powered out

143

rightwards from a little way up *Cave Route Right*. Defcon was a US military term, defining the level of threat of attack. Defcon 3 meant 'an increase to force readiness above normal'. That felt about right for Gordale. It wasn't all out nuclear war – not yet.

A few weeks after our honeymoon, Gill and I went back to Gordale with Chris Gibb. The idea was for Gibby to take some photographs of me on the Cave Routes for the magazines. To be honest, the pictures didn't work out so well, but the idea itself, in retrospect, is quite interesting. Since Al Evans began taking shots of me back in the early 1970s, I understood, partly through Pete, that good photographs were a surefire way of promoting the routes I was doing and, ultimately, my own profile as well. Pete had no obvious motive for this, other than propaganda in the cause of Pete Livesey. I think he enjoyed getting history on his side, even if that history wasn't always accurate. Pete, however, had a regular salary, while I was still living in near penury.

Now that I was married I was going to have to take life more seriously. Having finished her course before we left for Yosemite and my ascent of *Phoenix*, Gill had wanted to move back to her native Derbyshire, and we'd rented a farm cottage above Monyash. It was in a horribly exposed position. That winter of 1980 and 1981, the wind would blast round its limestone walls while Gill cooked dinner on the open fire. There was no proper stove. Living like that might not faze someone who lived to go climbing, but it was no way to go on as a couple. I was going to have to start planning ahead.

Since no one was going to pay me to go to the crag, the most obvious thing to do was leverage my name, such as it was, into some kind of moneymaking enterprise, which allowed me to carry on climbing as much as I had over the last few years. These days, the notion of professional extreme athletes is so commonplace it seems inconceivable that I would have struggled to make this work. It's a much more commercial world.

Now, young men and women who do anything significant have at least an idea of how to make money out of it, but in those days I didn't have a clue. I'd done all these big routes and had lots of exposure in the climbing media and on national television, but joining the dots to make some cash for myself out of that wasn't obvious in 1981. Getting married and later buying our own place in Eyam meant that I had to start learning fast. That November, I had some headed notepaper printed up with my name at the top and the words 'Rock Climber' underneath. However, as I would learn over the years, there's a lot more to being a professional athlete than simply being good at your sport. Some climbers don't mind standing around at trade fairs, chatting to complete strangers about how good they are, but I was never one of them.

I also had some tough lessons to learn about the integrity of a small minority in the outdoor trade. To start with, I'd been very lucky. I'd got to know Tony Howard, who was part owner of the harness and webbing manufacturer Troll Safety Equipment Ltd. Tony is one of the good guys, a dedicated climber who has travelled all over the world and done a lot of good things for the people he's met along the way. He didn't ask me if I'd like to work with Troll; I approached him. I got a small amount of money from Troll and worked with the company for almost five years. When I was dealing directly with Tony things went well. Then in the late 1970s Trevor Jones was brought in to deal with marketing and I became increasingly frustrated as he delayed payments for work I'd done. An Italian clothing company called Bailo offered me a lot more money to go and work with them, but Trevor told me Troll would match that. 'Don't worry,' he promised, 'we'll sort you out.' Reluctant to leave Tony and Troll, who had been so good to me, I hung on, turning down what would have been the biggest deal of my career. It was one of my more foolish commercial decisions.

At the same time as all this was happening, I was withholding my membership fee of the Climbers' Club, because of what

I regarded as an unfair hike in dues. I'd been a member for some time and relied on the huts the club owns for cheap accommodation when I was climbing away from home. Those of us on a limited income felt the CC was getting too expensive. Trevor was a bigwig in the Climbers' Club, and next time I was in the office he told me not to worry about my dues for the club; he'd take it out of the money Troll owed me. I quit more or less on the spot.

If I had my time over again I would develop the professional side to my climbing differently. But at the time, there was nobody to ask. Nobody else had made the mistakes I found myself making because there had never been a professional rock climber before. Maybe I wasn't the right person to blaze that particular trail. I just felt really privileged to get money for doing something I enjoyed. Work to me was what my parents did. It was something that cost them. I understood that the companies hiring me wanted something in return, and I would go to shops or trade shows. Sponsors want more than just a talented athlete. You don't just have to cut it on the crag, you need to have the right sort of personality too and the confidence to project yourself. Over the years I developed a kind of public persona, which I could use at work or meeting strangers on the crag; but I'm not one of nature's extroverts and found that aspect – being the public face of a company – something of a trial. What I never felt, however, was that the climbing industry, such as it was, owed me a living. These days, it seems to me, many young climbers assume they're going to be rewarded simply for climbing well. I suspect they're still being disappointed.

If I was struggling in the dark – and I was – over how I could make a living and keep climbing full-time, then I picked up some useful pointers that spring when I accepted an invitation from Andreas Kubin, editor of *Alpinismus* magazine, to travel to Germany for an international climbing festival. This wasn't like the previous exchanges I'd been on, like those organised by the

British Mountaineering Council here in the United Kingdom, or the French meet organised at Verdon by the FFME (French Federation of Mountaineering and Climbing) in the late 1970s. This was to be a public demonstration of top climbers in action for the benefit of the paying public.

Gill and I packed our rucksacks and caught the train to Munich, our fares paid by a huge sports chain called Sports-Scheck, sponsors of the event. When we arrived we discovered the festival now had a name – Sportsklettern International. This was, I think, the first time I'd heard the phrase sport climbing, albeit in its German form. Climbers from all over Europe and a couple of stars from the United States had been brought together at what I can only describe as a Bavarian version of Stoney Middleton, a steep limestone crag called Dohlenfels close to a road in the Frankenjura region. We arrived a few days before the festival began to find huge marquees being erected and scores of beer kegs being rolled into place for the expected hordes.

Before the crowds descended for the weekend festival, Gill and I managed to get some climbing done. All the existing routes were equipped with pegs and bolts, meaning we only had to climb with a rack of karabiners, quite a new experience for me back then. There didn't seem to be anything harder than English 5c, all of them superbly protected, but I spotted a couple of superb lines that hadn't been done as free climbs yet. One of them, *The Blue*, crossed a huge roof while the other was a beautiful wall, rather like High Tor, capped by a five-foot roof that had already been christened No Holds. Only it turned out to have just enough of them to give a satisfying 6a pitch.

On Friday morning the public arrived – more than five thousand of them. At the very least, this made Dohlenfels one of the most famous crags in Germany. I wouldn't have believed that so many people would travel long distances just to stand around watching other people climb, but they lapped it up. The organisers had told us that we were forbidden from starting until we got permission, and that we should only climb on those parts of the crag closest to the road. Gill and I watched them marching through the crowds, speaking into their walkie-talkies and looking important. The notion of waiting at the bottom of a cliff for permission to start climbing suddenly seemed ridiculous to me, so I told the closest official that I'd had enough of standing around and was going to climb *The Blue*.

Instead of being put out by my anarchic English ways, he got tremendously excited and rushed over to the public announcer's tent so the news could be relayed to the crowd. There was some excited chat through the loudspeakers and I heard my name, and the crowd surged forward to where Gill and I were waiting. Suddenly my partner disappeared into the crowd, and I was left facing a sea of faces with no one to belay me. Gill wasn't someone to put up with being shouldered to one side, but it took some sharp elbow work before she had the space to pay out some rope. I jogged up and down the route a few times, mostly for the workout but also to show off. The crowd went wild. All this for what was essentially a French 6c.

The explanation for all this excitement lay in the programme notes for the festival. More or less every hour through the day, the big names brought over for the weekend would be demonstrating what was called 'Clean Climbing', essentially free climbing. German climbers, it seems, were so used to pulling up on pegs and bolts, the notion of just using the rock had to be introduced in a mass-education project. In later years, the festival was acknowledged as a watershed in German climbing, a bit like Woodstock. Everybody seems to have been there.

This, of course, was in the years before the end of the Cold War and the fall of the Berlin Wall, so when the Swiss filmmaker Ruedi Homberger showed the festival his film of sandstone climbing in Saxony, then part of East Germany, it was as much a surprise to the locals as it was to me. Nuts weren't allowed on the sandstone, let alone pegs, so climbers relied on knotted ropes wedged into cracks for protection. Chalk was banned, which would have pleased the Clean Hand Gang, and climbing in the rain was also forbidden because the rock was so soft and easily damaged in the wet.

I knew some of the climbers who'd been invited from outside Germany. John Bachar was there, over from the United States, and Jean-Claude Droyer, who'd been staying with us that winter in our icebox outside Monyash. Some of the German and Austrian stars were less familiar including a quiet, friendly young guy called Wolfgang Güllich, who was clearly on his way to being great. He'd been in Yosemite the year before, where he'd done some of the harder routes like *Crimson Cringe* and the eighth ascent of *Astroman*. That evening the organisers gave us all a Helly Hansen pile jacket with our names on and asked us to take the podium to answer questions from the public. Through interpreters each of us was quizzed about climbing in our native countries. I was gripped with fear at speaking in front of such a large crowd expecting me to say something intelligent. People mostly wanted to know who was the best climber in Britain, who was the second-best and so forth. I tried to explain that hundreds of people were now climbing 5.11 and 5.12 – they seemed to find American grades more impressive than our British market garden variety – and so talking about who was best didn't really mean anything. Looking back, I can see that German climbing liked the idea of stars more than we did in Britain. Categorising climbers made more sense of things for them. Get a few headlines in Britain and you're there to be mocked by your mates. Do the same in Germany and someone will give you a BMW.

Next morning it rained, but we still managed to get some climbing done. Once again, however, the organisers insisted we only climb during our allotted slots so the crowd wouldn't miss anything. It was *Jeux Sans Frontières*, with the French looking truculent and the British contingent giggling about German efficiency and sneaking off without permission. Luckily the Luftwaffe arrived to give a demonstration of helicopter mountain rescue. Unluckily, the helicopter hovered over the campsite, where equipment manufacturer Salewa had put up several hundred tents to rent out to people staying for the festival. Half of them simply took off across the campsite in the downwash from the chopper. We retired to the marquee where we drank huge tankards of lager for the benefit of the half-dozen television crews who were covering the event.

The Bavarian climbing festival was an eye-opener for me. Lots of the star climbers were wearing clothes from their sponsors and looked on the event as an opportunity to promote the brands they worked for. I'd rocked up without any kind of agenda other than curiosity. There seemed to be a whole new commercial world out there that I knew very little about. I'm sure that seeing all this influenced my decision to start calling myself a professional. I was clearly good enough, so why not? I could also see the huge potential for growth in rock climbing in Europe. There was real enthusiasm from the huge number of climbers at Sportklettern International for what we were doing – essentially the kind of fixed-gear climbing most climbers in Europe now practice – and it marked something of a watershed in the sport's development in Germany. The resulting tidal wave of interest would see European standards soar, along with the turnover of climbing businesses.

I developed a real affection for German climbing and became good friends with Wolfgang. Whenever I came over for a festival, I would stay on for a few days afterwards climbing with him at different crags in the Frankenjura, repeating the latest hardest routes. Of all the climbers I've met over the years, I'd have to say that Wolfgang impressed me more than any other. It wasn't just that Wolfie was an outstanding climber, he was a wonderful person too. It blew me away to think of him pouring his energy into something like *Action Directe*, his super-route in the Frankenjura, and then doing routes on the Trango Towers in Pakistan's Karakoram. What was so exceptional about him was how he could switch from being courteous and thoughtful with his friends, to being utterly focused on whatever he was climbing. Very few top climbers I've met were able to do that. It was like the world just fell away for that moment, and then when it was over he'd instantly switch back and insist everyone joined him for coffee and a slice of cake.

Towards the end of 1982, eighteen months after the revelation I'd experienced at Sportklettern International, I was meeting Andreas Kubin once again, this time at Munich Airport, and this time as the guest of a Bavarian climbing film festival. After my first trip to Germany, I had signed a sponsorship deal with boot manufacturer Hanwag and now had a much higher profile in Germany. As I walked down the steps from the aircraft, I noticed a film crew on the tarmac. I looked round to see who'd they'd come to meet, and was amazed when they stepped forward to interview me.

Wolfie was waiting in the car when we got out of the arrivals hall, so I knew at once that even though it was December, there would be some hard climbing as well as the hard partying film festivals usually involve. Wolfie had spent the previous summer in California doing some incredible ascents and was already on his way to becoming one of the best sport climbers of the 1980s. Next morning we were fighting through Munich's rush hour traffic in Wolfie's mum's Volkswagen Golf, on our way to the Almühltal nature reserve and the saw-toothed limestone towers of Prunn.

It wasn't inspiring weather, but Wolfie soon had me creakily working my way up a couple of E5s; first a thin slab route where I had to plant my foot next to my fingers on a matchstick ledge, and then the complete opposite, a route called *Müsliweg* – Muesli

Way – that took a crack full of in situ nuts. Having tumbled off the crux, Wolfie took over and, after a fall, powered up through the crux to the top.

'Ron, I am just finding the abseil point,' he called down. I shouted back that I'd keep him on belay while he figured out how to get down.

There was a long pause. 'Ron, I am still looking for the abseil point,' Wolfie said.

'No problem!'

More silence, which was eventually broken by a torrent of German swear words. Or at least, I assume they were, not speaking any German.

'Scheiß! Verdammt!' That kind of thing. Next, there was a squawk and finally a loud, piercing cry: 'Aargh!' At which point Wolfie came flying back over the top of the crag, like a ski-jumper, though somewhat less stylishly, his arms and legs flapping urgently. With his last runner over twenty feet below the top of the crag I knew at once he was in for a monster fall. So I stepped backwards quickly to bring in some rope and prepared for impact. Wolfie came to a halt around twenty-five feet off the ground, having taken a cool fifty-footer.

'Crikey, Wolfgang, are you alright?' I asked him, when the dust had settled.

'Ja, this is normal.' He explained that if there was nothing to belay off at the top of the route it was standard procedure in the Frankenjura to jump back down, often dropping between bolts. I was always amazed at how casually Wolfie would treat being a long way off the ground. When it was my turn to lead the route, I recovered my gear in a more conventional fashion.

That evening, we pulled up outside the huge Alabamahalle in Munich. This wasn't the back room of a pub, the kind of place I usually gave lectures, but a concert hall. Pink Floyd had sold the place out the week before. There were climbing movies, including one by the British filmmaker Leo Dickinson, a rock band and even a comedian, who for some inexplicable reason was dressed as a priest with a chalk bag hanging off his waist. Thousands of people had bought tickets and I was reminded once again how different the scale of the outdoors was in Germany compared to the United Kingdom.

In the morning, after sleeping off a heavy night's partying, Sepp Gschwendner, technical consultant for a raft of German outdoor brands, including the boot manufacturer Hanwag, picked us up to go climbing. Wolfie and I stood on the pavement outside Andreas' apartment admiring Sepp's shiny new red Porsche, smothered in sponsors' stickers. He used to wear a red one-piece racing suit to drive in. Not long before I had traded in my old Yamaha for a Reliant Robin, the outmoded three-wheeler vans favoured by Del Trotter in the sitcom Only Fools and Horses. This was mostly my Yorkshire sense of thrift at work. I didn't have a full driving licence and the thought of forking out for expensive lessons was too painful. I could drive the Plastic Pig on my bike licence and Gill wouldn't complain about freezing on the back of the bike.

Now I was about to be driven to the crag in a top-perfomance sports car. It was like climbing inside the Starship Enterprise, and Sepp, a former racing driver, soon took us to warp factor, powering down the autobahn, heading back to the Frankenjura.

We parked above the Danube, just south of Kelheim, and walked down to the river under leaden skies, threatening rain. It was also freezing. I couldn't see much sense in going on but Sepp kept insisting that he had a big surprise for us. After fifteen minutes' walk, I saw what he meant. A gigantic limestone roof, some twenty-two feet wide, overhung both the path and the river. Sepp turned to us beaming with pride. He'd discovered the roof and the crack that split its length a few weeks before and spent two days figuring out the moves before climbing it. Named, perhaps inevitably, *Bavarian Reality*, after the route's Yosemite twin *Separate Reality*, it was graded IX- under the German system, perhaps hard E5 in Britain, and was still unrepeated.

Having travelled a thousand miles to be here, I thought I'd better give it a go. Warming up on a couple of boulder problems showed me just how cold it was. Still, in the spirit of Anglo-German relations, I felt obliged to give it my best effort. The first moves involved wet hand jams in the back of the deep, wide crack. I had to fight tooth and nail to make them stick. I found I could get my feet above my head, and then shuffle my hands along the crack in poor jams in the general direction of the lip. Eventually, it all went horribly wrong, my hands slid out of the crack, my legs got tangled and I found myself back on the ground, inspecting my bleeding numbed hands. It might have been named after *Separate Reality*, but it was harder, the climbing was far more complex and the jams weren't comfortably smooth, but covered in rugosities that left my hands mangled. After a couple of efforts, both Wolfie and I had the route ticked, so we celebrated at a nearby riverside café, drinking hot chocolate and listening to Strauss. I felt almost civilised. There was time for one more route that day, a much more subtle affair called *Rumplestiltskin* that was half a grade harder at IX – solid E6. For once, I got lucky and Wolfie didn't, probably the last time anyone got the better of him. Then, with darkness falling, Sepp raced us back to Munich in time for the lecture I was scheduled to give. As always before a lecture, I began to feel sick with nerves, literally, and tonight's audience were several thousand strong. I was glad when it was over.

Among the celebrities I met that evening was Mathias Rebitsch, the brilliant rock and ice climber from the 1930s, who had attempted the North Face of the Eiger in 1937 with Ludwig Vorg, and Nanga Parbat in 1938. He showed a film of climbing in the 1930s and proved to be the star of that evening. As a young man, Mathias and his friends had cycled for hundreds of miles back and forth to the Kaisergebirge and Brandenberg Alps from his home in Innsbruck, climbing grade VI routes with the minimum of equipment – or fuss. Mathias, or Hias as he was known, was now over seventy, but still living alone in the mountains. He was amused, and I think a bit saddened too, that the routes he'd climbed in the 1930s in such a clean style were now over-pegged and often climbed by artificial means. He remained at heart a dedicated free-climber. Even in the 1930s he took training seriously, doing pull-ups and bouldering to improve his power and technique. Some young Austrian climbers had recently repeated some of his problems and admired their difficulty for the time.

Hias told me that when he was young he was desperate to climb full-time. Even though he was poor, he would do whatever it took to visit the mountains, working part-time at odd jobs to get enough money for his passion. Older mountaineers, he said, despised him for his dedication, believing that climbing should just be a pastime, not an occupation in itself. But as well as studying chemistry at university, Hias had read widely in philosophy and became deeply attached to the work of Jean-Paul Sartre. Hias liked to climb hard, but he wasn't competitive. He just wanted to be as strong as he could be, outside in the mountains. He'd had a bad motorbike accident in the early 1950s that curtailed his hard climbing, but he'd still been on expeditions to the Karakoram and had gone back to university to study early human history, becoming an archaeologist and leading research expeditions to the Andes. Throughout the 1950s and 1960s he'd watched the rise of aid climbing with a sense of disappointment, but had been heartened by the resurgence of free climbing in the 1970s. I felt incredibly lucky, to have spent the day climbing with Wolfie, the best free-climber in Germany, and the evening with one of the free climbing stars of the 1930s, Hias Rebitsch.

NINE

Peak Performance

THERE ARE CLIMBERS WHO HAVE SPENT a lot more time than I have at Raven Tor in the Peak District, but the drive there is still sharply familiar to me, like the journey to school. Through Litton, out of the village, turning left, and down Tideswell Dale, down the hill to Miller's Dale and then sharp left past the Angler's Rest and along the left bank of the Wye to the crag itself. In the early 1980s, if I wasn't climbing here, or further downstream at Rubicon Wall, then I was often running along Miller's Dale with our dog Bill.

In my memory, the sky above Raven Tor is somehow always grey and flat and the holds polished and unfriendly, ready to spit you off. You could never claim the crag as a place of majestic beauty, although the steep prow overhanging the rest of the crag does make it impressive. I've always thought of the crag as being a bit of a scruff. There's a story – I don't know if it's true – that visiting American climber Alan Watts drove past Raven Tor on his first visit, discounting the place as not worth the bother. He just kept going, expecting something more worthwhile round the corner.

I've never made it a secret that I consider Yorkshire limestone far superior to the version found in Derbyshire. The crags are more impressive too, with the possible exception of High Tor. That said, you can't ignore the sheer concentration of hard routes at Raven Tor. Since the early 1980s, the continual advances in standards at Raven Tor suggest the crag has something going for it you can't find anywhere else, other than the fact that it's close to Sheffield, home to the greatest concentration of climbers in Britain. It comes down to the nature of the rock, I think, which lends itself to fiercely technical climbing, on holds so sharp and small that your fingers at the end of the day feel permanently crimped. Raven Tor suited the next stage in climbing's development. As climbers reached the boundaries of training, a new approach was required to push technical standards. In the 1970s, climbing fitness meant having enough stamina to outlast a climb. As the 1980s wore on, the hardest climbs began to require something extra – power.

I can't in all honesty say I saw it coming. In the early 1980s, interviewed for the film *The Fingertip Phenomenon*, I talked knowledgeably about how technical standards had reached their natural limit and future developments would rely on climbers achieving a higher level of fitness to link more of these moves together. That did happen, but it was training for power which really raised standards. Increasing a climber's power required a change in training techniques, a change pioneered by climbers like Wolfie in the Campus Gymnasium in Germany and Jerry Moffatt in cellars and homemade training facilities in Sheffield. Raven Tor would be a focus – perhaps the main focus – for this newest wave in British rock climbing. It was also a development that would eventually see me withdraw from climbing's front line.

To begin with, however, I was part of the growing obsession with Raven Tor. I was still travelling and still doing new routes in other areas. In 1982, the year I did *The Prow*, Gill and I went down to the sea cliffs round Pembroke and did a clutch of fantastic new lines. I never lost my enthusiasm for different styles of climbing and was still nipping back to Wales, doing repeats of John Redhead's new slate routes. But Raven Tor captured a lot of media attention in the early 1980s, particularly from Geoff Birtles, whose magazine *Crags* had grown into a new, bigger title, *High*.

He would always give Peak District routes a big billing, and I wasn't so naïve that I didn't go for the objectives that Geoff would give a lot of space in the magazine.

I'd already done a few new routes there, notably the girdle *Cream Team Special*, when Geoff and Al Evans had followed my lead. I'd also done away with the remaining aid point on a route we'd almost freed around that time called *Hubris*. But the real breakthrough came in 1981, soon after we moved to the Peak from Wales. *Sardine*, climbed in the 1960s by Bob Toogood, looked like it might go free but it had a tough reputation and the gear was awful. There was an old bolt, near the crux, and I replaced that, but even so it was quite a bold climb, perhaps E6 6b. Once it was properly bolted and some of the holds fell off, it became a good sport route at French 7b+, both harder and safer. It boggles me that *Sardine* has become so popular, with several tiny variations, its holds now more polished than a mirror. But it was this route that really switched me on to the potential for free climbing at Raven Tor. Now that I was based just up the road, it became an obvious place to keep fit and push the limits. The following year, climbing's interest in the crag really took off.

There were several big aid lines to go at, including the *Cambridge Bolt Route*, which Jerry Moffatt freed that spring and renamed *Rooster Booster*. Around the same time, I freed another aid climb, called *The Prowler*, and renamed it *Indecent Exposure*. *The Prowler* had two pitches originally, but the second was loose and not that hard and a real contrast in quality to the first. It never saw much traffic as a free route. The first pitch, however, became a classic. It started memorably, from the high branch of a young ash tree, a necessary manoeuvre because the lower section was usually both wet and covered in a horrible slimy ooze that made climbing it almost impossible. Like a stick insect, I angled my way up the swaying tree and then rocked backwards and forwards until I had sufficient momentum to reach some thin flake holds.

I changed instantaneously into a gecko, clinging to the wall, immediately committed as the tree sprang backwards without me.

Indecent Exposure was a terrific find, but it seemed clear to me that the plum line to go for was the aid route to the right of *The Prowler*, *The Prow* itself. Unlike *Sardine*, this had plenty of old aid bolts and other fixed gear so although the wall leered over me, it felt okay once I was on it. If I looked too carefully, however, all that aging ironmongery left me feeling a bit spooked. Some of the studs were threaded with old cord and any bolt hangers seemed disturbingly thin, like the ring pulls of a beer can.

Inspecting the route on abseil, it was clear I couldn't follow the true line of *The Prow*. Quite what the true line was is a little confusing after all these years. Crossing the rocky prow overlooking the road was the obvious challenge for aid climbers at Raven Tor. The first team to take it on started up an existing aid route called *Mecca*, well to the right of the prow itself. They then traversed a long way until they were underneath the looming beak of the prow itself. It's possible no one ever repeated this feat and Bob Dearman added a direct start a few years later, which superseded it. This is the line that Jerry Moffatt climbed later and called *Revelations*. I thought getting onto *The Prow* this way was too difficult, relying on a pocket I could barely use. But when I was climbing *Indecent Exposure*, I'd spotted a traverse line out of that route that bypassed *The Prow's* original start. I banged in a couple of pegs to protect this new section.

Higher up on the wall, after traversing twenty feet or so, I could move up on thin face holds to a good flake and worked out a sequence to the right of the original line leading up to a break and the first belay. In 1992, Malcolm Taylor freed this section, which he called *Rage*. Raven Tor is like that, little fragments of lines that represent sometimes months or even years of effort. Like the start, this section is two or three grades harder than my version of *The Prow*. The second pitch of my line then moved back left to rejoin the aid route in a powerfully overhanging groove leading to the second belay, a foot ledge and a huge number of decrepit pegs banged into a horizontal crack and all wrapped up in rotting thread. You needed a bit of faith that something in that lot would hold. The final pitch reared up the jutting prow itself, over some loose blocks, which, when I cleaned the route, I'd wanted to clear more forcefully. But it didn't seem fair to bomb the car parked right underneath me.

In 1982 yo-yoing remained standard practice, and that's how I climbed *The Prow*, taking a long session for each pitch. It was like clocking on for work each morning. Between attempts, Gill and I would nip up the road to the Green Shack, the little café further up Miller's Dale, for a brew and a chat while my fingers uncurled. Then it would be back to the factory floor. The route got steadily harder, but at least the pitches got shorter and the ropes more manageable. To get to the second pitch on the second day I had to climb the first pitch again, and then Gill prussiked up the rope behind me to belay. She had to hang in space for hours, something she loathed more as each hour passed, hanging off dodgy pegs on an overhanging wall. Tea breaks at the Green Shack became a kind of reward.

The climbing was incredibly powerful. Starting the second pitch, I laybacked off thin calcite fins of rock and tufa-like pinches in a wildly exposed position, creeping back left, levering myself up, feet braced on very little, into the bottomless corner. To be honest, I was too busy to think about where I was, perched above the road and relying on a lot of dog-eared protection, to worry about the constant exposure. I was just fighting all the time to stay on. Hanging in the corner, gasping and moaning, I had to reach up and left again around the prow to reach the next stance where I grabbed the tat and hung there blowing hard, my arms rigid with fatigue and my back and legs aching.

To reach the third pitch, I climbed the first two pitches again, running them together to save time, and then Gill prussiked up to join me. Both of us were now desperate to get the climb done. The consensus these days is that the third pitch is the hardest with a really powerful start to reach an overhang. Beyond that, the holds are good, but it's so steep and after so much strenuous climbing below it's not surprising people found crossing it the living end. Geoff Birtles took some shots of me on the upper section for *High* magazine, wearing a stripy t-shirt he'd loaned me that would stand out against the white rock.

The Prow got a huge amount of coverage, pumped up by its description in High as the 'hardest route in the world'. Of course, I knew perfectly well this wasn't true. Some wags pointed out that it wasn't even the hardest route at Raven Tor, an accolade they claimed for Moffatt's route *Rooster Booster*, climbed a few weeks before. As for myself, the crux move on *The Prow* didn't seem to me as hard as that on *Cave Route Left*, which I'd done the year before. But I can't pretend that the coverage wasn't useful. It reassured sponsors and kept my name in the public eye.

Becoming a professional climber did sound fun. For the past fifteen years all I'd done, and all I'd really wanted to do, was climb – every day, all day. Now I was getting paid for it. Jerry Peel, interviewed that summer for the film *The Fingertip Phenomenon*, said: 'He eats and sleeps climbing. That's Ron all over. He's not bothered about anything else. Or he doesn't seem to be. He's not bothered about possessions or a fancy motor.' All that was true, but in a way the magazine coverage and sponsorship deals were recognition for all those years of effort, for driving a Reliant Robin and living in a house without a cooker. Now that I was married, wanting to buy my own house, I needed to plan ahead beyond which crag I would visit next. But Gill proved to be far more adept than I was at managing the business side of things. Turning climbing into a job brought responsibilities that in retrospect I didn't feel like taking – if, in fact, I even could. I had to be extrovert, even brash, and talk myself up.

That sort of thing didn't come naturally to me. I felt deeply self-conscious at the best of times, and found generating media interest embarrassing. I look back at the interviews I gave to camera in those days, and I look and sound a lot more sure of myself than I remember feeling. I felt confident in my own ability, but putting myself on a pedestal made me uncomfortable. I had too thin a skin for the flak it drew. Mostly, this was good-natured ribbing from friends who had known me a long time, like Jerry Peel. Others saw me as needing to be taken down a peg or two. People would spot me on the crag and give me grief. Perhaps, in retrospect, I should have taken more control, or learned how to laugh off what was often just the product of envy. If you're splashed across magazines, you've got to take the good with the bad. Either ignore it or get out altogether.

Public scrutiny was an important aspect of climbing at Raven Tor in particular and the Peak District in general. You were watched, and it wasn't always a pleasant sensation. The sense of competition, the controversy over grading, changing ethics – it was all getting more intense and I began to feel under pressure. Chris Gore was one of the young climbers who emerged in the early 1980s, who saw it from the perspective of the next generation: 'Ron initially had a disservice done to him by the profile and hype given him in *Crags* magazine. He was expected to be the best, but really it was more political. The magazine deliberately associated itself with its own created star, and obviously the star believes in the image he's been given. He was taking on himself these imagined expectations of the people watching, in whose eyes he should have been flowing up the routes. Because he'd just become a media machine, his character didn't come out.'

That sense of the pack closing in made for good copy, and to an extent it was how I felt. I climbed with Jerry Moffatt in those early days and it was pretty obvious that he was talented and was going to get much, much stronger. And I knew I wasn't. I knew from then on there was only one way things could go and that was downhill. It wasn't hard to deal with. Jerry was fiercely ambitious and very hungry for success. Not only did he want to be the best, he wanted to be seen as the best. He had a much more businesslike approach to the commercial side of being a full-time climber. I thought getting paid for being talented at something I loved too good to be real, especially when I think of what work meant to my parents. Jerry, I think, took it as his due, and was confident he'd get the support he needed. He thrived on meeting people and argued his own case brilliantly. He was competitive to his fingertips – I can see why he liked racing cars – and zeroed in on challenges that would create a stir.

Later that summer, after filming me repeating *The Prow* for his Channel 4 television series *Pushing The Limits*, Leo Dickinson had asked me what next? It was clear that Raven Tor had a great deal of potential, and I nodded at the groove and wall that leads straight up to the first stance of *The Prow*. This was the direct start Bob Dearman had climbed in 1965. A few of us had been sniffing round this groove, but getting into it was hugely powerful. I couldn't get much more than the tips of my chunky fingers into the crucial pocket, which was often wet and became quite glassy after climbers started using a blowtorch to dry it out. The gear was also crap, a problem Jerry solved by adding a bolt and drilling a thread. Using a knee bar, he figured out a sequence no one else had spotted and did the first ascent around the time Leo's film aired, in the summer of 1984. This was *Revelations*, the first French 8a+ in the country. When I came to repeat it, I had to figure out a different way of doing it, to suit my hands.

Revelation is the last book of the Bible and full of prophecies about the future, not all of them good. Redpointing – practising a route and then climbing it without falls – had arrived. Standards rocketed and training intensified. *The Prow* became a training route. We used to tie two 50m ropes together and top-rope the whole thing in one go, doing laps on it. Jerry quickly had competition of his own. A year after the first ascent of *Revelations*, widely acclaimed as Britain's hardest route, the French climber Antoine le Menestrel nipped over from France and soloed it. Antoine was brilliant at Fontainebleau and had become incredibly powerful climbing there. I remember watching him lead *Revelations* before his solo ascent; it was effortless. There was a sense that everything in climbing was accelerating. At the start of the 1980s the top grade was around French 7c. By the end of the decade, Ben Moon had climbed *Hubble* at 8c+. A few years later, I held Malcolm Smith's rope for him as he climbed *Hubble* for the photographer Heinz Zak. He made it look easy. I don't think I've ever seen anyone so strong climbing. I've got huge admiration for Steve McClure too. The things he's done are incredible, adding a 9a to Raven Tor. But it wasn't for me, that style of climbing. I couldn't sit on a rope for day after day. I got bored if a route took more than a morning. For a kid who started climbing in the 1960s, not long after the golden era of Joe Brown and Don Whillans, things were getting silly.

At the same time, I quite liked being the old fart, even though I wasn't yet thirty. Suddenly there were all these young kids around, who were sprinting through the grades, and becoming ferociously strong. And there were still some of the older generation around too, dossing in Stoney like they'd always done. It made for a great crack. 'Dirty' Derek Hersey was often in the café, wearing his trademark greasy duvet, in the years before he became a stalwart of the Colorado scene. Mark 'Zippy' Pretty was, and is, a guru of Peak Limestone climbing, with an encyclopaedic knowledge of public transport. Andy Pollitt would be floating around, doing nothing or everything. There was Dave 'Chesters' Lee, a mate of Derek's and John Conn, who was a real character, a binman from Chesterfield who just liked hanging out in the Peak and doing the odd climb.

It was one thing to be climbing the hardest routes, but it gave me as much satisfaction to do new routes that people loved. I've fond memories of *Body Machine* for that reason. *The Prow* might have got the publicity, but *Body Machine* was for me the highlight of all the routes I put up at Raven Tor. It takes the same start as *Indecent Exposure* and *The Prow*, swinging out of that poor ash tree, and then moves right before going straight up the wall above. People would come up to me and say: 'Flippin' 'eck, Ron, that's a good route.' I think sometimes climbers forget that you're creating something for other climbers to follow and appreciate. It means a great deal to me that all three routes get three stars, confirming their quality. Standards will always progress, making today's hardest yesterday's news, but the quality of a route lasts. Your favourite new routes are a bit like your kids; they don't belong to you, but you want people to think well of them. It was bitterly disappointing when someone cut down the little ash tree below the crag in 2008, changing the character of *Body Machine* forever. The fact that so many climbers were so upset by the fate of one tree – almost a sacred tree by that stage – shows how much commitment the place inspires.

Still, it was a strange era, particularly for those of us who had developed their climbing ethics in another age and were trying to figure out what should be preserved and what should change. Sport climbing hadn't quite become the accepted norm for hard limestone climbing. Jerry Moffatt might have practised *Revelations* before leading it, but he did the second ascent of Ben Moon's *Statement of Youth* at Pen Trwyn in North Wales yo-yo style. Malham, on the other hand, had quickly become a sport climbing venue. In those days climbers still went up there for days at a time, camping out on the ledges like I'd done back in the early 1970s. A whole crowd of guys would be working on the hardest routes, all at the same time, all of them committed to the new ethic of redpointing.

I was still dipping my toe in both worlds at Malham, doing the first free ascent of my old childhood friend Phil Webb's route *Yosemite Wall* at E5, later bolted to give a straightforward sport climb. When we were kids, we'd wondered if a route like that would ever go free. Now it was three grades off the pace, but it felt more of a challenge before it was bolted. No one asked me if it was okay to change the route and, at the time, things like that annoyed me. I still had a foot in each camp, traditional and sport climbing, and thought the past should count for something. But I also started doing routes that seemed more modern, like *New Dawn* and *Mescalito*, and perhaps best of all, *Zoolook*, the first 8a at Malham. Even then, I yo-yoed these routes, although I later did redpoint ascents of them too. The main thing is that they were all three-star routes.

Being at Malham at that time did change my outlook on things, partly from hanging out on the catwalk, the broad ledge around the bottom of the crag that became more like a fashion catwalk, with all these skinny young lads squeezed into lycra. It was a long way from my Helly Hansen breeches, and thick socks in my EBs. Suddenly there was a big crowd all climbing the top grades, like Ben Moon, always laidback and doing route after route, and Andy Pollitt, also very cool. Steve Lewis was there, doing lots of new routes, and Martin Atkinson was another, like me from a village outside Skipton and powerfully built, in my mind an underrated talent. Sport climbing in Britain really took off at Malham.

The ethic in other areas wasn't so clear-cut. Raven Tor might have been turning into a sport climbing crag, but Chee Tor was still a traditional bastion and I had a score or two to settle there. Having been beaten to the first ascent of *Mortlock's Arête* by Tom Proctor and Geoff Birtles in 1976, another great line had been snatched from under my nose in 1980. One of the last new routes Pete Livesey climbed was *The Golden Mile*, a superb line just to the right of *Mortlock's*. I'd known it was there, just waiting to be done, and I knew Pete was interested. 'Don't worry kid,' he told me on the phone. 'I'm off to Blackpool for the weekend.' I was busy in Wales and so relaxed a little. What a mistake. Pete spent the weekend at the amusement arcade of Chee Tor, grabbing one of the Peak's best E5s. He named it after Blackpool's famous attractions, just to rub it in.

To the left of *Mortlock's*, however, was a beautiful, clean leaning wall that looked even harder than *The Golden Mile*. I was desperate not to miss out again, and because the route looked so bold, I decided, as I had done on *The Cad* four years before, to place a couple of bolts, the minimum I needed to get the thing done. There was some hard climbing to reach the first of these, protected by a poor wire, so it was by no means a sport route. I called it *Tequila Mockingbird*. Jerry Moffatt took a long fall off the crux trying to make the second ascent and suggested my grade of E6 7b should be more along the lines of E7 6c. (It was around this time that I gave up experimenting with the grading system, partly because French grades were starting to arrive.)

With *The Cad*, the bolts were quickly removed and a traditional ethic at Gogarth reasserted; at Chee Tor the opposite happened. First, a French climber called Jean-Pierre Bouvier repeated the route using the redpoint style of climbing, practising the moves and then leading it with no falls. He then tried to claim the route as his own, calling it *Gandalf Le Magicien*, arguing that using yo-yo tactics, as I had, wasn't a proper ascent. It seemed outrageous at the time, but in retrospect he had a point. Especially looking back on what happened next. Mark Pretty, arguing that if you're going to put two bolts in, you might as well do a proper job and make it four, drilled two more holes and turned the route into a sport climb. It was the only time I think I seriously lost my rag over a climb, and Mark and I fell out over it. There was a lot of huffing and puffing in the climbing media and a few sharp words.

The bolts were chopped, and have stayed chopped despite an attempt to replace them, and I'm pleased about that. There are so many great traditional limestone routes at Chee Tor, but it's a kind of climbing that doesn't get the kudos it deserves. Climbing a bold limestone E5 like *Autobahn*, another Chee Tor route of mine done around the same time, takes more skill and a lot more courage than a pumpy 7a+ at a sport crag. It would be a shame if a different and more exciting way of experiencing climbing were lost for good. Mark and I became good friends again, although I bet he still thinks there should be four bolts in *Tequila*.

The other great change in climbing during the 1980s was the emergence of organised competition. Anyone who's spent time around top climbers would know there has never been any shortage of disorganised competition, but the compulsion to come up with a definitive answer to the question who is the best climber in the world proved too strong. A combination of continental representative bodies, entrepreneurs and media interest gave organised competitions enough impetus. I guess competition was the logical conclusion to the new wave of sport climbing and a handy way for commercial interests to get involved. Each to his own. My feelings about them were mixed. I'm not a huge fan of being indoors generally, let alone for climbing, and since artificial structures are where competitions should be held, they don't hold much appeal, certainly not as a spectator. I'd sooner watch paint dry.

I went to one of the first European events at the Italian ski resort of Bardonecchia in 1986, along with, I think, Martin Atkinson and Ben Moon, who was sporting a gigantic set of dreadlocks. It was the second year the event had been held. The idea was to create publicity and some summer business for the little town by inviting the world's top climbers to pit their skills against each other. I had no idea what to expect and was gobsmacked when I arrived to find thousands of spectators milling around. Unlike modern competitions, the Bardonecchia events were held on the local crags, and in order to create new routes that locals and visitors alike would have an equal chance of climbing any notion of respect for the rock had been tossed out the window. Holds had been glued, drilled, chipped and hammered into existence. It was pretty much everything I'd been brought up to frown on, and with good reason. I made it to the semi-final, and arrived at the crux overhang to discover that the Michelangelo who drilled the crucial pocket over the lip had used quite a narrow drill-bit. I poked my fat fingers at it and discovered they didn't fit. And that was that. I spent the rest of the trip climbing on the magnificent crags around the town. If this was the future, and everyone seemed to be saying it was, then I wanted nothing to do with it.

Not all my experiences of competitions were so negative. In late 1984, eighteen months before Bardonecchia, Gill and I were given two round-the-world air tickets by Mont Bell, the Japanese importer of Clog, one of my sponsors. The idea was we'd spend a few days in Japan meeting Mont Bell executives and climbers around Japan and then be free to go on to America. The Japanese end of things was a real eye-opener. Mont Bell's founder and director Isamu Tatsuno had been the second Japanese climber to do the North Face of the Eiger, but was also passionate about Japanese culture, like the ancient tea ceremony and bathing. After the long flight, with an overnight stop in Hong Kong, we arrived jet-lagged and confused at Isamu's house. His whole family were there to greet us and his wife explained which pair of slippers we should wear around the house, which to use in the bathroom and how we shouldn't use any at all in our bedroom. She'd also prepared a bath for us, and feeling grimy after the journey we wondered who should go first. The bath, it transpired after a lot of smiling and nodding, was huge, fifteen feet square and full of boiling hot water, and since we were married we could go in together. We had no idea this was a ceremonial bath, not to wash in. It was purely for relaxation. By the time we'd finished, there was a scummy layer of suds on the surface and a look of horror on our hosts' faces.

The rest of the trip went a lot better as we travelled the country, climbing everything we were shown. Travelling in Japan was something I would never have done were it not for climbing. I'd never tried sushi, and saki was a real eye-opener. I teetered constantly on the verge of inflicting another cultural disaster on our hosts, but I loved it all. Chris Gore and Jerry Moffatt had been guests in Japan a few weeks before us, so when we were presented with a stunning, unprotected arête they hadn't been able to complete, I couldn't resist. I'd not long done *Master's Edge* at Millstone, a similar problem the Japanese had read about in the magazines. Would I oblige? Luckily for me it seemed to be a reach problem, and with my huge span I managed to claw my way to the top. There was lots of smiling and nodding. Would I like to give the route a name and a grade? *Edge of Extinction*, I suggested, and certainly 5.13. They were delighted. It was the first route of that grade in the country.

Leaving Japan, we stopped for a few days in Hawaii and then flew on to Los Angeles where I hired a Pinto station wagon from Rent-A-Wreck. As we drove on to the freeway east to Joshua Tree, Gill asked me where the ashtray was. 'You're sitting in it.' In town we stocked up on food and water, and drove out into the desert, suddenly released from all the smog and chaos of travelling halfway around the world. It seemed heaven to me, a place of endless sunshine where I could wander around all day in shorts doing some of the best and hardest granite climbs in the world. We did a hatful of 5.12s and 5.13s during our few days in Joshua Tree, including *Equinox*. My contract with Hanwag had ended – they never took off in Britain, not really being an advance on EBs

– and I revelled in the superb friction of my new sticky boots.

We found the Americans on our campsite kept themselves pretty much to themselves. But a group of German climbers proved much more friendly. The star of the group was a lad called Stefan Glowacz, who I knew had repeated Jerry Moffatt's German super-route *The Face*, aged just 19, the year before. We hung out together in the local bar, the Captain's Tavern, and even had a mass trip to the movies to see the first Terminator film. You don't put up a route called *Body Machine* and not have an interest in bodybuilding, so when John Long showed up and told us he worked out at the same gym as Arnold Schwarzenegger we were beyond excited.

Stefan told us that he'd been invited to a bouldering competition at Mount Rubidoux in the San Bernardino mountains just outside Los Angeles. I'd never heard of a bouldering competition before but Stefan suggested we went along and take a look. To save money, we decided to sleep in the Pinto. We drove over one evening to Riverside, the neighbourhood where the competition would take place, parked up and crawled into the back. We barely slept a wink. In the middle of the night a crazed Hell's Angel started riding round the parking lot on his bike, waving a gun in the air. It wasn't the best preparation for my first competition.

Still, I had nothing to lose and the atmosphere seemed incredibly friendly. As Gill said, she'd seen more competition on a wet midweek afternoon at Stoney Middleton. We paid our three dollars and were given a sheet marking the location of two hundred problems on boulders strewn across the rather scruffy hillside. Most of them were protected by a top-rope, since in those days nobody had a bouldering mat. The difficulty of the problems ranged from one to twenty, the latter being next to impossible and the idea was to climb eleven problems with ten to score. If you failed to climb the problem inside three minutes then you scored zero, if you did it first go then you got maximum points for that problem. More than three hundred people had turned up, including a bunch of local heroes who had the problems wired. Stefan made the mistake of picking problems with a high tariff that he couldn't manage to complete, and got knocked out. I was a bit cannier and arrived at my final problem with the chance to win if I could just get up it.

My mistake was to pick a slab route that I soon realised was hideously glassy and smooth. Word had got around about the Brit who was threatening an upset and a bunch of locals had gathered to watch. The mood of easy-going Californian warmth had dropped by several degrees as they realised some blow-in might walk off with the title. They were looking daggers, and I was starting to think there was no way I could get up the slab, which seemed to be utterly lacking holds. With the seconds ticking down, and the crowd starting to relax, I decided to make a dash for it, running up the slab and slapping for the obvious big hold and caught it, winning the competition outright. The locals were pissed off. Stefan was pissed off. But I walked off with first prize, which with perfect logic for a bouldering competition was a portaledge made by the big-wall expert Mike Graham and worth £300, quite a lot of money in 1984. We sold it immediately, thus funding our return to Joshua Tree. But the atmosphere at Mount Rubidoux had impressed me. Later, when I started fell racing, I found the same sense of camaraderie among competitors.

Two years after my bad experience at Bardonecchia, I was asked by the British Mountaineering Council to go as an observer to the Crimea where the Soviet climbing federation was organising a climbing competition. Russians had for years competed in speed climbing competitions but for the first time they had decided to include an event based on difficulty and had invited French route setters to come and 'create' routes, just as had been done in Italy. More out of curiosity about life behind the Iron Curtain than any real interest in the event, I agreed to go.

Arriving in Moscow, where I'd been told someone would meet me to put me on a plane to the Crimea, I found the flight's luggage piled in a heap in the arrivals hall. I couldn't find my gear anywhere and there was no indication of how to deal with this. I saw a well-known BBC foreign correspondent heading for the exit, so I asked him if he could offer any advice. He just brushed me off with his hand. After a couple of hours of wondering what the hell I was going to do, a beautiful Russian woman approached me, flanked by two stern-looking men.

'Come with us,' she said, and smiled. I instantly fell in love. 'I am Irene, your interpreter. You will leave tomorrow for the Crimea by plane. I will follow by train. Now, come with me.' She took me into town to a special sport's hotel. I'd had a tip to change my money on the black market, and with Irene's help found myself in a dodgy neighbourhood changing a thin wedge of pounds for a fat one of roubles. If I'd known how little there was to buy I wouldn't have bothered.

On the flight south next day, I flicked through some magazines I'd brought with me to pass the time. It slowly dawned on me that people were peering over the back of the seats to have a look at what I was reading. Clearly, a magazine from the West was too good to miss. So I passed the magazine back and a small crowd gathered round to have a look. As the aircraft, a colossal and rather dodgy Tupolev, came into land, the magazine was passed back. All the advertisements featuring cars and watches had been torn out. I should have warned them that consumerism isn't all it's cracked up to be.

I loved the Crimea. It was like the south of France, with lots of limestone crags, vineyards and sunshine. There were huge sea cliffs, some the size of Gogarth with a huge potential for new routes. The competition itself was an eye-opener. Once again I was shocked by the outright vandalism committed by the French route-setter and felt it was wrong that their version of climbing should be the one the isolated Ukrainians should have to endure. If there were too many holds, he'd whip out his lump hammer and knock some off. Too few, he'd cement some on, or drill some edges. The idea of nature setting the challenge had been thrown out the window. The Russians had no idea what Western climbing was all about and assumed this was all that was on offer.

I was more intrigued by the speed climbing. This had clearly been going on for years and the organisers had a well-practised system going. An old winch with a drum of wire cable was fixed at the top of the crag, like most of the climbing gear apparently homemade, although more likely nicked off the front of a ship. It didn't gather the cable in as fast as competitors climbed so if anyone fell off they took a huge fall. Luckily the blokes standing on the winch were quite large and wouldn't be shifted.

At the end of the week, Irene took me to the airport for my flight home. I'd had a lot of fun and barely put my hand in my pocket the whole time I'd been there. As a consequence, I still had a huge wedge of black market roubles in my wallet. It seemed pointless to try and change them back again – it's not like I had a receipt – so I just handed them over to Irene when I said goodbye, quite an unusual sensation for a Yorkshireman. It's just a shame I didn't have anything without holes in to read on the plane.

TEN

Taking Flight

MANY YOUNGER CLIMBERS I've come to know around the Peak District in the last ten or fifteen years assume that climbing gritstone is my great passion. It certainly became that, over the years, partly through necessity. When I was growing up, gritstone was my daily bread, the rock I climbed midweek, when I couldn't find a partner or didn't have the time to go on the big limestone crags. I worked out circuits of routes that I would solo routinely, and even did some shorter new climbs in this way, like the free ascent of *Small Brown* at Crookrise. When I moved to the Peak District in the early 1980s, I developed a similar programme, a way of keeping fit, climbing alone and doing as much mileage as I could physically manage. Ultimately, all this experience would lead to that day in 1986 when I soloed a hundred routes graded Extremely Severe.

A favourite venue for midweek soloing was the disused quarry at Millstone Edge, above Hathersage, where, to be honest, things would get a bit crackers. I'd solo up the thin, sixty-foot groove of *Green Death*, come down the blank neighbouring arête of *Edge Lane*, that sort of thing. This was solid E5 5c climbing, technically not too bad but requiring a lot of confidence. Quarried gritstone is a very different experience to the naturally weathered stuff you find at Stanage or in Staffordshire. The face holds are sharper and often more positive, but there are fewer

175

flaws in the rock where you can stick your feet and know you'll get some purchase.

Looking across from *Edge Lane* it was impossible not to wonder about the even blanker arête to the right. Tom Proctor had climbed its upper section, called *Great Arête*, in the 1970s. It's not as steep as the lower section, and much easier technically, but it still sees very few ascents. Fall off high on the lead and you'll most likely die. It seemed unlikely to me that its more difficult first half would be climbed any time soon, and I didn't bother to abseil down it. It wasn't my habit to top-rope things and there didn't seem to be any gear to protect what was obviously going to be a desperate climb. It simply remained as an outstanding project for somebody else's future.

For much of 1983 I was busy making films and moving into our own house, a pretty little cottage in Eyam, bought with the proceeds from all that hard work. I'd had a fabulous trip with Wolfgang Güllich, first in Germany and then at a climbing meet in France where we polished off all the hardest climbs there at the time. I'd then spent some time injured, having broken my leg falling off the grit and spending the last part of the year in plaster. Desperate to climb, but with winter drawing in, I went up to Yorkshire to have a look at a route I'd spotted on Kilnsey, which would later become *Dominatrix*. But it wasn't in condition, and neither, to be honest, was I. There was a particular move, a sort of powerful rock-over onto my injured leg. There simply wasn't any power in it.

When I got back to Derbyshire, somebody mentioned that Jerry Moffatt had been looking at the lower half of *Great Arête*. He'd done the route with the safety of a top-rope a few times and was just waiting for the right conditions to solo it. There was even a name for it – *Master's Edge* – because whoever climbed it first would have earned the right to the title.

I felt the familiar surge of competitive energy. Jerry had spent 1983 doing some fierce routes in Germany, the first ascent of

Master's Wall on Cloggy and climbed the beautiful gritstone arête of *Ulysses* at Stanage. His face was everywhere. I'd barely done a new route all year, and was becoming a bit of an old fart at twenty-eight. I was starting to feel part of an earlier generation whose time was passing. *Master's Edge* might give me the chance to turn back the clock a little.

Spurred into action, I made plans to go straight up to Millstone with Gill. Knowing the rock well, I packed a secret weapon I'd picked up from Geoff Birtles, a strange new camming device that he'd been sent to review in *High* magazine. Called an Amigo and manufactured by Edelrid, it was a strange contraption, a kind of sliding nut that you needed three hands to place. Looking at it, I wondered if it would fit the shot holes that are found all over Millstone, drilled by quarrymen for dynamite. These were of a standard size, and I'd become very familiar with them over the years.

It was a gloomy day at the end of December when Gill and I drove up to Millstone from Eyam. There'd been a lot of rain around over Christmas and I wondered if it was worth the effort, since the rock would most likely be damp. When we reached the crag, however, I could see at once the arête was dry, even if there was a huge wet streak down the groove of *Green Death*. I soloed to the top of the crag to warm up and threw a rope down the sharply defined arête. I thought it likely that chalk Jerry had left on the route would have absorbed some of the moisture in the air over the last few days and made sure I brushed the holds vigorously with a toothbrush. The arête itself looked rather enigmatic, particularly near the top, but I tested the holds and tried the Amigo in one of two shot holes at half height. I wasn't totally convinced, after tugging on it a few times, but it looked promising. That's all the preparation I did.

Back on the ground, I tied Gill firmly down to a nearby boulder off to the right. Over the years, plenty of climbers have been saved from hitting the ground on *Master's* by their seconds scampering backwards to take in some rope before their falling leader weighted the route's only protection at just below half height. It occurred to me this might be an advantage, but Gill was much lighter than I, and I was worried she'd be hauled backwards into the air, resulting in me breaking a leg – again. Better to keep her firmly on the ground. As long as she watched me carefully then I shouldn't hurt myself and she shouldn't move. Still, it all felt very marginal.

A couple of easy moves took me onto the arête. From here, an awkward technical series of moves leads up to the shot holes, but the climbing wasn't obvious. Bouldering mats were still far in the future, and I'd have to be careful not to snap an ankle. I soloed up and down a few times to work out the sequence and then tied in. Things went smoothly, I placed the Amigo and clipped in, and then moved up again, without any clear idea of how I was going to climb the upper part of the arête. It was a bit of a puzzle. I got one of my feet into the shot hole without the gear and placed my other foot onto the lip of the hole with the Amigo in it. Then, figuring I would need my feet the other way round to move up the arete, I skipped them around. But there was moisture on the lip of the free hole and my foot greased off. I fell. The gear held. I stopped a few feet from the ground and lowered down for a think, heart racing. It was obvious that if I fell from much higher on the arête it was going to be a close call. I thought about the long weeks of inactivity caused by my last accident. I would have to get this right.

Climbers these days, usually with the advantage of top-rope practice, know there's a neat solution to the crux of *Master's* on the right of the arête. You pull yourself in with an undercut and step high with your right foot, bringing within range a good edge and the finishing flat hold. Having watched videos of subsequent ascents, I'm pretty confident I didn't do *Master's Edge* like that at all. I wouldn't have had time to work out such a complex sequence. Looking at the photographs of my ascent, there isn't any chalk whatsoever on the wall right of the arête, only on the arête itself. I simply lay-backed the sharp-edged arête, using my big hands to pinch holds and make a sequence of teetering moves, always on the verge of swinging helplessly round and off for the long plummet onto the Amigo. I remember a definite smear on the arête where I could almost stop, but it wasn't close enough to reach the flat hold from that position. My reach, almost eight and a half feet from tiptoe to fingertip, must have helped.

There weren't many people at the crag that day. It was late December, after all, but John Conn was there and he'd brought a mate who took pictures of the first ascent and later sent me them. I had no record of his name, and still feel a little ashamed that his shots appeared, and have continued to appear, without a credit. But the last of the sequence shows me on easy ground above the flat hold. I've got the biggest grin on my face, mixed with a look of utter relief. Thank God that was over. Clearly, I hadn't done the route on-sight, but I felt I'd done it in pretty good style without any top-rope practice. *Master's Edge* was one of the first routes I did that stuck solidly at E7 – a grade harder than *Ulysses*, which I'd quickly repeated – and with a technical grade of 6b/c too. It's now more than a quarter of a century since the first ascent, and it still hasn't had an on-sight ascent. No wonder I was smiling.

Some people seemed surprised that I'd stepped in and taken Jerry's project. The man himself was pretty upset. But to be honest, I didn't think twice about it. It had to be done. In the mid 1970s a large number of climbers were operating around the top grades – probably the last time the upper ranks were so crowded – and competition for routes was fierce. We all watched one other, conspired, fibbed and dissembled – very light-heartedly – to make sure it was us who got to a plum unclimbed line ahead of the pack. It was part of the fun. No one owns a piece of rock.

I can see how when climbers started putting in lots of bolts then some issues of ownership might arise, but on something like *Master's* it was a free-for-all. Chalk one up for the old boy.

The first ascent pictures reveal something else about that day – what I had on my feet. After my contract with Hanwag came to an end, I had started wearing Firés, the boots everyone was talking about with the amazing sticky rubber. I wore my very first pair on *Master's Edge*. People roll their eyes when they see pictures of me climbing in Hanwags and sympathise. They do look clumpy, certainly compared to modern footwear, but they were no worse than EBs. I climbed some pretty hard routes in them, so they couldn't have been that bad. But Firés were something else. Overnight, it seemed, everyone's climbing standard went up by a full grade. On gritstone they made a significant difference. Many of the routes climbed in the mid 1980s would have been almost impossible without them.

Looking at the new routes I was doing on grit, there was an obvious rise in their technical difficulty around this time. It seemed that while I'd developed a modern body, I had been labouring with antique footwear. In the late 1970s and early 1980s, I'd done a lot of serious new routes around the E6 mark, like *Desperate Dan* at Ilkley, and *One Step Beyond* at Curbar Edge in the Peak District. With sticky rubber, I found I could do routes that were similarly bold but fiercely technical too. Routes like *Neon Dust* and *Toy Boy* at Froggatt still have technical grades of 7a, the latter being E7 as well. *Moon Madness* at Curbar was another one, and possibly E8. I was a better climber by then, but no doubt the boots helped. I wonder how I would have got on with *Strawberries* in sticky boots. It certainly adds credit to climbers like Johnny Woodward, who did the stunning *Beau Geste* at Froggatt in 1981, and Daniel Lee, with *Cool Moon* on Curbar, that these fierce gritstone problems were solved wearing EBs.

Living close by and with time on my hands midweek,

I reverted to my schooldays habit of climbing on gritstone when I didn't have the option of tying in with a partner. Long days soloing and bouldering became routine. Without doubt the highlight from those years spent on the grit, certainly in terms of difficulty, was a tiny route up the arête of an undercut boulder at Stanage Edge called the Grand Hotel, so named for the shelter it used to offer climbers dossing underneath it. It would become the last truly significant hard route of my career.

Halfway along Stanage is an area of boulders called the Plantation, a pilgrimage site for the world's bouldering faithful with an extraordinary number of hard problems. One of the most famous, called *Not To Be Taken Away*, runs up the middle of the Grand Hotel boulder and is what boulderers would term a high-ball these days because of its height. At the time it was graded HVS and was a regular part of my soloing circuit, long before the arrival of bouldering pads. I couldn't fail to notice the blank-looking arête to the left and began to play around on it. Starting on its right-hand side, I got my feet on a jutting block under the boulder's lip and threw my left hand up onto the blunt edge of the arête. For my right hand there was a sloper, and using this I'd get whatever I could – knee, toe, whatever – onto the arête and then go again with my left hand. It was a desperate move and it took weeks before I could do it, trying it again and again each time I went up to Stanage. This kind of behaviour was unprecedented for me.

Once it became clear I might actually be able to do this move onto the arête, I started wondering about the move at the top. I wasn't sure what I'd find when I got there and the fall looked horrible. So I took a rope up to the crag and hung off it over the top of the Grand Hotel to look at the holds. There was a massive bucket of a hold just short of the top, but the move to get that was a worry, off balance and thin. And there was no comfy mat waiting for me at the bottom. To prepare myself for what could be an awkward fall, I started jumping off *Not To Be Taken Away*, climbing a little higher each time to find out at what point jumping off became uncomfortable. I do daft things like that. But it was such a stunning line I became obsessed with it. It's only eight or ten moves, but it's a fabulous problem and still gets Font 8a as a grade, which was pretty good going for 1987. I called it *Careless Torque*. It's been repeated maybe only ten times, and only recently has had ascents without the benefit of a top-rope inspection.

From the mid 1980s soloing on the gritstone edges became much more important to me than it had been when I was younger. Moving into my thirties, I didn't burn with the same enthusiasm I had when I was starting out. Having done my fair share of hard routes on limestone over the years, latterly at Malham and Gordale in the mid 1980s, I could see that things were only going to get tougher and that meant just one thing – more training. For years, I'd been doing huge amounts of climbing in a day, setting up ropes on hard limestone routes to do laps, building up more and more stamina. Just maintaining that level of fitness took a colossal amount of time and I was finding it more and more tedious. I almost dreaded going climbing.

Worse, in order to attempt the hardest new routes being done in the mid 1980s, I was going to have to train differently – and more intensively. This was the era when British climbing went underground, into cellars where custom-built wooden boards offered specialist training techniques to increase power rather stamina. Being underground wasn't for me. I'd been brought up in the country and was only truly content outside. I would rather be out running across the moors in the winter months than inside a stuffy cellar working problems on a wooden board. Part of the whole appeal of climbing been the pleasure of being in a natural environment: the smell of bracken, the feel of rock under your hand, the breeze on your face. It wasn't just hard moves I found inspiring, but the line of a route, its architecture. You could look up at a crag and think that you'd created something. There was little aesthetic appeal in the lines being done now. In order to push the boundaries of rock climbing, it seemed, you had to turn your back on so much that was pleasurable and enriching about the sport.

I couldn't avoid the fact that I was now older than almost all the leading rock climbers in the country. I'd been doing it for ten years more than most of them. I felt myself wearying of the public side of being a professional, jockeying for position and keeping up my profile in the magazines. I had never felt comfortable with all that anyway. I felt foolish demanding attention so I could make a living. It was difficult for me to detach myself from all of that, and just treat it as a joke.

On top of all that, my marriage to Gill broke down. This wasn't altogether surprising. It's true we shared a passion for climbing, but Gill wasn't going to focus on it in the same way I did. And outside climbing, we were very different people. She was ambitious for things I didn't care about. I remember an agonising telephone conversation in France, where I was shooting photographs with John Beatty, when it became clear our marriage was over. She'd left by the time I got home and only returned to clear out her things. Our separation left me feeling defensive and reluctant to engage with the world. I kept myself to myself and stayed away from crags where I knew there would be a big crowd. It's part of the reason I spent so much time soloing on gritstone.

All these factors, splitting from Gill, my own indifference to how climbing was developing, meant my relationship with the sport began to change. At some fundamental level I'd had enough. Not, I should add, of climbing itself. At no stage did I think of giving the sport up and doing something else. Climbing is a deep part of who I am. In that regard I think I'm different from some of my contemporaries. When Pete Livesey decided he couldn't be top dog anymore, he walked away from the sport pretty much altogether. I know he looked back with pride on what he had achieved, as do I, but he didn't seem to need the sensation of climbing, of moving up rock, in the same way that I did. But I have to admit I was emotionally exhausted. The feeling that I had something to prove had started to make me anxious. Letting go of that feeling was simply liberating.

I had no problem adjusting to not being top dog anymore. I found I could easily live without being on the cover of a magazine. As time went on I began to take more and more pleasure in going to the crag without feeling any pressure or expectation about what I would do there. When people came up to talk to me at the crag it was no longer to discuss the latest controversy, or find out what I was planning to do, it was just to say hello or talk about the routes I'd done. I started to get a better perspective on things.

There were new things in my life as well. In the autumn of 1986 I started working for Wild Country, who had just bought out my previous sponsor Clog, the North Wales hardware manufacturer. I'd been happy at Clog, not least because when founding director Denny Moorhouse sold up, I got his old car – a Ford Capri – thus saving me from the indignity of driving a Reliant Robin. I was catapulted into the category of boy racer. Working for Wild Country meant renewing my friendship with Steve Foster, with whom I'd shared a lot of adventures in the 1970s. I also started paragliding, mostly through the influence of Geoff Birtles, an early convert to the sport who opened one of the first paragliding schools in Britain. Parascending – being towed into the air while hanging from a parachute – had been popular in Britain during the 1970s but paragliding was something altogether new. The idea of launching a parachute from a steep slope or a cliff-top had been around since the 1950s. During the development of parachute recovery systems for space capsules, NASA scientists developed the practice of 'slope soaring' to test their canopies. Reading about the practice in a magazine, three

TOP LEFT AND RIGHT Making the first ascent of *Master's Edge* (E7 6c) at Millstone. BOTTOM On top of High Tor after soloing *Darius* (E2 5c) live on daytime TV. Al Evans is to my left, with Chris Johnston filming.

TOP LEFT Gill and I dressed as H.M. and Martha Kelly at Laddow Rocks in the Peak District. TOP RIGHT With Sid Perou in the Verdon. I was midway through soloing *Ula* (F6b). Sid is hooked up to the 'talking rope'. BOTTOM Preparing to paraglide in Snowdonia. The peak top left is Snowdon, and the impressive crag of Clogwyn Du'r Arddu can be seen top centre. OPPOSITE Cutting loose high on *The Prow* (F7c) at Raven Tor. I'm pretty sure John Allen and Steve Bancroft are part of the crowd barracking from the road!

OVERLEAF Sid films me climbing *Chrysalis* (F7b) in the Verdon, for the film *The Fingertip Phenomenon*. TOP LEFT A proud moment: me with Natasha on the day she was born. TOP RIGHT Dad with the girls in Embsay. BOTTOM With the girls in Australia.

TOP LEFT Hanging out on the 'collapsing ledge' high on the Aiguille du Midi, above Chamonix. TOP RIGHT Me (left, without moustache!) and Brian Molyneux in a snow cave on the Eiger. I played the role of Dougal Haston, and Brian played John Harlin.   BOTTOM In the thick of it, running up Ringing Roger in the 2007 Edale Skyline race, part of the English Championships that year.

TOP Climbing *Not To Be Taken Away* (Font 6c) at Stanage. *Careless Torque* (Font 8a) is the striking arête in the foreground.　BOTTOM With the girls in the Ardèche. Jasmine on my right, Tasha to my left.

French friends, Jean-Claude Bétemps, André Bohn and Gérard Bosson from Mieussy in the French Alps, wanted to find out if a modern, 'ram-air' parachute could be inflated simply by running down a slope. On a June day in 1978 they tried out their idea on the mountainside above their village. Bohn managed to glide over a thousand metres down to the village football pitch and land safely. They called their new sport 'parapente', 'pente' meaning slope in French, a nod to the originators of the idea of 'slope soaring'. Within ten years the sport was attracting thousands of new enthusiasts and the first world championships were underway.

Flying teaches you to look at the sky in a completely new way. It becomes a place of constant movement, columns of warm air rising, wind flowing across the line of a ridge and swirling into chaos on the far side of the hill. As you slowly gain experience, you can feel how the air changes as you fly through it. You learn to predict where danger lies and where you can find lift. I began to explore afresh the Derbyshire crags I thought I knew too well. I'd fly the length of Stanage with my rock shoes and chalk bag, land and do some climbing, and then take off and fly back to the car. It was great fun.

Ordinary parachutes, like those used by skydivers, weren't ideal. Geoff had a friend who was trying to paraglide in the Peak District with one, but normal parachutes are designed to bring you down, not keep you up in the sky, so much of the time he was skimming the grass. So Geoff started manufacturing canopies that incorporated the new designs emerging to improve performance for paragliding. He also opened his paragliding school, but although he qualified as an instructor he was too busy editing *High* to run courses. He knew that I was enjoying the sport and asked me if I'd like to train as an instructor and work for him.

At the time, the Army ran the only certified instructor course recognised by the British Hang Gliding and Paragliding Association. I was packed off down south to Dartmoor for a long weekend of being barked at by men in uniforms, which I loathed. They kept insisting on getting up early. These days, beginners learn to fly in a dual paraglider, strapped to an instructor. Canopies are more reliable too, making novice flying far safer. Not in the 1980s. Then you ran through some basic theory and very soon had beginners running along a gentle slope with the canopy inflated over their heads, trying to keep it level. Once they had mastered these very basic skills, we took them to the top of a hill and launched them into the sky. It was like preparing pilots in the Great War, brave young fellows on the crest of a technological wave. We gave students radios at first so we could talk to them and offer advice, but after a while we realised they were just slavishly following our instructions and not learning the necessary skills to be independent.

The school operated from a field on the slopes of Win Hill in Derbyshire, where, according to legend, Northumbrians rolled stones onto the advancing Mercians who had charged over from nearby Lose Hill. Now we were sending down paraglider pilots. Geoff had negotiated an annual rental fee with the local farmer to launch off a spot called Hope Brink. We'd meet students in the Woodbine Café in the village of Hope and walk them up there. It was a boom time in paragliding. The sport proved an instant hit and lots of people wanted training. There were students coming through every week and for me the work was not only well paid, I could fit instructing around my other commitments.

Still, it was often terrifying, watching the latest batch of fledglings take to the air. My heart would be in my mouth as the latest novice sprinted down the hill and took to the air. You could get fantastic lift from Hope Brink, and easily gain a thousand feet from take-off. We'd tell students to turn right on take-off into the wind. Invariably, however, the odd one would forget all about that and carry straight on out into the valley, or even worse turn left. Occasionally there would be a serious accident. One student landed in power cables at the bottom of the hill. The canopy was frazzled, but the pilot dropped to the ground unharmed. All the communities in the Edale valley lost their electricity. The insurance bill for that one must have been quite large. Another student, who became a good pilot, crashed through a roof just a hundred metres from where I live now in Hathersage. Luckily the neighbour was a doctor and was able to offer immediate first aid.

After a while, apart from the moments of blind terror, I began to find instructing a bit passive. I'd get to walk up the hill once in the morning and then I'd be standing around all day. It was frustrating too, waiting for the right weather conditions. That frustration might have played a part in my own serious accident. At the end of a long day, in strong winds, I decided to fly to the bottom of the hill to save time rather than walk down as I should have done. Perhaps I wanted to show off a little, too. In the late 1980s all kinds of new paraglider innovations were happening and I was flying a particularly fickle new canopy made by Fall Hawk. Performance had been improved, but at the cost of stability. Almost without warning one end of the canopy would fold underneath the wing, and you'd start tumbling. If that happened close to the ground then you'd get hurt. Around this time, lots of my paragliding friends were having crashes, including Geoff, resulting in broken bones and worse. I suppose it was only a matter of time before my turn came.

To be honest, I can't tell you what happened because I don't have any memory of that day, but clearly my canopy failed and I hit the ground at speed. Despite wearing a helmet I was knocked out, hence the memory loss, and snapped my right wrist in two. I woke up surrounded by lots of anxious students and fellow instructors, including Geoff, wondering what to do. At the time I was seeing a girl who worked close by at an outdoor education centre. She was an ex-nurse and happened to be there. She bundled me into her car and took me to hospital. The pain was indescribable.

Luckily the surgeon who stuck my hand back on the right way round was a climber. He knew who I was and just how important it was that I keep some kind of mobility in the damaged wrist. Still, it was touch and go. The injury refused to heal, and there was a threat of embolism. I was hooked up to the anti-coagulant heparin twenty-four hours a day and spent more than a month in the Royal Hallamshire in Sheffield waiting for the bones to knit. I still can't straighten my hand or rotate it fully. It's made some undercut moves difficult, but otherwise I feel very lucky that my wrist more or less recovered completely. It took a long time, however, and coming when it did, in my early thirties soon after I'd climbed *Careless Torque*, the injury was something of a punctuation mark closing my best years as a climber.

It seems amazing even to me, but I went back to flying, at least for a while. It was soon after returning to work that I met a young aspirant flier called Zanna. She was a junior doctor working in Liverpool and was completely different to any woman I'd been out with before. Tall and slim, with bright red hair, she had grown up in Africa and enjoyed a wild and adventurous childhood. She was also fiercely intelligent, and always prepared to try new things – a paragliding course was pretty typical. I introduced her to climbing, and as our relationship developed she began using my little cottage in Eyam as a base while she continued her studies down south. We went to Chamonix together, to go flying and climbing. In the spring of 1989 Zanna found out she was pregnant and we got married. Jasmine, our first daughter, was born in January of the following year. Our second daughter, Natasha, was born in February 1992.

Becoming a father changed my life completely. I was more than a little reluctant about the whole idea. I knew it would mean a complete break with a lifestyle I'd enjoyed for years. But when Jasmine came along it was like a switch had been thrown in my head. When this tiny little scrap of a human was put in my arms,

I thought, this is me. Everything that had gone before, as much as I loved it, was done with; I'd started a whole new chapter in my life.

With Zanna's career blossoming, it made sense that a bigger proportion of childcare would fall to me, something that I didn't mind at all. It was perfectly natural, even if, in those days, stay-at-home dads were thinner on the ground. Everything about the kids I just absolutely loved; changing nappies, bath-time, waiting at the school gate at half-past three in the afternoon to pick them up. I got used to the gang of mothers gathered in the playground looking slightly askance as I barrelled up with seconds to spare, still dressed in my cragging clothes and with chalk and grazes all over my hands. One of the last climbing lectures I did was a fund-raiser for the after-school club, compèred by Paul Williams, who was now living in Sheffield. With his connections in the trade, he blagged lots of free gear for a raffle and we managed to raise a few grand. After that I think the mothers appreciated that I did have another role in life, beyond being a slightly chaotic dad.

Fatherhood didn't stop me climbing. All sorts of influences made me reduce my involvement – injury, mental exhaustion, the passing years – but I felt very differently about the world when I became a parent. I kept climbing though, even if I was no longer at the highest standard. We'd frequently take the girls with us. One of our favourite activities was bouldering at Fontainebleau, the stunning sandstone boulders south of Paris that I'd visited en route to Verdon in the 1970s. Jasmine and Tasha would explore the woods, kicking through the leaves and scrambling over small rocks, while Zanna and I took turns to go climbing. For a while Tasha got interested in climbing and became quite good at it. I don't think I've ever been happier than when sharing all that with my children.

ELEVEN

Making Movies

ANY SECOND NOW I was going to have to step out of the helicopter onto the lower summit of the Aiguille des Drus. This was not a good moment to lose my nerve. Below my feet the west face of Le Petit Dru disappeared for hundreds of vertical metres into shadowy gloom. Moraine banks below the wall caught the morning sunlight. Deep in the valley the town of Chamonix still looked half asleep. Through the side-windows of the chopper, the summit of the Aiguille Verte was vibrating slightly, in time with the rotors. Beyond the pilot's head, Mont Blanc filled the windscreen. It was a shame I couldn't just sit there in my seat and admire the phenomenal view, but I was there to work.

The pilot brought the helicopter's left-hand skid to rest on the summit rocks of the mountain and nodded at us to step out. Being on a mountain like the Dru feels exposed even when you've started at the bottom and climbed up. But stepping out onto its narrow summit – no bigger than an armchair – sent adrenaline pumping through my system as I swiftly stepped down and hugged the rocks. It was too soon after breakfast for this kind of stunt: from drinking *café au lait* to perching on top of the most dramatic mountain in the Chamonix Aiguilles in a matter of moments. The rush was incredible. I bent my face into my jacket as the helicopter surged into the air, and then set about fixing a belay.

It was the summer of 1993. With me were Stevie Haston, the charismatic and fiery legend from North Wales, and filmmaker Rob Parker, a man who seemed to be able to do anything he chose. Russell Brice, the veteran Everest guide, was also along to keep an eye on us. We waited impatiently for the helicopter to return. Slung beneath its belly was a net full of ropes, bivouac gear and camera equipment we needed to begin rigging for that day's shoot. A large amount of money, together with Leo Dickinson's credibility, was riding on what happened over the course of the next few hours. If high-performance climbing can be close to the edge, creating a network television series about high-performance climbing was even more intense.

We were there to recreate an ascent of the route Walter Bonatti pioneered in 1955 up the Petit Dru's west ridge; not Bonatti's own climb, but an attempt from almost thirty years later by Joe Simpson and Ian Whittaker. They were bivouacked high on the pillar in July 1983, when the ledge they were sleeping on collapsed. Joe and Ian were left hanging from some rather dodgy protection until a helicopter arrived to whisk them to safety. Two years later of course Joe was back in the near-death business with his epic descent from Siula Grande in the Andes, immortalised in the bestseller *Touching the Void* and later an award-winning movie.

We were recreating what happened on the Dru for an ITV series called *Dead Men's Tales*. Stevie and I were acting asstuntmen, climbing the route for long shots that would be cut with scenes played by actors. I was also acting as safety officer, keeping the actors secure in situations that, while not as risky as being dropped on the Dru, were potentially dangerous.

At night, we stayed in a plush hotel in town, living a life of luxury far removed from my usual experience roughing it at campsites and eating in cheap cafés. Zanna and the girls came over for a few days during filming, but I couldn't give them as much attention as I would have liked. The schedule was demanding and there wasn't time to disappear into the hills for a few hours paragliding or climbing, like we had before the children were born. Zanna was by now well on her way to being a consultant surgeon, and didn't see herself as the kind of person who sat around waiting for her husband to finish work. She'd become the over-achiever since the girls were born and was perhaps surprised to find me caught up in such a glamorous enterprise. Perhaps I was a bit surprised myself, but like many shy people, I'm secretly intrigued by the extraversion of show business, even adventure show business. It was exciting, and I was having the time of my life.

Working for Leo on the Dru was a dream job and the highlight of my involvement in adventure filmmaking. Ever since the success of *Rock Athlete*, I'd continued to work on films, either as the featured star or behind the scenes as a stuntman or safety officer. I wouldn't call it a career, but for around fifteen years I had a parallel life in movies. The journey that ended on the summit of the Dru in 1993 was a long one.

My old friend Al Evans had moved into television after co-founding *Crags* magazine, and we worked on a couple of projects in the early 1980s, including a Granada documentary about the history of climbing called *Great Escapes*. He brought in a bunch of climbers to reconstruct scenes from the past. Dominic Lee and John Stevenson were dressed up in tweeds and pointed at something old school, while Martin Veale and Chris Gore, two leading Peak District climbers in their day, took on the role of Rock and Ice heroes from the 1950s. I was featured climbing *Sardine* to show how far the sport had developed.

Al also brought me in for a programme on ITV called *Live at Two*. Live outside broadcasts were still something special in the early 1980s, relying on technology that would seem prehistoric to modern filmmakers. The planned segment was on risk and the producer, knowing Al was a climber, had asked him if he could film one of his mates doing something dangerous live. Al quickly settled on High Tor as the best venue. The crag is spectacular but easily accessed for all the paraphernalia the technical guys would need and straightforward to rig for the climbing cameramen. Then he called me. Would I be happy soloing something on the crag's main face? Something like *Darius*? I'm pretty sure I'd never soloed *Darius* before, and while I felt it was well within my capabilities, the idea brought me up with a start. The only doubt in my mind was the technical crux, right by an old bolt, some hundred feet or so off the ground. But I thought I could clip an eight-foot sling into it and then reach down from above the hard move to unclip and move on. Al thought that would be fine.

All sorts of strange, risk-taking activities were planned. A stuntman would jump off a tall building and land on an air bag. Someone else was a drug-taker, and would be interviewed about the dangers of life as a heroin addict; that kind of thing. I remember particularly an oldish chap called the Great Geezely, a variety performer who put a ferret down his trousers and did other strange tricks. He looked a little bit like a tramp, with a long, straggly beard and a shabby coat. I decided I'd be happier soloing *Darius* than having some needle-sharp teeth hovering around my essentials, but each to his own. The idea was that the Geezely would start off with a bit of ferret-legging, as it's known, then the director would cut to me soloing up High Tor before coming back to the studio so viewers could see the Geezely, assuming he was still functioning, stick a four-inch nail up his nose. This was daytime television at its finest.

On the morning of the broadcast we had a rehearsal to make sure everything was working. Al and another cameraman set up ropes either side of *Darius* so they could jumar alongside me as I climbed, taking it in turns to move up. Cables connected their cameras to a vehicle parked at the top of the crag, which transmitted the images back to the studios in Manchester. Computers barely existed in those days, and there was no such thing as a mobile phone or a digital camera. Compared to what's available now, broadcasting technology was huge, clunky and awkward to use. I had a radio microphone clipped to my shirt and hung its weighty transmitter and battery around my waist. Mick, the sound engineer, was a bit worried that he wouldn't be able to pick up the signal, telling Al he needed a clear line of sight to make the system work.

Al suppressed a giggle. 'Don't worry, Mick,' he said, and pointed to an obvious tree at the bottom of the route. 'Just climb out along that branch and you'll keep Ron in sight.' Shouldering all his gear, Mick swung up into the tree and then edged nervously out until he could get a fix on the line of the route. There he perched with his scanner, listening to his headphones. With Al and Chris, the second cameraman, in place, I started to climb, moving slowly enough so that whichever of them wasn't filming could get ahead of me. I reached the bolt – although it was in reality more a stud than a bolt – took out the sling and clipped it.

'What's he doing?' the director asked.

'Potentially saving his life,' Al replied from behind his camera.

'He can't do that,' said the director, sitting in the van at the top of the crag, 'this is a programme about risk.'

'We're coming up,' said Al, who started jumaring furiously. There then followed an argument between the cameramen and the director about what was and wasn't acceptable risk-taking. Considering how paranoid television companies are about safety now, it seems incredible that someone who knew nothing about climbing should demand to have his way over an issue like that, but the clock was ticking and tempers were fraying. We'd soon be on air.

'No problem,' I said. 'I won't clip the bolt.' Al tried to talk me out of it, but once I agreed to carry the sling so that I could clip in if things got scary, the broadcast went ahead. Al went very quiet as I moved through the crux. He knew better than anyone what was involved. But the climbing felt more than comfortable and I didn't think for a moment of clipping in the sling to the bolt. The thing broke not long after anyway, under the weight of a falling Australian lad.

The same year as I tussled with the Great Geezely for the nation's amazement, I also appeared in a short programme made for ITV's education strand, in the pre-Channel 4 days when ITV was still required to do that kind of thing. Gill and I were hired to act out the husband-and-wife climbing partnership of Harry and Martha Kelly. H.M. Kelly – none but his closest friends ever dared call him Harry – is best remembered for *Kelly's Overhang* at Stanage and the first ascent of *Moss Ghyll Grooves* on Scafell in 1926; Martha Emily Kelly, commonly known as Pat, was one of the founding members of the all-female Pinnacle Club. H.M.K. was quite a character and sometimes irascible. He'd started climbing as a kid, scrambling up some of Manchester's bigger landmark buildings. He favoured climbing in plimsolls over nailed boots and this allowed him to put up routes that were incredibly technical for the day, including the eponymous Overhang, a top-rope problem still graded hard 5b.

An insurance agent by day, Harry Kelly was a notable guidebook writer at a time when publication of rock climbing guides was just getting into its stride. He ditched the flowery writing previously used in journals and kept only what was useful. His rope was even marked so he could give accurate pitch lengths. The idea behind the film was to show children how essential it is to write clearly when people in a potentially dangerous situation are relying on that information. The scriptwriter was Peter Tabern, who as a writer and director went on to win several BAFTAs for children's television dramas and created the hit television show *Demons*. The cameraman for the shoot was Simon Kossoff, brother of Free guitarist Paul Kossoff, who has also had a long and successful career in television. Acting as a kind of outdoor consultant and fixer was John Beatty, a talented photographer who had recently struck out on his own. Over the next few years we worked on several projects together.

Peter's script required us to recreate the first ascent of one of Harry Kelly's routes, an awkward Very Severe at Laddow Rocks in Derbyshire called *Tower Face* that still gets a technical grade of 5a, despite being climbed at the height of the Great War in 1916. To be convincing, we had to dress up in old-fashioned clothes and ditch all our modern climbing gear. The producers found a traditional hemp rope at a chandler's yard in London and, despite H.M.K.'s innovative use of plimsolls, stuck me in a pair of nailed boots. My tweed jacket came from a charity shop, along with a bright white sweater and a battered trilby hat. Gill was given a hairdo more appropriate to the era and we set off in Land Rovers up the Chew Valley before trudging over the moors to Crowden Great Clough and the towering gritstone rampart of Laddow, set high above the steep-sided valley.

Not surprisingly given the route's difficulty, Kelly had an awkward time on *Tower Face*. Contemporary accounts tell how he 'set his teeth and went for it, hell for leather,' getting up the pitch on his second attempt. While I performed for the cameras, following H.M.K.'s advice that you should be able to climb down anything you could climb up, the film crew shooed nylon-clad walkers on the Pennine Way out of shot. Pat Kelly only lived another six years after following H.M.K. up *Tower Face*. She died in a fall from Heather Ledge high on Tryfan in the summer of 1922, just a year after the Pinnacle Club was founded.

Working on the Kelly film was fun as well as rewarding, but I was in my professional rock climber phase at the time, and the fastest way to raise my profile was by starring in my own projects.

The following summer I was back in the sunshine of Provence, climbing in the Verdon Gorge with some old friends. Having had a big success with the *Rock Athlete* series, Sid Perou wanted to make a climbing film that was more technically accomplished. I wasn't the only one who thought that the opening sequence of that first series had caught the physical appeal of rock climbing, and Sid felt that with the guaranteed light in France, along with the stupendous location, he could go one better. The film, called *The Fingertip Phenomenon*, was structured as a portrait of my life as a professional climber, but that was really just the glue to stick together some beautiful sunny climbing sequences. These were inter-cut with interviews recorded in grim winter weather at a crag in Derbyshire. It was the usual story. Hunched inside my jacket against the cold, I could barely look at the camera and seemed a bit defensive explaining about my life. But moving up the warm limestone of Provence, happy to be in my element, you couldn't shut me up.

Sid enlisted some familiar faces, including Gibby, who had been working regularly with Sid as a sound recordist on caving films. He had even survived a bout of histoplasmosis, a fungal lung infection contracted from inhaling dried bat guano in a cave in Mexico. It was great to be back in France with Gibby. Also there was Jerry Peel, looking as handsome as ever for the cameras, and Gill; they would be my climbing partners.

Sid developed chicken pox soon after we arrived in La Palud, so Jerry and I were left to our own devices for a few days while he recovered and tried not to scratch. We used the time to free *Pichenibule* at around French 7c, along with another new route and several more hard repeats. When Sid's spots started to subside and he felt able to start work, Jerry and I jogged up the classic *Necronomicon*, the route Pete and I had been sandbagged on all those years before. It gave us the chance to test out our new talking rope, a regular *kernmantel* design with an inner core and

197

sheath, but with a wire through the middle of it all and a jack plug on either end. The theory was Jerry and I would be able to talk to each other and the crew and so co-ordinate our efforts. Sid had hired a two-ton winch to lower him down the crag into the best camera positions, so it was important everyone knew what was going on. None of us realised that the long wire through the rope would act as a giant antenna. Every so often, the rope would pick up Radio Monte Carlo, and our conversations were punctuated by intermittent bursts of pop songs.

'Bring me up,' Sid demanded.

'Baby, now that I've found you...'

'Who said that?'

'... I won't let you go...'

'I need to go up.'

'... I built my world around you...'

'I need to go up NOW!'

'... I need you so...'

'Bugger. Too late. Lower me back down. We'll have to do that again.'

Despite the interruptions, *Necronomicon* was in the can. My next challenge was to solo the classic *La Demande*, not a difficult route but steep and, in the hot Provençal sunshine, prone to being greasy. Several pitches above the ground, I found myself a little off route, less certain of where the line went than I remembered. I knew I had to leave one crack system and traverse into another but I wasn't sure whether I'd moved across at the right place or if I was even in the right crack. It was more like a tight chimney than a crack, and horribly flared so that I felt myself in danger of being spat out like a cherry stone, a thousand feet above the ground. Anxious about my predicament, and forgetting my radio microphone was switched on, I started cursing the rest of the team for allowing me to end up in such a position. Below me, to one side, was a small tree. Maybe if I jumped I could reach it.

My hands were greasing up against the hot limestone as I chuntered on about my imminent death and what I thought about Sid and Gibby and the rest of them. I finally pulled myself together and climbed out of danger. At the top of the gorge, however, everyone was very quiet. John Beatty told me he'd had to look away. Gibby had recorded everything, and played it back to me. I'd forgotten everything I'd said by then, and quietly apologised.

The highlight of the film was a repeat of our recent free ascent of *Pichenibule*, which took three days of filming to complete. Look in the local guidebook, however, and you'll see it doesn't credit us. I had done it using the yo-yo tactics I'd practised all my climbing life, an approach not recognised by French climbers. Redpointing was now the only acceptable method. The retro-bolting of Verdon was also underway, with lots of single-pitch routes at the top of the crag being done that saved people the hassle of reaching the bottom of the gorge. I didn't mind the first development so much, but it's a shame that the true scale of Verdon is no longer appreciated in the way it used to be.

Looking back at those interviews in *The Fingertip Phenomenon* and how uncomfortable and shifty I look, it's blindingly obvious I didn't enjoy being the centre of attention. So it's not surprising that recreating other people's climbs for the cameras became a speciality of mine. After Verdon, my next foreign assignment was working on Leo Dickinson's hour-long documentary about the Eiger, using as its central narrative the first British solo ascent of the North Face by Eric Jones in 1981. Over the years, I'd become good friends with Eric, the world's boldest café proprietor, who regularly worked as a safety officer and stuntman for Leo, one of the world's foremost adventure filmmakers. Eric introduced us when Leo was making a series on extreme sports for Channel 4 and was looking for a rock climber to star in one of the programmes.

Leo is not a tall man, and I'm over six foot so we must have looked an interesting pair. I tend to appear self-contained and quiet, while Leo is compact and intense, a fizzing bomb of energy, constantly thinking and planning how to do the next impossible thing. Sometimes the bomb would explode and you'd cop it. I remember on the Bonatti shoot forgetting to double-clip one of the Swiss-made 16mm film cameras into a belay. Leo got cross. 'These things are worth a fortune,' he said, 'you've got to be more careful.' Ten minutes later, while fiddling with the camera before shooting a sequence, he dropped it. All that expensive mechanism and glassware exploded on a rocky ledge. Back in the valley, Leo shot off to Geneva and bought another one.

During the early 1980s, I worked on a couple of projects with Leo, including the Eiger film, arguably Leo's best and widely regarded as a classic. He recreated the tragic attempt of 1936 when two Austrian and two German climbers died, one after the other, the last of them, German Toni Kurz, succumbing just a few feet from rescue. Leo also wanted to include a reconstruction of the first ascent of what became known as the Harlin Route, or the Eiger Direct, in the winter of 1966. During the ascent, American John Harlin, the inspiration behind the route, fell to his death when a fixed rope he was climbing high on the face broke.

Leo had the brilliant – but controversial – idea of filming a skydiver dressed in 1960s climbing gear falling in front of the face, an idea that was if anything too realistic for some of those involved with the climb. But he also had a few climbing stuntmen hanging around the North Face to get close-ups of these historical figures. That's where I came in. Life on a big mountain was quite a change for me. Although I'd spent weeks on end on monster cliffs in Yosemite and Verdon, my alpine experience was limited. I didn't mind the exposure, but the objective dangers of mountaineering – falling rocks and so forth – took some adjustment. Worst of all, I had to shave off my moustache.

My introduction to serious alpine climbing was essentially that moment when I emerged from the railway tunnel inside the Eiger onto the lower half of the North Face. Leo, who moved all problems out of his path like a bulldozer, had got permission from the Swiss authorities to stop the train and exit by this tunnel, but the entrance was full of snow that had to be cleared first. I was handed a shovel. Once outside on the face, I was soon swarming up the Difficult Crack, the first significant technical climbing on the Eigerwand, and then swinging across the Hinterstoisser Traverse, the critical linking pitch of climbing that opens up the middle section of the face. I felt happy enough to move around unroped half the time, which left Leo a little anxious.

Leo had shot a lot of footage during Eric's epic solo, but in order not to compromise his friend's achievement, had lowered out of helicopters onto the face and filmed him from a distance. Now Leo wanted to humanise what looked on screen to be a rather cold-blooded achievement with, to the uninitiated, little obvious drama. Hence the introduction of the Eiger's sensational history. He also wanted some close-up shots of Eric at different points on the climb to cut with wider shots that would show armchair viewers just how courageous Eric's achievement was. Eric, however, had twisted his knee skiing during the shoot and so I was drafted in as his double, with my face discretely tucked out of camera shot. I was unaware at the time, but Eric didn't like the idea of someone masquerading as him in a film about his greatest adventure. It didn't seem right. But, as he told Leo, 'Ron's the only person I'd like to be me.' That was quite a compliment.

I also got to play one of the team forcing the Harlin Route in 1966 – I can never remember if I was the Scottish legend Dougal Haston or John Harlin himself – jumaring up fixed ropes dressed in 1960s gear. My daily commute on this job was fairly unusual. The Swiss tourist board had provided us with a chalet in Grindelwald to use as a base; I'd do a couple of thousand press-ups before breakfast to keep in shape, then we'd walk down to the station, catch the train to work, get off at the tunnel and start jumaring our fixed ropes to the location of that day's shoot. We became part of the local scene and friends with some of the local guides, especially Hannes Stähli who did many extraordinary rescues on the North Face. He was a lovely guy. He enjoyed working with his hands and had a sideline in stonemasonry. One of his jobs was making headstones for the local graveyard.

Hannes was also the coach for the Swiss women's alpine skiing team and was always encouraging me to have a go. I'd never been on skis in my life but he didn't seem to think that would be a problem. On a day off from shooting, he said he was going to take me up to Kleine Scheidegg but first we needed to borrow some gear. 'So, Ron, take zese,' he said, handing me some boots in a ski rental shop owned by a mate, 'und here are your skis. Now, off you go, und good luck!' Outside, I stood at the top of what seemed a very steep slope and began cautiously snow-ploughing down the mountain. The day before I'd been swinging around the North Face. Now small children were zooming past me. I felt a little foolish. Near the bottom a large group of German skiers surrounded me.

'You should not be here,' they told me angrily.

'Now then, lads,' I said, drawing myself up to my full height. Then, having jostled my way out of the mêlée, I slid cautiously home.

Suddenly, so-called adrenaline sports were all the rage. While he was still wrestling with his colossal Eiger project, Leo was commissioned to do a series for Channel 4 called *Pushing the Limits*, featuring different adventure sports and athletes. I guess that's what they mean by someone being a hot property. Two of the programmes focussed on climbing, and in the summer of 1982, through Eric's recommendation, I found myself repeating one of my hardest climbs, *Strawberries*, for Leo's camera.

First Leo lashed himself halfway up the *Vector* buttress, so I could solo the route *Vector* as a warm-up before moving on to the headwall. It was interesting to contrast how Sid and Leo worked. Sid chose not to interfere at all with what I or any other athlete was doing. He just let you do your thing and hoovered it all up with his camera. Leo was much more involved, getting close-ups for cutaways and asking you to do sequences again and again until he was happy. I suppose Sid's approach was more documentary while Leo was always keen to dramatise the action, though he claimed later that he shut his eyes on *Vector* because he couldn't bear to watch. He loved sensational footage and I took some hugely exaggerated falls from the top of *Strawberries* to ham up the action. A postcard from that shoot sold steadily in Eric's café for years afterwards.

The other climbing film for *Pushing the Limits* was about steep ice climbing, then in one of its periods of rapid technological advance. I had done very little ice climbing over the years, being someone who lives for sunshine and hot rock. I've also suffered increasingly from Raynaud's disease, which affects the small capillaries at the ends of your fingers or toes. My fingers turn white and it often takes me hours to get them properly warmed again. But since we were in Switzerland anyway, shooting the Eiger film, when Leo suggested we try some icefall climbing I was all for it. Perhaps I was being naïve, but being with Eric gave me confidence to try something far out of my usual experience. And anyway, I was getting paid to go climbing. Why not?

Hannes Stähli was on hand to offer some advice about venues, and he suggested Kandersteg, easily accessible in the plush off-road Mercedes he had loaned us for the shoot. These days Kandersteg is one of the most famous destinations in the world for icefall climbing, but in the early 1980s the equipment that has generated such a huge new interest in winter climbing was only just coming to maturity. In each hand I had a smart new Clog axe, with its revolutionary curved pick, and to keep my feet warm a pair of plastic boots, then all the rage. But looking at the rest of my gear, it now seems rather antiquated: crampons with straps, rather than a modern clip-in binding, and old-fashioned ice screws. These days ice screws have a clever little handle to turn them into the ice and they are quick to place. Back then, you had to get the pick of an axe through the eye and lever the screw in while hanging off the other tool. It could take ages and consequently you only placed screws when they were absolutely essential. As for the theory that ice climbing was like having a jug in each hand, it never quite seemed to work like that, not for me anyway. The icefall was often plumb vertical and there was a lot of rubbish to clear off to get a good placement. Watching Leo's film more than a quarter of a century on, I can see myself visibly relax once I get onto ground with a bit of rock to hang onto.

Part of the difficulty was the state of the ice. It was melting fast as we walked up to the base of the route, and chunks of snow were sloughing off the bottom of the route. It's actually helpful if the ice is a little plastic, but the high temperature that day was taking things a little far. The place was falling apart. In the back of my mind was the real fear that the whole thing, all three pitches of it, would collapse, which is exactly what it did the next day. It might have contributed to my rather nervous performance. Lacking Eric's long experience, I found myself hanging with bent arms from my axes and panicking a little. It was a good job I was so fit. Equipped with the latest gear, and a decent pair of gloves, I think I'd enjoy ice climbing a lot more in the modern era. But at least my one ice climb was also one of the hardest.

Both the Eiger film and *Pushing the Limits* were big successes and I was grateful to Leo for having worked on them. Television, in those days at least, was a lucrative business and I made far more money working on films than I did as a climber, albeit less frequently. My stints with Leo allowed me to buy my own house, the tiny cottage in Eyam I shared with Gill, for £12,000. I daren't think what it might be worth now.

Yet the recognition films like *Pushing the Limits* brought me just showed how unsuited I was to life as an outdoor celebrity. It made me wonder why anyone would want to be famous. A job I did quite early on was working as safety officer on a film that featured the British mountaineer Alison Hargreaves climbing the South Face of the Aiguille du Midi above Chamonix. This was long before she became well known for her solo Alpine climbs and her amazing ascent of Everest. She seemed a lovely person, but desperate to be famous. She would ask me about how I'd become so well known. Partly, of course, it was through appearing in films, like the one we were then making. Almost by chance, I had become the first rock climber to use television to raise my profile. We also exploited the new market for home videos, which only became widely available in the early 1980s. Together with Al Evans, I made one of the first climbing videos released in Britain, called *Body Machine*. But I was never comfortable about the whole publicity machine. Perhaps I should have explained to Alison that it wasn't all it seemed.

Through television, however, I met plenty of people who did want recognition, sometimes above everything else. I appeared in a documentary on cheating in sport presented by the former Trotskyite politician Derek Hatton, who had just been expelled from the Labour Party for his role as deputy leader of Liverpool City Council and the adoption of an illegal budget. He was the man who hired taxis so his officials could go round handing out redundancy notices to council workers – and was then ridiculed for it by Neil Kinnock. Hatton was trying to forge a new career as a television personality, and his researchers had dug up Pete's dodgy first ascent of *Downhill Racer* to sit alongside the tales from other sports of eye gouging and ball tampering. The crew erected a pylon by the route so the camera could follow me while I soloed up it and Pete made excuses for himself, while laughing up his sleeve.

By the time I landed on the summit of the Dru in 1993 I must have contributed to more than a dozen television shows over the years. But working for Leo that summer was undoubtedly the climax. I felt really privileged to be included on that team, shooting drama-documentaries in the most extreme situations imaginable. It was like being on the inside of a James Bond movie, zooming around the Alps in helicopters and staying in top-notch hotels, rich banker types watching us at dinner because we seemed to be having a lot more fun than they were. Leo had gathered an interesting group of people, including Rob Parker, one of the world's best cave divers whose technological innovations and raw courage had pushed back the frontiers of what remains one of the world's most dangerous sports. Not only had Rob become a top adventure cameraman, he had also brought together the finance for *Dead Men's Tales* through his myriad contacts. He was one of those guys everybody likes. Rob was a good climber as well and one half of the team that opened the Bristol Climbing Centre. It was a tragedy when he died deep in an underwater cave system in the Bahamas.

My role was to perform the climbing stunts in two of the series, Joe Simpson's epic on the Dru, and Doug Scott's agonising retreat from The Ogre in 1977. Scott, the first Englishman to climb Everest as part of Chris Bonington's 1975 South-west Face expedition, broke both his legs near the summit of this desperately difficult Karakoram peak. He crawled down on his knees, hauling himself along fixed ropes where necessary, and all the time remaining an active part of the team, debating decisions and never giving up. He was clearly incredibly tough and determined.

But climbing the Bonatti Pillar on the Dru was definitely the highlight of that 1993 schedule. With miles of fixed rope dropped by helicopter on the summit, we abseiled down to the bottom of the route and then started climbing up so Rob and Leo, who was with Eric Jones filming from the bottom of the route, could get long shots of Stevie and me. We were dressed in gear from the early 1980s, which already, just ten years on, looked incredibly dated. Climbing with Stevie was great fun, such a huge personality on such a big mountain. Not wishing to be marooned on the summit after dark, we moved quickly up the pillar until the message came through our headphones: 'Slow down, you're not supposed to look that good.' I tapped the microphone against the rock and made crackling noises. 'Can't hear you, Leo! Comms must be failing.'

As it turned out, we missed the helicopter anyway. It was called out on a rescue mission on its way to collect us that evening, so we were forced to bivouac. It was no hardship. A huge amount of food – fresh bread, sausage, paté – and a few bottles of red wine had been left for us, together with thick sleeping bags, so we settled in for the night. As darkness drew in and the lights of Chamonix started twinkling, three climbers emerged from the Dru's North Face, two lads and a girl, exhausted from their long climb. They couldn't believe their eyes when we welcomed them with lots of fresh food and wine. Ironically, Alison Hargreaves was also on the face that day, climbing alone, although we didn't see her. Next morning, we were pulled off the summit by helicopter and were back in the valley for breakfast.

The critical scene in the Dru film was the recreation of that awful moment when Joe and Ian's ledge disappeared from beneath their dozing bodies. It must have been a terrifying shock. High on a steep rock wall, in complete darkness and not adequately belayed, the two young climbers suddenly found themselves hanging in space from doubtful protection, a heartbeat from joining the ledge that had just fallen to the bottom of the mountain. Capturing that sense of utter and terrifying surprise was going to be a key part of the film's success.

Leo hired actors to play the roles of Joe and Ian, and like many actors they had fluffed up their resumés to secure the part. Thus an afternoon's abseiling in the Scouts was leveraged into years of climbing experience. They certainly weren't prepared for the difficulties of the shoot. Even though the truly dangerous stuff had been done by climbing doubles, some of the close-ups were still pretty alarming, most of all the ledge collapse. To recreate this, Rob had placed a portaledge on a rock wall close to the Aiguille du Midi cable car station. Hung from a couple of bolts and rigged with hooks that could be opened by pulling a lever connected by cables, the ledge was then covered with polystyrene blocks painted grey. When the lever was pulled, the ledge would disappear and the blocks spin off into space. A long length of thin cord would prevent the portaledge from disappearing down the mountain. It was all a bit Heath Robinson but Rob seemed convinced it would work. There's no way anything like this would be allowed now.

The two actors playing Joe and Ian were quite different characters. One had the good sense to play down what he was happy doing, and he was excused from being on the ledge. The other was a little more full of it, but hopelessly out of his depth. Just getting him onto the ledge and tied in was awkward enough, but as the reality of his situation – hanging over a drop on a ledge that would disappear from underneath him at any moment – began to sink in, he became more and more agitated. Then he started screaming. I have to say, I couldn't help but find the whole thing quite funny. I think he'd rather taken against me for being a quiet Yorkshireman. Now I had my hand on the lever that would send us both into space. I may have been laughing as I pulled it.

TWELVE

Super Vet

IT'S FAIR TO SAY I'M A CREATURE OF HABIT, always have been, always will be. First thing in the morning, I'll make a cup of coffee and take it back to bed with a couple of digestives and listen to the news. Tasha does the same. When the girls were little, they'd jump into bed with me for a chat, and then spill crumbs everywhere. These days, I've gone wild and have chocolate digestives – own brand, mind, and only because they're almost as cheap as the regular ones. Then I'll get up and have another cup of coffee and a couple of bananas. I loved bananas as a kid. Grandad Bate sold them in his little shop in Embsay, and if there were any rotten ones left over we might get them. I'll have a couple of bananas for breakfast, as I have for years.

Then it's time to go running. It's as much part of my daily routine as the bananas and has been for the last fifteen years or so. How far depends on what day of the week it is, what I've done the day before and what I've got planned for the day. If it's Monday and summer, then most likely I'll have competed in a race the day before, so it will be a short distance, perhaps no more than an hour. I'll be out of the house around 9.45am. Later in the week, depending on whether or not there's a midweek race, I'll be running further. An hour and twenty is a medium distance, two hours is the longest I'll run. I have a sequence of regular routes I've built up over the years I've been living in Hathersage, in North-east Derbyshire, and I'll rotate them in turn. Like Embsay, Hathersage sits in a basin, overlooked by a circle of high moors and rocky outcrops, although the limestone country is a little further south, just over the horizon. Wherever I run, it's uphill. I should probably structure my training better, doing hill reps and speed work, but unless I'm doing a reconnaissance for a race I pretty much stick to regular routes that start from my front door. I know exactly how long each route will – or should – take and wear a watch to check my progress. I never wear one in a race, though. It seems daft to me. There's a whistle to start you off and they give you your time at the end.

Any stretching is very light. I prefer instead to start running gently and build up. I used to routinely take a couple of ibuprofen before I began, but I've read too many warnings about overusing anti-inflammatory drugs, so I've gone cold turkey, even though I'm often in a bit of pain. I've broken both ankles several times, and I can still feel a bad break in my right one when I'm running. I know there's a good chance that the injury will stop me at some stage. Cold and damp British winters aren't the best environment for an ageing athlete like myself. I notice that Joss Naylor, the fell running legend from Wasdale, now in his seventies, likes to spend his winters in Spain. He's still up on his Lake District fells in summer though.

Fell running is in my blood, in a way. Grandad Bate was a good runner in his youth, and locally very successful. There's a long tradition in the Dales and the Lake District of professional racing, dating back centuries. Local fairs staged all kinds of athletic competitions where men could test their strength and win a little cash. Such contests are mentioned in the legends of Robin Hood and in Walter Scott's novel *Ivanhoe*. For shepherds and gamekeepers working the fells year round, running across them was an obvious way to compete. The Grasmere Sports and Show is one such tradition, which still draws a crowd numbered in thousands. The fifth Earl of Lonsdale, Hugh Cecil Lowther, known as the Sporting Earl, was a big fan, although he's more famous for cleaning up boxing and instituting the Lonsdale belts. Large bets – the largest being Lonsdale's – were placed on fancied runners, which is how Grandad came unstuck.

There is a big race held in Embsay every year in September, organised by the British Open Fell Runners Association (BOFRA), and a story in the local press had tipped Grandad as worth a few quid at favourable odds. So a local bookie headed off a possibly disastrous day for the bookmaking fraternity by getting Grandad drunk. Like me, he barely drank at all, so I doubt it took much. Needless to say he didn't win. Nowadays, there's a strong amateur tradition in fell running, as administered by the Fell Runners Association, which has become a much bigger organisation than BOFRA. Grandad's racing was part of the professional circuit and beyond the pale as far as the Amateur Athletics Association was concerned. There was that little bit of pride that fell running was a working man's game, where the money you won could make a real difference to a shepherd's wages. No doubt gentlemen and university types looked down on it.

My own interest developed as my climbing career began to wind down. I'd always done a bit of running, plodding round when I needed a break from the rock, and I went out several times with John Beatty, who as a member of the Rucksack Club was a dedicated fell runner. John had helped the well-known distance runner Mike Cudahy with some of his record-breaking outings and had illustrated Mike's classic fell running book *Wild Trails to Far Horizons*. I got to know Mike through John and found him an inspirational figure. We went out running together once on Bleaklow, in north Derbyshire, on the foulest of days. After a couple of hours John and I looked at each other through the howling gale and wondered whether we shouldn't head back. 'I'll see you later, lads,' Mike said and disappeared into the mist for another two hours.

It was a bit of a shock having to start again as a near-newcomer to a sport and watch the top guys far in the distance, literally as well as metaphorically. But I stuck at it and was soon doing up to twenty miles or so a day. People think the pain of running such long distances across difficult terrain is an appalling prospect, but I actually revelled in it. I loved being that tired, experiencing a total body pump. It made me feel content, like I'd done something that day.

After my training run, I'll come home and relax a little before lunch, usually just a sandwich and a cup of tea. If I'm honest, I probably don't eat enough. When I was at my peak as a rock climber, I weighed around twelve and a half stone, which is quite light for a man of six foot three. But I had to work hard to keep that muscle on. All those press-ups, sometimes a couple of thousand in the morning, kept my shoulders comparatively large. These days, with my climbing training regime twenty years in the past, I doubt I weigh much more than eleven and a half stone. I never realised how much running took out of me until I weighed myself before and just after a race. I'd lost quarter of a stone. I couldn't believe it. My legs have always been pretty thin, and that hasn't changed much, despite the running. I've avoided cycling, which several older climbers I know have started doing seriously, and so my thighs have never bulked up. But I do have an indoor bike to work on for when I'm injured, without question the most boring activity known to man.

One of the great appeals of fell running is that self-reliance is still a big part of each race. Roadrunners expect a marked course with lots of marshals. You can't get lost. But in fell running if you get lost then it's your cock-up. That's just part of the crack. My running club, Dark Peak, give a prize called the Pertex Trophy to the man or woman who makes the biggest navigational error of the season. No one wants to win it, but it's fair to say the roll of honour includes some of the club's best athletes.

There's a phrase I like that sums it up – the trod. It means the vague hint of a path, maybe left by sheep or deer, but not a recognised footpath. It's the line you'd take as the most logical route across hilly terrain. That requires you to have a feeling for the hills, that they're your element, the place you belong. In a road marathon it doesn't matter how long you take. You can walk the thing if you want. But on the longer fell races, if you're not performing to a reasonable standard, then you're out. People can't fool themselves about what they're doing. That gives fell running a lot of integrity.

As I ran more regularly, I started going to a few local races as an unattached participant, meaning I didn't belong to a club. Every race, I discovered, has its own character. Some are famous for their prizes, good and bad, or the great cakes afterwards. At Chelmorton they give away butties and meat pies and thank you for turning up. I loved the atmosphere and often bumped into friends I'd made during my years climbing. Fell running seemed to me much like the climbing world was when I started. You could find yourself sharing a brew and a chat with the bloke or lass who had just won the race. No one gave the impression of thinking they were any better than the rest. I'm not sure it's like that in climbing anymore, and it's beginning to change in the fell running world. Several books have been published about the sport and it's becoming more popular. Many more runners with no real interest in the outdoors are taking it up as an alternative to road running. And for me running is about being in nature. Once the whistle goes at the start of an event then I'll compete as hard as I can. But racing is only a small part of it for me. It gives running a bit of an edge, a sense of purpose. But mostly it's like climbing was back in the late 1960s, another way to experience a world I've been exploring all my life. I've started birdwatching in recent years too. Sometimes I'll spot a bird I haven't seen for a while and then be thrown into a quandary about whether to stop running and look, or just keep going.

After a few races as an unaffiliated athlete I took part in the Three Peaks Race in Yorkshire, which takes in the summits of Pen-y-Ghent, Whernside and Ingleborough. I did well that day, perhaps because it was so warm, and beat most of the lads in my category, which attracted the attention of the Dark Peak Fell Runners, the famous Sheffield club. They invited me to join them. I don't train with the Dark Peak, because they meet at a pub in the city, but I'm very proud to compete in their famous brown vest.

Like most runners, I have my quirks. Being tall with long thin legs I struggle uphill compared to shorter lads with a bit more muscle in their thighs. I'm quicker on the flat, however. I'm also known for being reckless in descent, which is tough on ankles that are rather battered after so many breaks and strains. I'm always going over on them and then have to rest up for a while. My Raynaud's disease is a bit of an issue as well, and in cold weather I have to wear gloves, and have even resorted to mountaineering mitts in harsh conditions. On longer races, where I'll need some sugar to keep me going, I like to carry some jelly babies in my bumbag. Not the black ones though. The food colouring in them makes me belch, which hampers my breathing, so I'll pick out all the black ones and give them to the girls.

If there's a winter race, like the Mickleden Straddle held in February, then I'll try and run that, but the calendar really starts building in the spring. Smaller events, barely advertised and aimed at local runners, might have fifty or sixty competing. Larger events will attract a field of three hundred or so. In the summer I might have three races in a week. That's the limit my body can take. On the Tuesday it might be Calver, then it will be Castleton on Friday and the Edale Show on Sunday. That's a short sharp shock of a race, straight up the slope of Kinder Scout and with the steepest descent in the Peak District racing calendar at the end. Races, like climbs, have categories and the Edale Show race is 'AS', the 'A' meaning it has lots of climbing in it, at least

250ft per mile and the 'S' meaning it's a short course of less than six miles.

One year the Edale Show race was the English Championships, and being a short course, the women and men ran separately. So if you're competing you get to watch the elite women at work, which is quite a rare occurrence. Normally, they disappear at the start and are home and showered before you see them again. Normally, you're just following along behind, so it's a treat to see the elite athletes. On the steeper sections, where the rest of us are walking, they seem to be sprinting. It's unbelievable what a human being can run up. I suppose there must have been climbers looking at me thinking something similar; it's good to get that perspective. Sometimes the bigger races will produce a video of the event, and I'll sit there in front of the television waiting for the split second when I'm on the screen. Tasha will look at me and say: 'You sad old man.' I have to confess, I keep all my medals and little trophies on the mantelpiece in the front room.

Fell running has its stars just as climbing does, but this time I'm looking up at them and wondering what it takes to be that good. One of my heroes is Rob Jebb, just a regular Yorkshire chap who works for BT, wins lots of races, has been British champion a couple of times and likes to go for a pint afterwards. Unlike me, Jebb doesn't run in winter, but competes in Cyclo-Cross. Starting in 2000, he won the Three Peaks Cyclo-Cross race seven years in a row. It would have been eight if the moors hadn't been closed for foot-and-mouth disease in 2001. It was a bit of a shock for everyone when he came second in 2009. Excelling at two sports like that is very impressive.

I do win races, in my category at least, which is now the over-fifties veteran's group. There's a lad in the Peak District called Mike Egner, who is world class. If Mike shows up, then I know there's no chance, but if not, then I often prosper. I've taken part in some fantastic competitions like the Masters World Mountain Running Championships in Keswick in 2005, the summer I turned fifty. I was chuffed with that. It was like being at the Olympics, with over a thousand runners taking part from all over the world. Fitz Park in Keswick, where the race started, was packed with thousands of people. They had the biggest marquee ever erected in Cumbria. It was even on television. The course was fantastic, onto Latrigg and Skiddaw and up Lonscale Fell before coming back to Keswick. I didn't win but I put in a creditable performance. In 2008 I was part of the Dark Peak's over-fifties team that won the Gold Medal in the English Championships for an aggregate score taken from the best short, medium and long-distance races. I just went along to make up the numbers, but it was great to be involved.

I did win an event outright once. Almost. It was a race called the Hope Moors and Tors, taking in several hills above Derbyshire's Hope Valley. It wasn't long after I'd started competing and I was still a bit wet behind the ears. The race offers two courses, one of eight miles and another of twenty. Typically for me, I wanted to do the twenty-mile event, but there were rules about what you had to wear as protection against bad weather. I'd turned out in my usual skimpy running shorts and a vest but the organisers said I needed full-body cover, waterproof top and bottoms. I had no choice but to enter the shorter course. Both routes start by heading up the valley to Castleton then onto to Mam Tor where the long course splits off and heads north to Kinder. The short course heads for Lose Hill. When I arrived at the summit I had no idea I was in the lead, but did know that I needed to punch my card with a 'dibber' to show I'd passed through the correct route. But the dibber was nowhere to be found, so I asked a bloke who looked like a race marshal where it was hidden.

'Oh,' he said. 'There's no dibber here.'

And so I ran on, crossing the line in first place, with spectators cheering me home. I felt immensely pleased with myself. But when I came to hand in my card to the race officials, they asked me where the mark from Lose Hill was. I told them there wasn't a dibber there.

'Oh,' they said, looking stern. 'Yes there was. I'm afraid you're disqualified.'

'But what about the race marshal?' I huffed.

'What marshal?'

Occasionally, the weather and terrain take over and any notion that you're in a race is lost as you find yourself in a fight for mere survival. The Edale Skyline in 2007 was that sort of event. Climbing up Ringing Roger above the village and heading to Kinder Scout we could hear the wind getting louder and louder. When we reached the edge of the plateau it felt as if I'd stepped into a hurricane. There was a noise like a jet engine wound up to full power and I could barely stay on my feet. I'd had the good sense to wear more clothing than usual, including my mountaineering mitts in an attempt to keep my fingers from turning blue. Other runners had started in shorts and vests, and were suffering horribly. The race is well organised by the Dark Peak and help was on hand to sort out those more badly affected. Race marshals had put up tents at checkpoints for runners to shelter in and several runners at a time would crowd in to warm up. It's the only time in my life where I was in genuine fear of being blown off my feet. Running along Mam Tor, above a long and nasty drop, I felt myself being shoved towards the edge, no matter how hard I pushed my shoulder into the force of the wind.

Sooner or later, hopefully later, all the breaks and strains my body has endured over the years will stop me running. I really can't complain if I'm a bit creaky on winter mornings. What I've been through was worth it. My dad, as he got older, suffered a bit too, but his aches and pains were from a lifetime of work, of endless early mornings, lighting the fire in a cold house in the depths of winter before going out into the darkness to collect milk churns. Whatever happens, I'll still be going outside, and I'll still be climbing if I can, and if not then watching birds and walking. I went birdwatching as a lad, an interest I shared with Dad and my brother Clifford, so in a way I'll just be reverting back to childhood habits.

Running kept me going when the girls were younger, at a time in my life when things seemed most difficult. After ten years, my marriage to Zanna began to break down. While she was training as a surgeon our life together worked well. My little cottage in Eyam was a base for her to come back to when work took her off to different parts of the country. When Jasmine was born we lived for a while in Bamford, and then bought a house in Hathersage. Zanna became more settled, getting a job as a consultant in her specialist field at the Royal Hallamshire in Sheffield. At the start, she had loved being outdoors doing things. As our relationship continued and her work situation changed, she put down more roots and started to widen her circle of friends. She wanted to hold dinner parties and go to the theatre, situations that were not my natural habitat. She was becoming connected to a world that filled me with dread.

Then on a work trip Zanna met someone else, a woman she had known before she met me, and they began a relationship. Eventually she moved out and we agreed to joint custody. The girls spent half the week with their mother, but after a few months Jasmine decided she wanted to live with me full-time, and a few months after that Tasha was back home too. It was obviously a tough time for everyone concerned. People are much more open about all sorts of things now, certainly compared to how society was when I growing up in Embsay. But I can't pretend that the fact Zanna had left me for another woman didn't make a difference. It knocked my confidence. However losing the children was the worst thing. When I dropped them with their mother, I'd be back home on my own. For around six months after she left, I found myself in a deep pit of depression, and at times I felt suicidal. I began to drink much more than I had, and started running obsessively. Running was, quite literally, mind numbing. It was the only time I could forget my pain. Being a single parent meant I had a lot to focus on, and I poured a lot of my energy into that. But like any single parent, I've found starting a new relationship too difficult. It's not something I'm sure I could do anymore.

We'd booked a trip to Zambia before Zanna left, so she could show the girls, who were now finishing primary school, where she'd grown up. Her sisters were going too. Since we'd paid for it, and since the girls wouldn't go without me, I agreed to tag along. That was one of the strangest times of my life. Leaving aside the stress of our failing relationship, I felt uncomfortable staying in luxury safari lodges owned by rich white people, being waited on all the time. To escape the tension, I'd put my running shoes on and disappear off into the bush. Folk at the safari lodge were astonished I did that, but I found it liberating. I got chased by elephants once, but by running I found I could make my own connection to what I was seeing, rather than being led round by the nose. The kids loved seeing the animals at first, but soon got a bit fed up seeing the same thing every day. They liked visiting local villages better, seeing real people.

Since we separated, Zanna has bought a house in Hathersage and lives nearby. My world became entirely focussed on the girls and my old life of travelling and climbing was no longer possible. Even before Zanna left, I'd wanted to spend time with my family. You want your kids to be happy and that means staying around. I had to be at the school gate at half-past three, and everything else was made to work around that. Things haven't always gone smoothly. It's fair to say I have a jaundiced view of our laws on issues like divorce and children living with fathers, something the state seems to frown on. Money has often been tight. For years I worked with rope manufacturer Marlow as part of their sales team, but when they bought out a European climbing rope manufacturer, they ended their domestic operations and I was laid off. Work became more piecemeal after that. It's a good job I'm cheap to run.

Mostly, however, I'm just grateful to have had the chance to be a father to Jasmine and Tasha. Family has always meant a great deal to me, even though through my twenties I was rarely at home. Mum died in 1992 of cancer, still only in her sixties, not long after Tasha was born. She said: 'I'm not going to die until I've seen the baby.' A few days after Tasha arrived I drove up with Zanna and the girls to see her, and a few days later Mum died. After that Dad and I saw more of each other and talked more than we ever had when I was young. I think in the end he was proud of everything I achieved, even if he wasn't the kind of man to say it out loud. My sister Alison, who has been a wonderful aunt to the girls, took care of Mum when she was ill, but couldn't go through it again when Dad was diagnosed with the same cancer ten years later. He went into a hospice near Halifax, where I'd visit him often. It was an amazing place, Dad was looked after with so much care, right up to his death there in 2002.

You can't get to your mid fifties without losing a few close friends along the way. But it's not easy to see your contemporaries die prematurely. I still miss Paul Williams, his endless enthusiasm and warm-heartedness. The weekend he died, in early June, he phoned to try and persuade me to come out with him soloing at Froggatt. 'Cruising the grit,' as he called it. Soloing gritstone at the weekend wasn't for me. I felt too self-conscious for that but Paul loved the theatre of it all. While climbing *Brown's Eliminate*, a route well within his capabilities, a hold snapped perhaps only twenty feet above the ground, but the landing was hard and Paul fell awkwardly. He died in hospital later that day. You'll still often see flowers or a candle in a little niche in the rock near where he fell, almost fifteen years after his death. Through his guidebooks, you can get a sense of the man, but he's still keenly missed. Solo climbing is such an unforgiving discipline. Apart from Paul, several other friends have perished in this way, including John Bachar and Jimmy Jewel. I know how lucky I've been. I still see Paul's son Chris from time to time.

Pete Livesey died in 1998 aged just fifty-four, the age I am now. After he dropped out of the climbing scene at the end of the 1970s, the decade he had dominated, I would often see him out running at Malham or Gordale and would sometimes drop in at his café for a brew. The idea of Pete being ill was so bizarre that I couldn't believe it when I heard he had cancer. He'd been feeling poorly, went to see his doctor and collapsed in the surgery. There was more or less nothing to be done. I believe that at the time of his funeral he was still leading his veteran's category in the orienteering championships, despite having been ill for some weeks. Pete had been quite a wild character in his youth, but after he married Soma and they had a child he mellowed and became a much more thoughtful person. All the posh newspapers carried obituaries of him. I think he would have had a good laugh at that, the rebel from Huddersfield. There was a memorial for him in Skipton, with the great and the good giving speeches. I think he would have chuckled at that too. I went along, and read out a little piece I had written. For myself, I'm not the sort of person who would want a big send-off like that. I'll just have my ashes scattered on a good strong wind up on the moors somewhere.

Other friends have passed on. Wolfgang Güllich died in a car crash in 1992, most probably having fallen asleep at the wheel of his BMW on his way home from an early radio interview. I felt a real affinity and admiration for Wolfie. He was so considerate of others, and often, because of their egos, and because Wolfie was quite reserved, other top climbers failed to notice his qualities and even abused his hospitality. Tom Proctor, that gentlest of giants, succumbed to cancer, again aged just fifty-four, in 2001. Tom had pretty much quit climbing after his expedition to Cerro Torre in 1981, but he was still busy in Peak District cave exploration, using those huge arms of his to dig out hidden passages.

Some of my friends seem the same as ever. Gibby married a Thai girl a few years ago and spends a lot of time in South-east Asia. He's still larger than life. We sometimes have old fart reunions, with friends from the Sadcocs days, like Brian Swales and Terry Birks, when we talk about the past. Now the girls are growing up and moving out, perhaps I'll have more time again to get around some favourite old haunts. Jasmine now lives and works in Buxton and Tasha is thinking about becoming a lawyer. She's a great one for the party scene though, the complete opposite to me. It's exciting to watch how their lives develop. When Tasha's gone, I'll sell the house and move somewhere smaller, near enough the girls to be in touch. I've sometimes thought of moving back home to Yorkshire, but I'll wait and see.

As for climbing, I can't see it not being part of my life. There was a time in the 1990s where I continued to go out more through habit than desire. I suppose I went through a period of still wanting to climb but no longer knowing what it was for – what role it played in my life. When you've been very good at something, when it's been the purpose of your whole existence, it feels a bit odd carrying on at a lower standard. I can understand why lads like Pete and also Jerry Moffatt moved on to something else. I suppose I did too, in a way, with my running. Raynaud's made it very difficult for me to go bouldering in winter, when conditions are best on the grit. And running seemed to be a better use of time when the girls were growing up. I could get more done in the few hours I had available.

In recent years, however, I've started enjoying my climbing

more and more. Partly this happened with the opening of the Climbing Works in Sheffield, a new bouldering wall, the biggest in the world apparently, in an old industrial unit. Now I have somewhere to go in the winter where I can climb and not worry about my fingers, although it can get pretty cold in there. With more time on my hands again, I've started pushing my grade a bit more. I'll do problems up to Font 7b+, and be trying 7cs, not far off my top limit of twenty years ago. A couple of years ago I wouldn't have been anywhere near that. In modern terms, perhaps, it's no great shakes. The top grades now are Font 8c or 8c+. But it's not bad for a bloke in his mid 50s. I've got a fair amount of stamina; I'll do up to three hours or so a visit, four or five days a week.

Given the damage my body's sustained over the years, I'm mostly just grateful I'm climbing at all, so to be pushing my grade is almost incredible. It also puts me back in the company of climbers. I've never felt too happy being inside, but a bouldering wall is much more sociable than a leading wall, where either you or your partner is usually up in the air and busy. There'll be a few people around who'll stop for a natter, giving me the latest gossip about who's done what. And in the summer, when it's warm enough for me to climb outside, the extra strength and stamina allows me to do some hard things again on the crag. It's mostly bouldering or soloing. I don't tie onto a rope much these days. But who knows what might happen in the future.

I suppose, deep down, the same thing motivates me now that motivated me when I was a young lad, living in Embsay and driving my parents spare. It's that urge to be out the back door and up onto the moors. There's something uplifting about it, a sense of liberation, whether I'm running or climbing. As I grew older, I felt I had a lot to prove, to show everyone that I could use the talent I'd been given. Eventually, the effort I put in brought rewards. I travelled to places I never expected to see and have enjoyed a life that was always full of new experiences and excitement. But through it all I needed that sense of space and freedom to be myself, and that's as true now as it was then. Always, even during the toughest times in my life, the moors and the crags were just up there, with the promise of a new horizon.

SIGNIFICANT ASCENTS AND DATES

This list is a collection of selected highlights from Ron's climbing career, together with other key dates in his life. An extended list of all of his climbs and achievements would fill another book.

1955, 6 May	Born Ronald Norman Fawcett in Embsay, near Skipton, West Yorkshire.
1969	Introduced to roped climbing at Rylstone Crag by Arthur Champion, with an ascent of *Dental Slab* (S 4a, FA: Bill Bowler 1935).
	Spends winter aid climbing.
1971	First recorded new route, *Problem Wall* (E2 6a) at Malham Cove, climbed solo.
	First ascent (FA) of *Cove Crack* (E2 6a) at Malham Cove.
	First free ascent (FFA) of *Mulatto Wall* (E3 5c), aged 16, at Malham Cove. The first of many new routes known as much for their quality as their difficulty.
	Numerous new routes, particularly on local gritstone crags like Crookrise and Deer Gallows, climbed around this time, often solo. Includes *Ron's Crack* (E3 6b).
1973	First visit to Verdon Gorge with Pete Livesey and friends, aged 17. Free ascents of *Le Triomphe d'Eros* (F6c), *Solanuts* (F6c) and *Necronomicon* (E4 6b, F6c).
	First ascent of *Slender Loris* at Malham Cove, with one point of aid. Freed by Fawcett in 1979 at E4 6a.

227

Inspired by Al Evans' discovery of Trowbarrow in Lancashire, makes first ascent of *Alladinsane* (E1 5a).

First visit to Yosemite. Makes fast ascent of *The Nose* (5.9, C2, 2900ft, FA: W. Harding, W. Merry, G. Whitmore, 1958) on El Capitan with John Long.

1974   Second trip to Yosemite, with Livesey. Made first ascents of *Crack-A-Go-Go* (5.11c), The Cookie Cliff, and *Bircheff-Williams* (5.11b), Middle Cathedral.

1975   Near-free ascent of *Cave Route Right-hand*, Gordale Scar, Yorkshire, with Livesey.

1976   FFA of *Liberator* (E3 6a) at Bosigran with Livesey.

FFA of *Cream* (E4 6a) with Livesey during BMC International Meet.

Turns 21.

Second ascent of *Mortlock's Arete* with Livesey (E4 6a, FA: Tom Proctor and Geoff Birtles), Chee Tor, Derbyshire.

FA of *Cream Team Special* (E5 6b), Raven Tor, Derbyshire, with Geoff Birtles and Al Evans.

FA of *Supersonic* (E5 6a), High Tor, Derbyshire.

The bold first ascent of *Slip'n'Slide* (E6 6a), Crookrise, Yorkshire. Arguably the most serious gritstone climb in Britain at the time.

1977   FFA of *Void* (E3 6a). Early attempt on Strawberries, Tremadog.

FFA *Vulcan* (E3 6a), Tremadog.

FFA of *Citadel* (E5 6b), Gogarth.

Early ascent of *Astroman* (5.11c), Washington Column, Yosemite.

1978   FFA of *Milky Way* (E6 6b), Ilkley, Yorkshire.

FA of *Desperate Dan* (E7 6b), Ilkey. Some now grade *Desperate*

Significant Ascents and Dates

Dan as hard E6, particularly following the development of bouldering pads, but it is a contender for the first E7 in the UK. A direct start was added by James Pearson in 2009.

FA of *The Cad* (E5 6a), Gogarth, Gwynedd. Controversially places two bolts, which are later removed.

1979   FA of *Lord of the Flies* (E6 6a), Dinas Cromlech, Gwynedd.

FFA of *Carnage* (E2 6b), Malham Cove.

FFA of the Livesey classic *Doubting Thomas* (E5 6b), Malham Cove.

FFA of *Déjà Vu's* first pitch (E5 6b), Kilnsey.

1980   FA of *Strawberries* (E6 6b), Tremadog.

FA of *Atomic Hot Rod* (E5 6b), Dinas Cromlech.

FFA of *Dinosaur* (E5 6b), Gogarth.

FA of *The Big Sleep* (E6 6b), Gogarth.

FA of *Psycho Killer* (E6 6b), Clogwyn Du'r Arddu.

Rock Athlete broadcast on national television.

West Face of El Capitan (5.11c) with Gill Kent, free, in six hours. Likely the fastest ascent of the route at that time.

Three-day ascent of *The Phoenix* (5.13a, FA: Ray Jardine, 1977).

1981   Visits Frankenjura, making FFA of *The Blue Roof*.

Marries Gill Kent. FFAs of the Cave Routes, Gordale, while on honeymoon: *Cave Route Left-hand* (E6 6c), *Cave Route Right-hand* (E6 6b).

FA of *Piranha* (E6 6b), Rubicon Wall, Derbyshire.

1982   FFA of *Indecent Exposure* (F7b+), Raven Tor.

FFA of *The Prow* (7c), Raven Tor.

229

FFA of *Body Machine* (F7c), Raven Tor, completing a trilogy of high-quality routes of the hardest standard.

FFA *Scritto's Republic* (E7 6b), Millstone, Derbyshire.

FA of *Tequila Mockingbird* (E6 6c), Chee Tor. Use of bolts proves controversial both for being too few and too numerous.

FAs in Pembrokeshire: *Stennis the Menace* (E6 6b), *Yellow Pearls* (E5 6b) and *Boss Hogg* (E6 6b).

Significant ascents in Germany.

1983   Filming in Verdon.

Suffers serious accident soloing at Clogwyn y Grochan: *I had been working on the Cromlech; Gill was following a local lad up Left Wall, and Eric was soloing a damp Cemetery Gates. It was filmed and shown live on World of Sport, and I was helping the crew. Job done, the team headed off to the pub but I wanted to do a few routes so Gill dropped me and Bill – the dog – off at the Grochan. It was a damp evening and there was no one else at the crag. I don't remember much else, only waking up with Bill licking my face and a horrendous pain in my arm. Somehow I straightened it up, nearly passing out again with the pain, managed to get my gear together and hobble down to the road. I tried to get a lift into Llanberis – no chance – and ended up walking. Much to Gill's disgust she had to leave the party to take me to hospital!*

FA of *Master's Edge* (E7 6b), Millstone, Derbyshire. Although Fawcett abseiled down the route and checked out the holds, there was no top-rope practice.

1984   FFA of *Yosemite Wall* (E5 6b), Malham.

FA of *Crimson Cruiser* (E5 6a), Craig y Clipiau. Another Fawcett route know for its high quality.

FA of *Mescalito* (F7c+) and *New Dawn* (F7c) at Malham Cove, and *Defcon 3* (F7c+) at Gordale.

Significant Ascents and Dates

Travels to Japan and then the US, climbing *Equinox* (5.12d, FA: Tony Yaniro, 1980) and winning Mount Rubidoux bouldering competition.

Fast repeat of *Revelations* (F8a+, FA: Jerry Moffatt, 1984) at Raven Tor.

1985 — FA of *Zoolook*, the first F8a at Malham.

1986 — Solos 100 gritstone Extreme-grade routes in a day near his home in Derbyshire.

1987 — FA of *Careless Torque* at Stanage, one of the first Font 8a boulder problems in the UK.

Technique book *Fawcett on Rock* published. A collaboration with photographer John Beatty, and writer M. John Harrison.

Suffers serious paragliding accident.

1988 — Climbing in Morocco with Dennis Gray and John Beatty.

1990 — Daughter *Jasmine* born.

1991 — FA of Jasmine (E6 6b), Bamford Edge, Peak District.

1992 — Daughter Natasha born.

1993 — Filming on the Aiguille des Drus with Stevie Haston and Leo Dickinson for *Dead Men's Tales*.

2004 — Joins Dark Peak Fell Runners.

2005 – 2009 — Wins Dark Peak Over 50's Club Championships. *Since turning 50 I've been 1st Super Vet (Over 50) at many local races, including Castleton, Edale Skyline, Hope, Bradwell, Bamford, Hathersage, and more.*

2007 & 2008 — With fellow Dark Peak runners, wins Gold Medal for Over 50's team competition in the English Championships.

231

100 EXTREMES IN A DAY

FROGGATT

1 Downhill Racer (E4 6a)
2 Long John's Slab (E3 5c)
3 Tree Survivor (E3 6a)
4 Oedipus Ring Your Mother (E4 6b)
5 Cave Wall (E3 5c)
6 Cave Crack (E2 5c)
7 Heartless Hare (E5 5c)
8 Great Slab (E3 5c)
9 Artless (E5 6b)
10 Hairless Heart (E5 5c)
11 Synopsis (E2 5c)
12 Nutty Land (E1 5c)
13 Brown's Eliminate (E2 5b)
14 Armageddon (E3 5c)
15 Big Crack (E2 5c)
16 Stiff Cheese (E1 5c)

STANAGE

17 3D Wall (E2 6a)
18 Tip Off (E1 5b)
19 Dry Rot (E1 5b)
20 The Tippler (E1 5c)
21 Tippler Direct (E3 6a)
22 The Dangler (E2 5c)
23 Censor (E3 5c)
24 Yosemite Wall (E2 5b)
25 Topaz (E4 6a)
26 Easter Rib (E1 5b)
27 Ice Boat (E1 5c)

28 Coconut Ice (E2 5c)
29 The Actress (E1 5b)
30 Desperation (E1 5c)
31 Constipation (E3 6a)
32 Wuthering (E2 5b)
33 The Asp (E3 6a)
34 Don't Bark, Bite (E1 5c)
35 Dark Continent (E1 5c)
36 Acheron (E1 5b)
37 Blood Shot (E2 5b)
38 Old Dragon (E1 5b)
39 Plastic Cream (E1 5c)
40 Curving Buttress (E2 5b)
41 Monday Blue (E2 5b)
42 Left Unconquerable (E1 5c)
43 Milsom's Minion (E1 5b)
44 Crossover (E2 5c)
45 Nuke the Midges (E1 5c)
46 Esso Extra (E1 5b)
47 Cinturato (E1 5c)
48 Centaur (E1 5c)
49 Living at the Speed (E1 5b)
50 Archangel (E3 5b)
51 Giro (E1 5c)
52 Argus (E2 5b)
53 Shock Horror Slab (E2 6b)
54 Counts Buttress (E2 5b)
55 Daydreamer (E2 6b)
56 Nightmare Slab (E1 5c)

BURBAGE SOUTH

57 Millwheel Wall (E1 5c)
58 Pretzel Logic (E3 6a)
59 Zeus (E2 5b)
60 Above and Beyond the
Kinaesthetic Barrier (E4 6b)
61 Dork Child (E1 5c)
62 Pebble Mill (E5 6b)
63 Nick Knack Paddywack (E2 6b)
64 Old MacDonald (E1 6a)
65 Sorb (E2 5c)
66 Fade Away (E1 6a)
67 Recurring Nightmare (E5 6b)
68 The Knock (E4 6a)
69 Yoghurt (E4 6b)
70 The Boggart (E2 6b)
71 Boggart Left-hand (E3 6a)

CURBAR EDGE

72 Scroach (E2 5c)
73 Left Eliminate (E1 5c)
74 Right Eliminate (E3 5c)
75 The Toy (E1 5c)
76 L'Horla (E1 5c)
77 Elder Crack (E2 5b)
78 Canoe (E2 6a)
79 Finger Distance (E3 6b)
80 Kayak (E1 5b)
81 Kappelout Direct (E3 6b)
82 Vain (E2 5b)
83 Colossus (E1 5b)

84 Saddy (E1 5b)
85 Smoke ont' Watter (E1 5c)
86 Squint (E1 5b)
87 Fidget (E1 6a)
88 Afterbirth (E2 5c)
89 Birthday Groove (E1 5c)
90 Diet of Worms (E3 5b)
91 Deadbay Crack (E1 5b)
92 Deadbay Groove (E1 5b)
93 Black Nix Wall (E1 5c)
94 Rat Scabies (E3 6b)
95 Mister Softee (E1 5c)
96 Apollo (E2 5c)
97 Soyuz (E2 5b)
98 A.P. Jacket (E3 5c)
99 Unreachable Star (E2 6a)
100 Ulysses or Bust (E5 6b)

ACKNOWLEDGEMENTS

I'd like to say thanks to Jaz and Tasha for allowing me to drag them around the world when they were little without throwing too many strops, and in later years for putting up with me for being such an unorthodox dad. To all my old climbing mates who humoured this obsessive youth, particularly Gibby, Terry (Birks) and Brian (Swales). I wish Pete (Livesey) and Paul (Williams) were still around too.

Thanks to Sid Perou for giving me my big break in *Rock Athlete*, and to Eric Jones, the most humble of heroes, who introduced me to Leo's world of extreme mountain sports.

A massive thanks to Vertebrate for giving me this opportunity to tell my story and finally, to Ed, for going way beyond his brief and making this such an enjoyable journey.

Ron Fawcett
Hathersage, February 2010

Acknowledgements

When I was a kid just starting climbing, Ron Fawcett was God Almighty, with the emphasis on the 'Almighty'. He seemed peerless, which at the time, in 1981, he probably was. I was mates with two lads who lived in Great Longstone in Derbyshire, who were cousins of the immensely talented Lee brothers, Daniel and Dominic, then starting to rival Ron in the Peak. By 1982 I was hearing secondhand whispers that Ron was no longer King of the Hill and that new, younger climbers were stealing his crown. Not long after, he nipped ahead of Jerry Moffatt to climb Master's Edge at Millstone, so there was clearly life in the old dog yet. He was 28 at the time.

So to end up helping one of your boyhood heroes write his autobiography was beyond exciting, and thanks to Ron's openness and honesty, it proved a happy experience too. For a man who doesn't like chatting about himself, he stuck to the task with great patience. Because the Fawcett memory is not always of metronomic reliability, some of his friends stepped in with useful reminiscences and dates. I am indebted to old climbing partners and friends, including John Beatty, Arthur Champion, Al Evans and Jim Perrin, his teacher George Spenceley, filmmakers Sid Perou and Leo Dickinson, Matt Heason for providing me with copies of the Fawcett filmography and Colin Wells for offering up his interviews with Ron. Thanks also to Stephen Goodwin, who edited the manuscript and offered wise counsel and the team at Vertebrate who made the whole process so enjoyable.

Ed Douglas
Sheffield, February 2010

INDEX

Index

Index